ESSAYS IN
TWENTIETH-CENTURY
NEW MEXICO
HISTORY

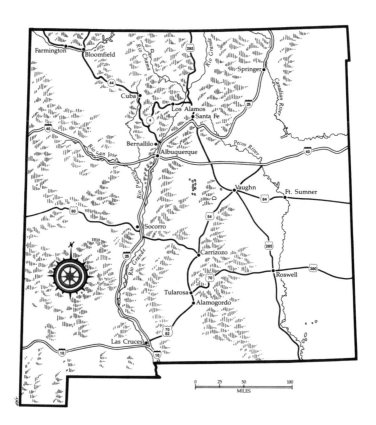

ESSAYS IN TWENTIETH-CENTURY NEW MEXICO HISTORY

EDITED BY
JUDITH BOYCE DEMARK

UNIVERSITY OF NEW MEXICO PRESS
ALBUQUERQUE

Library of Congress Cataloging-in-Publication Data
Essays in twentieth-century New Mexico history / edited by Judith
Boyce DeMark. — 1st ed.
p. cm.
Includes bibliographical references and index.
ISBN 0-8263-1483-X (pa.) :
1. New Mexico—History—1848–   . I. DeMark, Judith Boyce.
F801.E87   1994
978.9'05—dc 20
93–25178
CIP

In honor of William M. Dabney

CONTENTS

_____

ACKNOWLEDGMENTS

MANY people are involved in the compilation of an anthology. In addition to the fourteen contributors to this volume, I would like to give special recognition to John Grassham for his work in compiling and editing the photographs in this volume. I would also like to thank Darlis Miller, Byron Johnson, Cheryl Foote, and Ray Sadler for their comments and suggestions at various stages of the proposal and manuscript. The staff at the Computer Information Resources and Technology (CIRT) Department of the University of New Mexico provided invaluable assistance to a computer novice. Much gratitude is extended to Barbara Guth at UNM Press. And I would like to give a special word of appreciation to my husband, Ray DeMark, for his encouragement throughout not only this process but the long years of graduate school.

INTRODUCTION

JUDITH BOYCE DEMARK

NEW Mexico has a written history that stretches over 450 years. Archives are rich with diaries, journals, and government documents, yet most of the secondary literature on New Mexico history covers only the first 360 years. In fact, a perusal of state history texts and journal articles indicates that all but a few scholars have focused on the years before 1900.

As we near the close of the twentieth century, more historians must begin to do primary research and to publish data on the significant trends and events of the last 100 years. This book is intended as a springboard for more twentieth–century New Mexico scholarship.

Overlying themes of this anthology include major economic influences that have shaped the state, population changes in the first several decades of this century, cultural pluralism, the development of New Mexico from territorial status to statehood, and the experiences of the people of New Mexico. Some of the essays in this volume discuss several themes, while others focus on one theme or examine themes in the context of a particular group.

This anthology spans the years from 1900 to 1965. The reason for choosing this time frame is the impact of World War II on the New Mexico economy and population. Many of the essays cover the first forty years of the twentieth century, the period when the New Mexico economy set its present course and the tricultural population became multicultural. Yet the cataclysmic events of World War II, which proved so significant in transforming New Mexico, demand that any collection of twentieth-century essays include some information on the post–World War II years. The years from 1945 to 1965 provide a framework in which the reader can observe the changes brought to New Mexico by the war it was in this period that New Mexico finally became a full-fledged partner in the U.S. economy.

New Mexico became a territory of the United States in 1850. As a territory, New Mexico was a possession of the U.S. government, in a relationship that favored the wishes of the federal government over the needs and desires of the residents of the territory. For example, governors were appointed by the president rather than elected. This meant that in the entire territorial period, although Hispanics constituted the largest ethnic group, New Mexico had only one Hispanic governor. When the territorial legislature attempted to control the entry of non–New Mexico railroad companies in the 1870s, the Atchison, Topeka & Santa Fe (AT&SF) used outdated incorporation papers to evade territorial law.

With the arrival of the AT&SF in New Mexico in 1879, the future of the territory was dramatically altered. Just as with World War II over sixty years later, the coming of the AT&SF brought significant changes. The railroad led to an increase in the population, added to the ethnic diversity of the territory, brought jobs, and provided a new transportation and communication link with the rest of the United States. Many of the entrepreneurs who pushed for railroad development in New Mexico believed the territory was on the brink of new and spectacular growth. Although their expectations did not work out quite the way they had hoped, New Mexico did experience tremendous changes. And, like other western states, New Mexico was part of the boom-and-bust economic cycles caused by circumstances and events in the rest of the United States.

Boosters often referred to the cultural diversity in the state as tri-cultural, since Anglo, Hispanic, and Native Americans made up a large percentage of the population. Since the latter part of the nineteenth century, however, the state's population has actually been multicultural. There are many differences within the three major groups. The Anglo population includes people from diverse backgrounds. Thousands of today's Anglos in New Mexico are second- or third-generation Italian Americans, most of whom are Catholic. Also included in the designation *Anglo* are grandchildren or great-grandchildren of German Jewish immigrants who came to New Mexico in the late nineteenth and early twentieth centuries. Anglos came from such places as Chicago, Warsaw, Moscow, London, and Paris. Some were Jewish, some Catholic, some Protestant. In addition, smaller racial and ethnic groups have been in New Mexico since before the turn of the century. These include African Americans and Asians.

According to the census of 1900, there were almost 200,000 people living in New Mexico. The population was spread throughout the territory, with the largest concentrations in the still relatively small towns of Albuquerque, Las Vegas, and Santa Fe. Less than 10 percent of the population lived in towns, and over 90 percent were born in New Mexico. Thus, the population of New Mexico in 1900 was still predominantly rural and native-born.

Politics at the turn of the century was focused on the fight for statehood, which took sixty-two years to achieve. Conservative Republicans, including non-native-born Thomas B. Catron and Albert B. Fall, dominated the political structure because of their friendships with politically powerful national figures. But Miguel A. Otero, native New Mexico Hispanic and governor of New Mexico Territory from 1897 to 1906, was the major personality in the fight for statehood.

Statehood was achieved in 1912 at the height of the Progressive Era, a period of reform that affected all parts of the United States. The New Mexico state constitution, however, did not reflect this progressivism. Old guard politicians drafted a conservative document that disregarded women's suffrage, direct election of senators, and other progressive elements. The first U.S. senators elected by the New Mexico legislature were conservative Catron and Fall.

Between 1900 and 1910, the population of New Mexico grew by over 67 percent. Still, there were fewer than 3 persons per square mile in 1910 compared to 30.9 for the United States as a whole. Although their numbers were small, the minority populations were growing. For example, in 1900 there were only 8 Japanese in New Mexico, yet by 1910 there were 258. Due to such factors as the Chinese Exclusion Act, however, the number of Chinese in New Mexico dropped from 341 in 1900 to 248 in 1910.

The economy of New Mexico during the first decade of the twentieth century was dominated by agriculture. There were 35,656 farms in New Mexico in 1910 and over 30,000 persons listed as farmers, including about 1,500 foreign-born immigrants and 2,000 African Americans and other minorities, excluding Hispanics. Other major employers included the railroad, some mining companies, and manufacturing and merchandise firms. Most of over 300 New Mexico manufacturing enterprises listed in the census of 1910 were printing establishments and lumber mills. Ninety-eight mine operators employed almost 600 workers, with the largest number in coal mines. Although there was only one hospital in Albuquerque, the territory's largest town in 1900, the number of patients was steadily growing in Albuquerque and other communities as more people came to the Southwest hoping the climate would improve their health. Their increase soon created a health-care industry that became one of the major employers in New Mexico.

While agriculture continued to be the largest employer, a growing percentage of the New Mexico workforce was employed by railroad companies and their subsidiaries by 1910. The apex of the railroad years was 1914, when there were over 3,000 miles of main-line track in the state. Railroads brought health seekers from the East and the Midwest in large numbers after 1900. Many of those who recovered stayed in New Mexico and added to the population and workforce.

New Mexico's population almost doubled by 1920. The state was still overwhelmingly rural, and those employed in farming or ranching made up more than half the workforce. However, new industries were giving an economic boost to New Mexico after a post–World War I slump. These industries included tourism; health care, particularly tuberculosis sanatoriums; and new energy sources, especially oil and natural gas. The southeastern portion of the state was given a boost with the development of oil fields in Artesia and Hobbs in the 1920s. Although developed later, natural gas from the San Juan Basin in northwest New Mexico provided fuel for a small market as early as 1921.

By the 1920s railroads were giving way to a new form of transportation, the automobile. One of the primary reasons for the growth of the New Mexico tourist industry was the improvement of the now legendary U.S. Route 66, the major east-west thoroughfare across the nation, which crossed the state and passed through Albuquerque. Construction on the two-lane dirt road began in the 1920s, and the route originally meandered through Santa Fe, Albuquerque, Los Lunas and west. Throughout the 1920s and 1930s, the state of New Mexico increased spending on highway and road construction. Better roads brought more newcomers and led to the development of the trucking industry in New Mexico.

Transportation improvements brought another benefit for New Mexico—the growth of the tourist industry. Local boosters worked with the Santa Fe Railroad as early as the latter part of the nineteenth century to promote the advantages of settling in, or at least visiting, New Mexico. A major agency, the New Mexico Bureau of Immigration, led the drive. The tourist industry actually had its roots in such institutions as the Taos Art Colony. Founded by Bert G. Phillips and Ernest L. Blumenschein in the late nineteenth century in northern New Mexico, the Taos Art Colony—and the later organized (1915) Taos Society of Artists—helped advertise the culture of New Mexico by exhibiting art works throughout the United States. Writers such as Mabel Dodge Luhan and D. H. Lawrence helped attract other writers and artists to the state. As art colonies developed in Taos and Santa Fe, interest in Native American culture increased. The number of museums began to grow, and there was a revival of interest in Indian pottery making, rug weaving, and jewelry making.

The tourist industry also benefitted from New Mexico's unique blend of cultures and a campaign aimed at attracting those interested in learning about its art, architecture, and Native American population. Although boosterism often pandered to the unrealistic image of Indians held by many Americans, it lured thousands of visitors to New Mexico in the first three decades of the twentieth century. The presence of the tourists helped to create jobs in such businesses as motels, hotels, restaurants, and curio shops.

According to the census of 1930, the population of New Mexico had reached 423,317. In addition to the continued increase of the three major ethnic groups (Native American, Hispanic, and native-born white), New Mexico now had residents born as far away as the Philippines and India. And while the native-born white population continued to be overwhelmingly the largest group in 1930, there were almost 7,800 foreign-born whites in the state that year.

In 1930 New Mexico officially joined the age of air travel with the inauguration of the first regularly scheduled passenger and mail service to Albuquerque by Transcontinental & Western Air, Inc. (TWA). Several air fields were constructed in the state in the 1920s and 1930s. The largest and most successful was Oxnard Field, the site of the present-day Albuquerque International Airport. Oxnard housed major airline facilities by the 1930s and was used by aviation pioneers Wiley Post and Jacqueline Cochran. Although Oxnard Field's business declined by the late 1930s, it served another important function when it was transferred to the U.S. Army in 1942.

The federal government was another contributor to the economic and population growth of New Mexico. World War I created a need for military training camps, some of which were converted to regular military bases by the 1920s and 1930s. Franklin Roosevelt's New Deal gave a major economic boost to the state. When the Great Depression of the 1930s hit New Mexico, farmers were particularly hard-pressed. The value of New Mexico farmland was the lowest of any farmland in the United States, and ranchers faced drought, dust storms, and falling market prices.

Many farmers and ranchers lost their land when they could not pay taxes. Hispanic New Mexicans lost family lands at an even faster rate than Anglos. As a result of the efforts of Senator Dennis Chavez and Governor Clyde Tingley, New Mexico received more money per capita through several New Deal agencies than any other state. Chavez served on both the Senate's public works and appropriations committees. Thousands of New Mexicans—farmers, artists, and others—were put to work through the Works Progress Administration (WPA) and the Civilian Conservation Corps (CCC).

One of the changes in New Mexico that resulted from New Deal programs was a political shift. The Democratic party received credit for the measures of the New Deal, and gradually the Republicans, who had held power in New Mexico for half a century, gave way to the Democrats. The Hispanic vote was particularly significant in this process. Democrat Chavez was chosen to replace Bronson Cutting after Cutting's untimely death in a plane crash in 1935. Clinton P. Anderson was another leading New Mexico Democrat who represented New Mexico at the national level from 1945 through 1972, first as a member of the U.S. House of Representatives, then as secretary of agriculture, and after 1948 as U.S. senator.

On the eve of U.S. entry into World War II, several factors set the stage for New Mexico to play a larger role in the U.S. economy. The population of the state had grown to 531,818, an increase of 270 percent from 1900. The urban population had grown to about one-third of the total state population, and city boosters were trying to attract businesses to New Mexico. The cost of living was lower than the national average, and taxes were relatively low. Moreover, New Mexico lay in the Sunbelt, which received a major population influx in the three decades after World War II. The military was especially attracted to New Mexico for many reasons. For example, the sunny climate meant that the air force had more flying days.

The New Deal helped increase the power of the Democratic party in New Mexico, and its programs put people to work, but the New Deal alone did not end the Great Depression. It took a world war to raise the nation out of hard economic times. For New Mexico, World War II was a major turning point. When the United States entered the war in December 1941, thousands of New Mexicans joined the military. Some 50,000 state residents served in the armed forces during the war. Native Americans, who at that time were not allowed to vote under the New Mexico Constitution, nevertheless volunteered in large numbers. In fact, New Mexico had the highest volunteer rate and one of the highest casualty rates of any state. One reason for the high casualty rate was the Bataan Death March, in which the Japanese forced thousands of captured U.S. and Filipino soldiers and civilians on Bataan Peninsula to march sixty miles to a prison camp. Over half of the New Mexico Coast Artillery was lost on Bataan, and this included many Hispanic New Mexicans.

The Albuquerque Army Air Base was renamed Kirtland Field in 1942, and instructors trained crews for B-24s, B-29s, and gliders. Other bases opened around the state during the war, including Roswell, Clovis, and Alamogordo. Military personnel and other government employees added to the wartime population of New Mexico, and many service people returned to the state as permanent residents when the war was over. The increase in military facilities created jobs for New Mexicans, especially in construction and service occupations.

Other employment opportunities came with the increasing need for war-related technology. Two major facilities, Los Alamos and Sandia national laboratories, opened during the war and are still major employers in the 1990s. Los Alamos was the site chosen for the construction of the first atomic bomb, and the first and only test of that weapon took place at the Trinity site on White Sands Missile Range. The missile range is still an important employer for southern New Mexico. Sandia National Laboratories is operated by a private defense contractor under the direction of the Department of Energy and focuses on both nuclear weapons research and the development of energy resources. The availability of mineral resources in New Mexico also proved important for war-related technology, especially the discovery of uranium in western New Mexico.

By 1960 New Mexico's population had reached 1 million persons, four times the total in 1900. More than 200,000 people resided in Albuquerque, and the next three largest cities were Roswell, Santa Fe, and Las Cruces. Seventy percent of the state's residents lived in towns with populations over 2,500, so that by 1960 New Mexico was, indeed, an urbanized state.

This anthology demonstrates that many events helped change New Mexico from its former colonial status to an important force in the U.S. economy. One thread running throughout these essays is the creativity and energy of New Mexico's population. From the beginning of the twentieth century through the dynamic years of World War II, the people of the state have made a difference. The significant changes brought to New Mexico with World War II would not have been possible without the individuals and groups, newcomers and natives, that make up the multicultural environment that is New Mexico. By the 1960s New Mexico's role had shifted from an exotic colonial outpost to a participant in the political and economic process of the United States.

The first five chapters look at the various uses of land in New Mexico. Agriculture, mining, and water use have each played a significant role in the area's economy since prehistoric times. In chapter 1 Joan Jensen focuses on the traditional mainstay of the New Mexico economy, agriculture, as seen through the work of farm families. Ira Clark in the second chapter studies the use of groundwater in New Mexico in the twentieth century. In chapter 3 Christopher Huggard takes the history of copper mining in Grant County in the first decades of the twentieth century as a case study of New Mexico's mining industry. The fourth chapter focuses on a Depression-era federal program of livestock reduction among the Zuni Indians, intended to improve economic conditions on reservations. Susan Perlman follows the reactions of the Zuni people to government interference in their traditional life-style and examines the results of livestock reduction. The changes in the day-to-day life of twentieth-century ranch hands, both Anglo and Hispanic, are observed by Steve Cormier in chapter 5.

While agriculture dominated the first decades of the century, federal and local government employment became increasingly significant as a result of the New Deal and World War II. The next four chapters focus on the changes in various service industries from the beginning of the century through the post–World War II years. Included in this section are studies of the role of the military and other government agencies and an overview of the changes in labor history. In chapter 6 Barron Oder follows the growth of the military in New Mexico from the nineteenth-century militia to the twentieth-century professional military. Judith Johnson in chapter 7 examines the New Mexico Penitentiary and how it has changed over the years. Chapter 8 focuses on urban rivalry; Arthur Gomez discusses relations between Farmington, New Mexico, and Durango, Colorado, during the first two decades after World War II. In chapter 9 Robert Kern studies the changes in labor unionism from the turn of the century through the post–World War II period.

Four case studies comprise the third section, each study following a different type of newcomer to the state. In chapter 10 Jake Spidle, Jr., examines the tuberculosis industry from 1900 to 1940 and demonstrates the significant impact health seekers had on the economy and population of New Mexico. Sandra Schackel in chapter 11 presents another aspect of the rise of the health-care industry with a discussion of public-health nurses who worked with Hispanic and Native American families in New Mexico in the early decades of this century. In chapter 12 William Tydeman studies the work of a twentieth-century New Mexico photographer who captured thousands of images of Native Americans for use in the tourist industry in the 1920s and 1930s. Chapter 13, the final chapter, discusses one of the most tragic events in the history of minorities in the United States: the internment of Japanese Americans in prisoner of war camps during World War II. This event brought a large group of immigrants to New Mexico against their will. Richard Melzer considers life in the prisoner of war camp at Santa Fe during the war, as it affected both prisoners and local residents.

At the conclusion of this anthology is a brief annotated bibliography by Spencer Wilson, listing reference sources for studying twentieth-century New Mexico history. Although not many books and articles deal specifically with New Mexico in the twentieth century, Wilson shows that one can find relevant information in magazines, monographs, and local histories.

ONE

FARM FAMILIES ORGANIZE THEIR WORK, 1900–1940

⚜

JOAN M. JENSEN

AFTER interviewing Clara Coleman of Anthony, New Mexico, in 1937 for what was then the Works Progress Administration, Marie Carter wrote that Clara was proud of the fact that she paid for the family sheep ranch herself. Mabel Luke Madison told Carter, "I liked ranch life right from the start, for I rode the range with [my husband] Jim, learned to cook and eat chuck-wagon food and to ride and rope with the best of them." Ellen Grubs Reaves said, "I kept house and done the cotton picking too. . . . I enjoyed it." Jesusita Aragon later told Fran Leeper Buss, "I went all day on my horse with my dogs to watch the sheep. . . . When I'm just a little older I help to shear the sheep. . . . No other girls know how to do it, but I know how to shear, and I work outdoors like a boy. I don't like indoor work, but I have to do it too." Esperanza Salcido remembered, "When I was in the seventh grade, we moved to a ranch near Cimarron. I really enjoyed that. I was a tomboy, and I used to take care of the field with my brother. We'd go out and chop wood, bring it in, and saw it. I like that work a lot." Josephine Turrietta said, "We had to help my daddy cut hay, rake it and bale it. You name it, we had to do it."[1]

These women were part of the majority of women—86 percent in 1900 and 67 percent in 1940—who still lived in rural areas in New Mexico. Historians have often dismissed examples of such women's work as exceptional by using a model for rural areas of strict gender division of labor. According to this model, the work of women outside the household was an exception to the "normal" division of labor. Under this ideal division, women were in the household caring for children, preparing food, maintaining clothing, and keeping house. Men were in the fields plowing, planting, harvesting, and caring for animals. Children also divided their work along gender lines, with young boys apprenticing to their fathers in the fields, young girls apprenticing to their mothers in the kitchen. According to the model, these gender roles transcended most ethnic lines. One of the jobs of historians of women in the past few years has been to test the model. Using the concept of the gender division of labor as a tool rather than an assumption, a method rather than a stereotype, they have been able to develop more accurate models. With them, we can begin to probe the reality of labor in farm families in New Mexico.

My study of New Mexico farm families in the period 1900–1940 shows a reality far different from the stereotypical picture of most Hispanic and Anglo families. In fact, the stories with which I began this chapter are part of a pattern that tells us how farm families organized their work around economic and social realities. Women commonly performed such "unwomanly" tasks as those mentioned above. Not only did New Mexico women spend much more time outside the household than has been portrayed but in many cases they also assumed full responsibility for running farms. They did so within an economic climate that, especially in Hispanic communities, made it increasingly difficult to insure the survival of family farms.

Recent research has shown that farm women by their own definition performed work that fits into four different models. One model is that of a strict gender division of labor with women as homemakers. In a second, women do part of the work outside the house in busy times. Third, some farm couples have a work partnership. Finally, some women manage farms and ranches by themselves. Multiple models of this sort are valuable because they are based on the perceptions of farm people themselves and because they open up the question of how many women, and men, fit into each model—a question that is still undecided. This chapter does not state precisely how many farm families fit into each category. Rather, it identifies some ways to evaluate the factors that determine those numbers.[2]

Each farm family in New Mexico had certain external and internal boundaries that affected the lives of family members. External boundaries were set by rules embedded in social institutions that governed or reflected the values of society. The most influential rules were those reflected in legal, religious, and economic institutions. Internal boundaries were set by families as they adjusted their lives to various circumstances. Among the most important variables were the age of family members, the developmental stage of the family enterprise and the agricultural community of which it was a part, the types of work to be performed, the yearly cycle of agricultural work and its level of intensity, and the economic circumstances (class) of the family. Together these external and internal boundaries determined how farm families organized their work. How creatively a New Mexico farm family matched its resources to these boundaries also determined, to a great extent, how successful it was in remaining on the land.

The external boundaries of law established the formal rules by which farm families functioned. Law was in some ways the most visible boundary. At marriage, two individuals agreed to join their lives legally. Although many people were unaware of the intricacies of family law, it governed most New Mexicans because most were legally contained in a family.

Family law controlled both property and labor. New Mexico lawmakers revised the family law code several times between 1901 and 1915 but the main provisions remained in place as the state moved from territorial to state status. Not until the late 1940s did women began to demand changes in some of these provisions that made them, as Judge C. J. Smith wrote, "powerless during marriage." Young women and men were legally subordinate to their parents until eighteen and twenty-one, respectively, and thus legally owed them their labor and obedience. Parents had to agree formally before children under those ages could marry or work for themselves. Under New Mexico community property law, husband and wife formed a legal partnership agreeing that all goods accumulated would be divided equally when that partnership was ended by death or divorce. During the partnership, each agreed to work for and to support the other. The woman, however, agreed to give up part of her civil rights. As one judge put it, one partner "had larger power than the other." That person was the husband. He was legal head of the family, and he controlled the partnership's property. During most of the period from 1900 to 1940, the husband could dispose of the community property without his partner's signature, though she could not do likewise. He could also dispose of his half of the property by will, though she could not. He might will his property to her, to his children, or to someone else. At her death, her property went first to him to pay debts, and then to her legal heirs. The custom among Hispanic men seems to have been one of equal division of property among daughters as well as sons. The testamentary pattern among Anglo men is not yet clear. It is possible that, as was the case in most common-law states, men willed most of their property to sons. In common-law states, the idea that the man should hold most of the family property in his name was still strong despite property laws protecting married women.[3]

Next to law, religion was the most important external boundary for the farm family. For some, it was probably the most important boundary. Both Protestant and Catholic marriage vows established rules by which the pair managed their lives together. Normally, civil marriage was reinforced by a religious ceremony that stressed unity and caring for each other. The teachings of most churches at the time also stressed the subordination of the woman to the man through her vow to "obey" him. For Christians, the teachings of St. Paul still enforced this subordination of woman to man. In religion, as in law, Hispanic women may have had an advantage over Anglos because of the exalted place of holy women— saints and the Virgin Mary—in the Hispanic belief structure. Religion offered Hispanic women strong spiritual protectors, and they did not hesitate to call on them when necessary.[4]

Law and religion put families in a certain set of economic rules. Within marriage, the normal rules of trade and capitalism functioned only indirectly. Both the man and the woman expected to share their economic gains with each other, their children, and to some extent more distant kin. In Hispanic families, custom and religion reinforced this economic sharing. The *comadre-compadre* (godmother-godfather) support structure had an important economic function. So, too, did kinship credit networks, in which kin helped each other, expecting to be paid whenever possible but expecting no profit and no foreclosure if a family could not pay. Among Anglo Protestant immigrants, economic individualism was much more strict. The family had fewer protections from the outside world of capitalism, where everyone had to function in a profit-making economy. This economic isolation made many Anglo families more economically aggressive. A family that failed found itself much more alone than would have been the case in an Hispanic farm family. For this reason, also, Anglos frequently created formal community institutions. As the Anglo minority grew in the late nineteenth century, it began to support public schools, health-care institutions, farm cooperatives, and government assistance. Anglos supported federal land grants in homesteading, agricultural extension services, and most New Deal programs. Anglos also supported or allowed discrimination in how these institutions cared for Hispanic family members.[5]

Within external boundaries, then, farm families managed their special strategies. The family cycle was perhaps the most significant determinant of the female role. The age and health of husband and wife was an important factor. When a husband died while children were young, the woman often took over the man's job; likewise, a widowed man might take over the woman's job, caring for the children and house as well as his fields. These single spouses depended heavily on the oldest child for assistance. This was sometimes the case even if both parents were alive. If older children of both sexes were available, parents tended to divide their work by gender, but if there was only one older child, he or she often performed the work of both genders. Jesusita Aragon had to do both kinds of work because she was the oldest child. If the oldest son was the second child of the family, he might have to help his mother haul water, chop wood, care for younger siblings, and prepare food.[6]

Some types of work were fairly strictly divided by gender, others less so. Agricultural extension agents, who divided their own labor along strict gender lines, enrolled Anglo children in various kinds of activities. A tabulation of club members by gender in 1921 shows some overlapping, the most gender-segregated clubs being those for beef raising and clothing. Both sexes joined clubs for poultry, sow and litter, dairy, garden, corn, and canning.[7]

Cooking, according to later accounts, was a gender-mixed job in many places. Many young men joined cooking clubs when agents formed them. Cooking was a particularly useful skill for ranch men, for they were often on the trail and had to prepare their own food. One agent reported that she had asked a group of young men why they wanted to join the cooking club: "They answered me that when they left school they would be in charge of stations on the ranches and did not intend to live on beans." In Dona Ana County in 1930 there were two separate boys' cooking clubs where the boys learned camp cooking. Lillian Beach, who owned a small ranch, cooked for cowboys. Larger outfits generally had a male cook. In small outfits, men sometimes traded off cooking duties. Native American men often participated in food preparation, especially during special ceremonies. Anglo men likewise considered it important to be able to prepare meat for the large, almost ritual, barbecues in ranch communities. At *matanzas,* or butcherings, Hispanic men organized the cooking of meat, although women helped.[8]

The yearly cycle of work could also pull family members at certain times of the year into work commonly done by one gender. In ranching the yearly roundups, or drives to greener pastures, often drew the whole family into one working unit. Navajo families worked together in moving their herds to summer pasture. Mabel Madison remembered driving cattle. Clara Coleman drove pack trains back to Las Cruces for supplies while she and her husband kept their animals in the mountains for summer feeding. On farms, families harvested grain, hay, beans, or chile peppers. In Hispanic communities, women seem to have picked chiles more often than beans or grain, but young women helped with threshing and older women winnowed grain, dried chiles, and shucked corn. Children of both sexes sometimes helped in these tasks.[9]

Two main types of agriculture existed during the early twentieth century in New Mexico, subsistence and commercial. On larger operations, women often had little to do with outdoor farm work. Celestine Neale remembered that on her farm near Las Cruces, she spent her time working indoors at household tasks. Middle-sized commercial farms and ranches often included subsistence farming as well. On these farms and ranches, women often helped in the commercial operation and managed the subsistence farming. On subsistence farms, women often did most of the work because men worked off the farm to bring in cash. From 1900 to 1940, many Hispanic and Anglo farms were subsistence operations.

During the early twentieth century the subsistence type of farm increased, and thus women played a more important role in agriculture than they had previously. The first increase came with the homesteading rush on the eastern plains. These were poor families with little surplus wealth, looking for land. Homesteading laws gave families a chance to own land if they could live there and farm it for nine months out of the year for a certain number of years. With so little capital, the family often could not survive on income generated by the farm, so men commonly sought off-farm work in construction or road work, or on larger farms, while women stayed on the home farm managing it until such time as it could support the family.[10]

Likewise, on small Hispanic farms, where income from agriculture could not support families moving to a more consumption-oriented economy, women took over while men went out seeking off-farm work. In northern New Mexico, the most lucrative jobs for husbands and sons were in mining and sheep raising. Older daughters could contribute more to the family through school teaching than other family members could through any occupation except mining. By 1940 smaller subsistence farms were dependent on off-farm work and government assistance. In some northern villages, this occupational pattern developed before World War I; in others, it followed soon after. As Lorin Brown remarked of Cordova after World War I, the men sought seasonal work outside the village for six to eight months and the women took charge of planting crops. Direct government assistance began to arrive only in the 1930s, but the pattern had already been established by that time. The federal government simply provided new types of off-farm work and extended it to young women as well as young men. Susan Archuleta remembered that most of the money paid to young people went directly to the parents while the youths received only a small stipend. There was a wage differential in the work of young men and women. The youths' stipends were equal, but the family received more for the work of young men than for that of young women.[11]

The cause of the shift in patterns of work lay in the economic and political conditions of early twentieth-century America as well as in conditions in the West and specifically in New Mexico. Anglo farm families who homesteaded were generally fleeing the increase in tenancy that accompanied the lack of available land in the states farther east. As the economic boom ended in the 1890s, many farm families sought political solutions in the Populist and Socialist parties. When political challenges did not change the progress of commercialization of farming, poor farmers took their agrarian dreams of landholding farther west. New Mexico was one of the last safety valves of the rural American population. If families could not survive on New Mexico homesteads, they had few options except tenancy or day labor. The first choice of most families was to extend women's farm work while men worked off-farm. For many, the dream ended with the drier weather on the high plains in the 1920s and the terrible droughts of the 1930s. Subsistence farms never produced enough capital to make the major improvements necessary to survive hard times. Eventually, most of these farm families gave up and moved off the land. Only a few made the transition to large commercial ranches or farms.[12]

The Hispanic families, with their fertile and irrigated valley lands, should have been in a more favorable position to survive at the subsistence level. However, these families were as much affected by economic change as homesteaders were, although in a different way. The Rio Grande Valley consists of three parts—upper, middle, and lower. Long settled by the original Native American and Hispanic residents, the irrigated valley lands were seldom available to Anglo settlers. Between 1920 and 1940, Hispanic families in both the middle and lower valley lost much of their land, thus drastically changing the way they organized their lives.

In the middle and lower valleys, small irrigated plots had traditionally offered work for the entire family. Commercial agriculture was not practiced on most farms. Instead, families produced what they needed, with a small surplus to enable them to afford necessary purchases. Each year, like the Nile, the southern Rio Grande flooded the fields spreading rich soil but making it difficult for families to live near the river bottom. At first, families cleared small fields, organized irrigation, and allowed long stretches to remain in bosque or brush. There was plenty of land for communal grazing, houses were clustered in villages on high ground, and families went out to work separate plots near the river. In good years the system worked well; in bad years many crops were destroyed by flooding. In the middle valley, where the river was traditionally more mild-mannered than in the lower valley, similar problems began to develop in the twentieth century. Logging in northern New Mexico caused excessive runoff, leading to flooding and silting downstream. More and more land became unusable as the river moved and changed in response to environmental conditions.[13]

The lower valley was the first to be affected by Anglo settlement. Less populated than the upper valley, the southern riverbanks still offered opportunity for Anglo farmers who arrived in the 1880s and 1890s. Homesteading south of Las Cruces continued into the early twentieth century. Hispanics told those who came with the idea of developing

commercial agriculture that it was a waste of time because of the unpre-
dictability of the river. For example, they warned Royal Jackman against
it when he arrived in 1892. Nonetheless he hired Hispanics to clear his
172-acre homestead, planted 150 acres in crops, built an adobe house, and
bought twenty-five head of stock and some horses. When he lost everything in the flood of 1905, a local man told him, "Yacky, the more you
have, the more you lose." Such folk wisdom was born of the cruel experience of farming in the valley. Families with smaller farms patiently rebuilt
their farms and homes. Families with larger farms were impatient.[14]

Even before the flood of 1905, Anglos and some Hispanic farmers
had worked to get federal support to build a dam upstream and have the
Reclamation Service tame the river. After years of international and
domestic negotiation, construction of the dam began in 1911. During the
building of the dam, there was work for small farmers and homesteaders,
but once the dam was finished in 1916, it had to be paid for. The federal
government had farmers pledge their land as security for repayment of
the $7.2 million needed for the project. The establishment of the Elephant
Butte Irrigation District allowed the government to tax the farmers to pay
for the dam. Within the next twenty years, the Hispanic farmers who
owned small farms gradually lost the best land.[15]

The dam tax simply accelerated a process that had already begun.
Losing land was not new for Hispanics. From the time Anglo merchants
had first arrived, Hispanics had run up bills for consumer items they
needed but could not pay for with cash. Perhaps they expected Anglos to
act as kin, extending the time to pay. But Anglos were less patient than
kinfolk. They took land when farmers could not pay cash and thereby
acquired large holdings.

The custom of dividing land among all children equally also weakened the hold of Hispanics on the land. Small plots could not be used to
produce crops requiring extensive acreage. Most of the land lost earlier
was grazing land, and many farmers managed to hold onto their river
land until the dam was built. The new dam now had to be paid for with
taxes on these small plots. Most subsistence farmers could not afford to

switch to the more expensive commercial agriculture because they lacked sufficient capital to level their fields, build drains to remove excess irrigation water, and buy fertilizer and equipment. Those who could not pay became delinquent and had to sell out.[16]

Anglo farmers were able to buy out Hispanics for two reasons: they had easier access to financing through Anglo-owned banks, and they could use this financing to switch from food crops to cotton production. (Cotton was a profitable commercial crop if the farmer could afford the necessary machinery and fertilizer.)

As Hispanic men and women lost their land, many of them became tenants, sharecroppers, and day laborers. Women who did not work in the fields found work on Anglo farms and ranches, cooking and cleaning. Before the dam was built in 1911, 70 percent of the farms were owned by Hispanics. By 1929, 60 percent of the owner-operators were Anglo, 80 percent of the tenants were Hispanic, and most farm labor was Hispanic. Over 75 percent of valley acreage was planted in cotton. The Great Depression of the 1930s brought the final change from tenancy to farm labor. Hugh Calkins, regional conservator, estimated in 1936 that of the approximately 50,000 rural people in the Mesilla Valley, one-third had a family income of under $300 a year, 70 percent under $600, and 10 percent over $1,000 a year. The federal government had paid $250,000 in relief to maintain the seasonal labor force necessary for picking cotton. As in the middle and upper valleys, these farm families used relief as the cash income that supplemented subsistence farming. World War II swept most of the younger family members off the farm into the army or urban wartime jobs.[17]

The middle Rio Grande underwent much the same transformation as the south but over a shorter period. The result was much greater opposition. Until 1934 Hispanic landowners used violent confrontations and political organization successfully to defer their taxes. Then these families rapidly lost their land as well. Officials arranged for the federal government to absorb costs for the middle Rio Grande Valley conservancy district and worked hard to help families commercialize with the Farm

Security Administration (FSA). Most FSA plans were scrapped soon after the war. Few of the many marketing cooperatives financed by the FSA were successful, and apparently few subsistence farm families made the transition to commercial farming. Instead, they migrated to urban areas where the war, and then the economic boom of the postwar period, provided a new safety valve for rural discontent. Farm families organized their labor by exporting it. Children used part of their wage earnings to subsidize remaining subsistence farms and to care for aging rural parents.[18]

Was there an alternative? Would helping women make the transition to small-scale commercial farms and providing off-farm labor for men have been a better alternative? Perhaps. But such an alternative was not considered by government officials, given the deep gender division of labor they endorsed. Only dramatically new social experiments carefully keyed to the experience of rural farm families might have succeeded. Moreover, because Anglo families were waiting for a chance to use these lands commercially, it seems unlikely that such an adaptation of the new pattern of gender division of labor on the farm would have received Anglo support.

In the north, where agricultural land was most marginal and Hispanic population most dense, the farm families held onto their land. There government officials, many of them Hispanic, were able to help families on small subsistence farms survive depression and drought and remain on the land.[19]

In the south, many middle-sized Anglo farms were able to survive as well. A fifty-acre cotton farm in the Mesilla Valley could support a family.[20] The government helped buy more time for these middle-sized farms, about another forty years. The next generation of Anglo farm families faces the same problems Hispanic families faced earlier. Whether they will be more successful in surviving on the land remains to be seen. Much may depend upon the imagination and resourcefulness with which farm families learn to control the internal and external boundaries of their labor.

Notes

1. Interviews with Clara Coleman and Mabel Luke Madison, in Dona Ana County Pioneers, WPA Files, New Mexico State Records Center and Archives (hereafter cited as NMSR); interview with Ellen Grugs Reeves, Working Lives of New Mexico Women Project, Rio Grande Collections, New Mexico State University (hereafter cited as WLNMWP, NMSU); Fran Leeper Buss, *La Partera: Story of a Midwife* (Ann Arbor: University of Michigan Press, 1980), 23, 25–26; Nan Elsasser, Lyle MacKenzie, and Yvonne Tixier y Vigil, *Las Mujeres: Conversations from a Hispanic Community* (Old Westbury, CT: Feminist Press, 1980), 62, 29. An overview of farm women is given in Joan Jensen, "New Mexico Farm Women, 1900–1940," in Robert Kern, ed., *Labor in New Mexico: Strikes, Unions and Social History since 1881* (Albuquerque: University of New Mexico Press, 1983), 61–81.

2. Jessica Pearson, "Note on Female Farmers," *Rural Sociology,* 44 (1979): 189–200. See also Seena B. Kohl, *Working Together: Women and Family in Southwestern Saskatchewan* (Toronto: Holt, Rinehart, 1976), 100.

3. Theodore E. Jones II, "Community Property—Power of Testamentary Disposition—Inequality Between Spouses," *Natural Resources Journal,* 1 (1967): 645–49; Robert Emmet Clark, "Management and Control of Community Property in New Mexico," *Tulane Law Journal,* 26 (1952): 324–43. See also Barnett v. Barnett, 9 N.M.205 (1897).

4. Joan M. Jensen, "Pioneers in Politics," *El Palacio,* 92, no. 1 (Summer/Fall 1986): 12–19. Ramon A. Gutierrez, *When Jesus Came, the Corn Mothers Went Away: Marriage, Sexuality and Power in New Mexico, 1500–1846* (Stanford: Stanford University Press, 1991), discusses the role of the Virgin Mary in the earlier period.

5. Oliva Harris, "Households and Their Boundaries," *History Workshop Journal,* 13 (1982): 143–52. On discrimination in health care and education see Cecilia S. Miranda, "Infant Mortality Rates in Dona Ana County, New Mexico, 1900–1945: A Political and Social Perspective," Master's Thesis, New Mexico State University, 1992 and Joan M. Jensen, "Women Teachers, Class, and Ethnicity: New Mexico, 1900–1950," *Southwest Economy and Society,* 4 (Winter 1978/79).

6. Kohl, *Working Together,* 89, briefly discusses the oldest-sibling case.

7.   There was more rigid gender segregation in clubs earlier. See Joan M. Jensen, "Canning Comes to New Mexico: Women and the Agricultural Extension Service, 1914–1919," *New Mexico Historical Review,* 57 (1982): 361–86.

8.   Annual Narrative Report of Hazel C. Usner, District Extension Agent, 1929, Union County, New Mexico College of Agriculture and Mechanic Arts, State College, Agricultural Extension Service, Annual Reports, New Mexico, National Archives, microcopy T876, reel 11 (hereafter cited as NMCAAES, Annual Reports). Annual Report of Ezra Grimes, Home Demonstration Agent, Dona Ana County, 1930, NMCAAES, Annual Reports, Microcopy T876, Reel 11. Mabel Luke Madison remembered their cook as famous for his sourdough biscuits, Dona Ana Pioneers, WPA Files, NMSRC. Lillian Beach Interview, WLNMWP, NMSU. For *matanzas,* see Ida Gutierrez in Elsasser, MacKenzie, and Tixier y Vigil, *Las Mujeres,* 66.

9.   Lillian Beach Interview, WLNMWP, NMSU; Clara Coleman Interview, Dona Ana Pioneers, WPA Files, NMSR.

10. Interview with Celestine R. Neale and Esther Meerschidt, WLNMWP, NMSU. See also Sarah Dentsch, *No Separate Refuge: Culture, Class, and Gender on an Anglo Hispanic Frontier in the American Southwest, 1880–1940* (New York: Oxford University Press, 1987).

11. Lorin W. Brown, *Hispano Folklife of New Mexico: The Lorin W. Brown Federal Writers' Project Manuscripts* (Albuquerque: University of New Mexico Press, 1978), 190–91; Elsasser, MacKenzie, and Tixier y Vigil, *Las Mujeres,* 37.

12. Jose Orlando Arrom, "Decision-Making and Managerial Strategies in Human Adaptation: The Case of the Roosevelt County Cattlemen" (Eastern New Mexico University: M.A. thesis, 1973), 29–30.

13. Frequent floods are discussed by Dona Ana Pioneers, WPA Files, NMSR, and in Paul A. Lester, "History of the Elephant Butte Irrigation District" (New Mexico State University: M.A. thesis, 1977), 21–31.

14. Interview with Royal Jackman, Dona Ana Pioneers, WPA Files, NMSR.

15. Lester, "History of the Elephant Butte Irrigation District," 93–99; and Ira G. Clark, "The Elephant Butte Controversy: A Chapter in the Emergence of Federal Water Law," *Journal of American History,* 61 (1975), 1006–33.

16. See especially interviews with Nemecio Provincio and Sarah Bell Adams, Dona Ana Pioneers, WPA Files, NMSR.

17.   Hugh G. Calkins, "Reconnaissance Survey of Human Dependency on Resources in the Rio Grande Watershed" (mimeographed, USDA, Soil Conservation Service, Region Eight, Regional Bulletin No. 33, Conservation Series, no. 6, December 1936), 104–127; Lester, "History of the Elephant Butte Irrigation District," 95–103.

18.   Lester, "History of the Elephant Butte Irrigation District," 36–71, quote on 67; Bernalillo County, County Agent, Annual Report, 1925, 1930, and Valencia County Agent, Annual Report, 1929, 1930, NMCAAES, Annual Reports, reels 7, 12; M. Brian McDonald, John Tysseling, Michael Browde, and Lee Brown, *Case Studies in the Development of New Mexico Water Resources Institutions: The Middle Rio Grande Conservancy District and Urban Water Pricing* (New Mexico Water Resources Research Institute, Technical Completion Report, Project No. 1345640, 1981), 1–27. Papers of cooperatives and loans are in the Farm Security Records, National Archives, Record Group 96.

19.   Joan M. Jensen, " 'I've Worked, I'm Not Afraid of Work': Farm Women in New Mexico, 1920–1940," in Joan M. Jensen and Darlis A. Miller, *New Mexico Women: Intercultural Perspectives* (Albuquerque: University of New Mexico Press, 1986). For a more detailed study of these northern New Mexico farming communities see Sarah Deutsch, *No Separate Refuge: Culture, Class, and Gender on an Anglo-Hispanic Frontier in the American Southwest, 1880–1940* (New York: Oxford University Press, 1987); Sandra Schackel, *Social Housekeepers: Women Shaping Public Policy in New Mexico, 1920–1940* (Albuquerque: University of New Mexico Press, 1992), pp. 111–40; and Suzanne Forrest, *The Preservation of the Village: New Mexico's Hispanics and the New Deal* (Albuquerque: University of New Mexico, 1989).

20.   Interviews with Nina Griffin and Lucille Tatreault, WLNMWP, NMSU.

TWO

GROUNDWATER IN TWENTIETH-CENTURY NEW MEXICO

IRA G. CLARK

WHOLESALE exploitation of subterranean sources is the most significant water development of the century, and New Mexico is the focal point. A combination of factors turned the attention of water users toward this supply at this particular time and place. Precipitation was rarely adequate for normal demands, and practically all the surface supply had been appropriated. Owners of fertile lands could not put them into production because no water was available. Under these circumstances shallow groundwater suggested a tantalizing solution, but extensive use had to await technological advances needed to make it both possible and economically profitable.

Ownership of these waters had been a subject of considerable discussion from the distant past. At the turn of the century, the states were fairly evenly divided between two groundwater rules both of which were formulated at a time when few sound data were available. Under the English rule, jurists recognized the existence of underground streams and diffused percolating waters. Whether surface or subterranean, streams came under the same law while diffused percolating waters were considered part of the soil and, as such, belonged without restriction to the overlying proprietor. Waters were presumed to be percolating until proved otherwise. The American rule limited the right of the owner of overlying land to the reasonable needs of the tract, with due regard for the rights of other proprietors whose lands lay over the aquifer. New Mexico had never unequivocally committed itself to one over the other.

As hydrologists became more knowledgeable, they worked to change the law so that it would reflect more accurately newly acquired information on the nature of groundwater. They ran into opposition from proprietors who were fearful of losing control of the waters under their lands. By 1912 Samuel C. Wiel and Clesson S. Kinney, the preeminent authorities of the day, commented on the utter confusion of the law governing this potentially major source. Artesian flows were an exception. They were those whose sources were higher than the point at which they reached the surface and therefore emerged of their own volition. Legislators were well aware of the extraordinary value of this water resource and the certainty of its exhaustion if not regulated. The Roswell Artesian Basin was so richly endowed that it attracted nationwide attention and in the late 1890s territorial lawmakers enacted statutes for its protection. Even so, the decline in its flow became so pronounced by 1917 that the Federal Land Bank at Wichita refused to make loans in that area.

From early in the century, prospective irrigators in three areas did display interest in utilizing shallow groundwater. Residents of the Portales Valley bordering Texas turned to pumping because there was no surface supply. Their valiant efforts lasting several years proved fruitless because costs far outran returns. The outlook was much brighter in the vicinity of Deming where the underflow of the Rio Mimbres could be tapped at much less expense. A limited, but nonetheless permanent, development did take place there. Dry-land bean growers in the centrally located Estancia Valley got no further than drilling a few test wells. Pumping water for irrigation was therefore all but nonexistent prior to World War I.[1]

During the early 1920s, these same areas enjoyed a modest revival of interest in pumping but again acute water shortages in the Roswell Artesian Basin dictated the course of events. The shortage became so critical that prominent Roswell residents prodded the legislature into appropriating funds for a thorough study of their basin. Alfred G. Fiedler of the U.S. Geological Survey was the primary architect of the resulting plan. Long before statehood, territorial courts had committed New Mexico to the appropriation doctrine. Under this doctrine a prior appropriator acquired a right against all subsequent applicants to the use of that quantity of water which he had put to beneficial use so long as he continued that use. In New Mexico this was an administrative procedure. The prospective appropriator made application to the state engineer, who first had to determine if water was available. If so, the state engineer could approve it with the priority date relating back to the date of the application. Fiedler and his Roswell associates became convinced that nothing short of applying the appropriation doctrine would furnish adequate protection against wanton expenditure of this precious resource. They therefore ingeniously represented their proposed measure as simply putting existing law into statutory form. Designed specifically for Roswell artesian waters, it was nonetheless written in broad enough terms to apply in other areas and to other forms of groundwater which might require protection. A legislative majority bought this reasoning in 1927 as did the state supreme court which upheld the soundness of the principle while overturning the statute on other grounds. It was reenacted in acceptable form in 1931. The key section reads: "The waters of underground streams, channels, artesian basins, reservoirs, or lakes, having reasonably ascertainable boundaries, are hereby declared to be public waters and to belong to the public and to be subject to appropriation for beneficial use." This statute followed in every detail the act providing for the appropriation of surface waters and was the first effective legislation adopted by any state to protect groundwater. Quite possibly it is New Mexico's most significant contribution to western water law. It served as the model for the National Resources Planning Board's recommendations on the subject, and all prior-appropriation states have borrowed from it.[2]

Fiedler's foresight was amazing considering that in 1930 groundwater use was confined to areas of previous use and constituted a mere 15 percent of New Mexico's 527,000 irrigated acres. By the end of the decade, it had risen to only 140,000 acres. Besides the Roswell Artesian Basin, which initially encompassed a limited acreage, the only declared basins were the Mimbres Valley, Lea County, Hot Springs Artesian, and (arising out of a conflict with Arizona) the Virden Valley on the west side of the state. Each had to be administered with due regard to its own unique characteristics. Again it was the Roswell Artesian Basin that enjoyed the primary growth but from an extensive shallow water aquifer which had no connection with the artesian flow. When Fiedler suggested its use in 1934 there was such an enthusiastic response that within three years this aquifer had to be closed to further appropriation.

The termination of World War II was the watershed. Technologies were fully developed and more areas recognized the potential in exploiting this resource. The 320,000 acres using groundwater in 1950 increased in the following three years to 445,000 depending exclusively on groundwater (more than one-half of the total irrigated acreage) with an additional 131,000 supplementing the surface supply, a figure which has remained relatively constant.[3] The growth was statewide but particularly notable on the High Plains, and because of drought even spread to the Rio Grande Valley below Elephant Butte. These figures do not include industries and municipalities, both of which were almost wholly dependent on groundwater. Legislative awareness of one matter of deep concern was revealed by passage in 1949 of an act permitting only licensed drillers to sink wells in declared underground basins, thereby placing this invaluable resource in the hands of qualified and responsible developers. Their qualifications and equipment must first be approved by the state engineer, followed by payment of the license fee and the posting of bond. Such licenses were revocable if the grantee violated its terms.[4]

With no protection for subterranean waters outside declared underground basins, a continuing threat existed of surrounding states raiding New Mexico's groundwater resources; therefore, for purposes of that act alone, a law of 1953 declared *all* groundwater in New Mexico to belong to the public, and forbade its transportation for use outside the state from wells drilled either within its borders or immediately contiguous which would draw on New Mexico's resources. A slight relaxation occurred in 1959 when the exportation of a maximum of three acre-feet annually was permitted solely for exploring and drilling for oil and gas. The theory behind this legislation did raise a question of fundamental importance, namely: was the export ban a legitimate exercise of police power for the purpose of protecting from rapid exhaustion groundwater which, in an arid state, was a particularly vital asset, or was it interference in the movement of a commodity which under the interstate commerce clause of the constitution must be permitted to flow unrestricted through the normal channels of commerce.

This was the sole point at issue in the lengthy and acrimonious controversy between El Paso, Texas, and New Mexico beginning in September 1980 over whether the city had the right to tap the neighboring state's groundwater in order to avert a predicted acute water shortage by 1995. On learning of El Paso's intent to submit requests to drill 326 wells in New Mexico for pumping 296,000 acre-feet of water annually, New Mexico State Engineer S. E. Reynolds immediately brought the waters in question under his jurisdiction by declaring the as yet undeclared Lower Rio Grande Underground Basin and the Hueco Bolson. He then denied the applications. The folly of the proposal was self-evident because its proponents admitted that the tremendous overdraft in relation to re-charge would exhaust this source within a century, leaving El Paso in the same predicament as before. New Mexico's defense rested primarily on *Hudson County Water Co. v. Carver,* a 1908 decision upholding the right of a state to safeguard its basic natural resources without having to account to anyone for its actions. Certainly arid New Mexico's shielding of its limited groundwater resources represented a wholly defensible applica-tion of this principle. El Paso countered by asserting that this principle had been superseded by one ensuring that state law could not interfere with the transportation of water in interstate commerce, citing *City of Altus* v. *Carr* (1966) and later *Sporhase* v. *Nebraska* (1982). *Altus* was so ambiguous that it was impossible to determine the actual reasoning or holding of the court. In striking down a Nebraska statute prohibiting the exportation of groundwater, the court in *Sporhase* declared water to be an article of commerce, but with the admonition that the justices "reluctant to condemn as unreasonable measures taken by a state to conserve and preserve for its own citizens this vital resource in times of severe shortage" and conceded that a "demonstrably arid state conceivably might be able to marshal evidence to establish a close means-end relationship between even a total ban on the exportation of water and a purpose to conserve and preserve water."[5]

El Paso filed its suit to have the statute declared unconstitutional in the Federal District Court for New Mexico presided over by Judge Howard O. Bratton. Adhering closely to El Paso's reasoning and utilizing the narrowest of interpretations, he ruled that a state could exclude from interstate commerce only the quantity of water necessary for human survival; furthermore, the best use of New Mexico's underground water was in promoting El Paso's growth as the major economic center in the area. Viewed realistically, the decision appeared to encourage rapid exhaustion of groundwater regardless of long-term consequences, and to promote the unrestrained growth of a city having no reasonable expectation of ever having sufficient water to attempt large-scale industrial growth. This was destined to be El Paso's only triumph.

New Mexico's response was dual in nature: appeal of the decision while redrafting the circumstances under which it would continue to operate. These included safeguarding existing water rights and controlling activities contrary to water conservation or detrimental to the public welfare. El Paso filed a motion to have the amended statute declared unconstitutional as differing only superficially from its predecessor, but the judge refused to do so during the course of the appeal.

The lamentations of disappointed New Mexicans were short-lived because early in 1983 the 10th Circuit Court of Appeals vacated the judgment and directed a rehearing based on the amended statute. Judge Bratton recognized the criteria written into it as legitimate so long as the state engineer treated applications for water rights even-handedly and with no preferential treatment of the state's residents. Meanwhile, Las

Cruces and Alamogordo, the three affected counties, New Mexico State University, Elephant Butte Irrigation District, the State Land Office, and hundreds of individuals expressed opposition to the El Paso applications because of their obviously adverse impact on long-range water rights.

The state engineer announced late in 1984 that hearings on the Hueco Bolson applications would be commenced within the year and those for the more controversial Lower Rio Grande Underground Basin three years later. Shortly thereafter El Paso chose to challenge in state district court a regulation drafted by the state engineer much earlier which limited water planning to a maximum of 40 years. The state engineer reasoned that attempts to project water needs and shortage beyond that period became too speculative. The city ignored this regulation in making applications to run well over 100 years. The judge concluded that he lacked jurisdiction over such administrative regulations and held that El Paso must abide by them. Hearings on the Hueco Bolson then continued intermittently over nine months after which the state engineer deliberated for another three months before rejecting both the Hueco Bolson and the upcoming Lower Rio Grande Underground Basin applications at the same time. There was, he said, no evidence that El Paso would suffer a water shortage during the next 40 years. El Paso appealed this decision in both the state district court for Dona Ana County and Federal District Court for New Mexico. The U.S. Court rejected the federal action as a duplication of effort. The state action was moved to Deming where eventually the presiding judge dismissed the appeal on a technicality. The city then appealed to the New Mexico Court of Appeals to address the substantive issue.

The Court of Appeals was in the process of initiating the wholly novel concept of mandating settlement conferences to clear its crowded docket, with George Perez, a retired state judge, selected as the mediator for this controversy. Despite considerable general skepticism, Perez succeeded. The key terms were that both sides would terminate litigation, El Paso would withdraw all requests for New Mexico's groundwater, New Mexico would not challenge El Paso's right to drill wells immediately adjacent to their common boundary, and the two parties would form a joint regional commission to study available options for solving the area's water problems. After eleven years and legal costs estimated at between $11 million to $14 million, this bitter struggle terminated, leaving intact arid New Mexico's claim that its groundwater was a unique natural resource which the state had a right to protect.[6]

The circumstances under which New Mexico's groundwater regulations came into being dictated that they remain distinct from those governing surface waters. Even though the two sets of rules parallel very closely and all water users are drawing on the same source, certain differences have to be recognized. That is because the two types of water rights holders are appropriating water at two different stages of the hydrologic cycle. The holder of a surface right does nothing more than transport water from his point of diversion to the place of use; the groundwater appropriator, on the other hand, has to expend a very considerable amount of money and effort before his water becomes available for use. Such activities do present many more possibilities of impairment of the rights of others and must therefore be accomplished within a framework of laws to prevent this from happening. The one inescapable conclusion is that the two types of rights cannot be administered separately since each has a direct bearing on the other.

The bulk of the cases which collectively spell out present-day groundwater law have arisen from applications requesting a change in the method or point of diversion. In the absence of statutes the owner of a water right may change his point of diversion as long as by so doing he does no injury to others. New Mexico's requirement that his actions must first be approved by the state engineer was therefore a limitation on a preexisting right rather than the source of that right. The precedent-setting cases have been those in which the purpose for making the request for a change of diversion from surface to underground water or the reverse was to restore a full original water right which had eroded due to the activities of subsequent appropriators. This was an accurate description of the situation in which W. H. Templeton found himself when he requested a change in the place and method of diversion from his surface right to waters of the Rio Felix tributary of the Pecos to a ground water right by drilling a well in the Valley Fill. The Valley Fill was not only the primary source of water for Rio Felix but also the natural reservoir for the Roswell Shallow Water Basin, which the state engineer had closed in 1937 as fully appropriated. Templeton received sufficient water to take care of this surface right until 1952 when excessive pumping in the Valley Fill reduced the flow of the Rio Felix considerably below that right. The State Engineer rejected the application as a new appropriation in a closed basin. Templeton appealed and the court, in overriding this ruling, held that the holder of a surface right could trace back to their sources all waters which contributed to that stream's flow above his point of diversion. The one limitation was that he could not impair rights derived from an appropriations which were senior to his.[7] In other words, all waters within a basin deriving from a single source were one and the same and should be treated as such whether above or below the ground.

New Mexicans were so far removed from the reasons for passage of the Federal Water Pollution Control Act (FWPCA) and its various amendments that they were never really attuned to its primary end of cleaning up contaminated rivers. Their waters were of relatively high quality because there were few municipalities and industries to dump refuse into running streams in such quantity as to render them useless for other purposes. Nor did the massive amendment of 1972 address New Mexico's problems. It was directed towards improving the quality of the waters in states with sizable stream flows capable of furnishing recreational facilities as well as supplying domestic needs, with the ultimate goal of making those waters swimmable and drinkable. The trickles of water which were characteristic of New Mexico's streams were seldom of sufficient depth to be even wadeable, and the flow normally was destined to be diverted from the streambed to be put to beneficial use elsewhere. The state's attempts to salvage something from laws which obviously did not fit its problems frequently led to interesting results.

The FWPCA amendment of 1972 complicated rather than resolved the problems of appropriation doctrine states. It stamped with finality unquestioned nationalization of the pollution control program. The federal government assumed authority for drafting regulations of uniform nationwide application, and for their enforcement with little room for exceptions. The problem of the states which dictated the terms was excessive pollution of their rivers, and they were wholly oblivious to the existence of groundwater in their zeal to cleanse these streams. These states had also followed a long-time policy of disposing of contaminants by burying them without reflecting on the consequences. By now it was quite evident that New Mexico's future was tied to reliance on the underground waters to supplement its scant surface supply; nonetheless, the state was mandated to concentrate its energies toward improving the quality of waters already acceptable for domestic purposes instead of being permitted to devote its efforts to protecting the source upon which its future depended. Failure to successfully safeguard subsurface waters from pollution would most certainly result in costly cleanup operations with the potential for inducing irreversible damage.

Despite these barriers the arid states have made progress in protecting their all-important subterranean waters. One essential step was to identify the major sources of groundwater contamination. The Environmental Improvement Division (EID) in the Department of Health and Environment is the primary agency charged with this responsibility. It has summarized these sources in considerable detail under eight headings: household septic tanks or cesspools; urban runoff; agricultural chemicals such as pesticides; brine from oil and gas production; contaminants incidental to the marketing of petroleum products, particularly underground storage tanks susceptible to leakage; mining and mine tailings; nitrates from sewage plants, dairies, and similar activities; solvents used in manufacturing process; accidental discharges, spills, and leaks; and public landfills. Other water-quality agencies were simultaneously engaging in a multi-pronged offensive to point out the dependence of the state's economy on its underground water resources, repeat at every opportunity the need for appropriate protection of the quality of that resource, promulgate rules and regulations to carry out such a program, and enforce the various orders when necessary.[8]

Declining groundwater levels in some parts of New Mexico are symptomatic of serious problems in the future. The aquifers identified with the Rio Grande tend to recharge rather quickly and present no serious problems at this time; elsewhere, as a rule, the rate of withdrawal is far in excess of the recharge. This is especially true of the southeast quadrant which is the largest consumer for irrigation purposes since it has only a limited quantity of surface water. Even along the Pecos, which is essentially a spring-fed river, there have been declines of as much as 120 feet due to intensive drawing on the underground supply for use in irrigation. Where there have been relatively high concentrations of agricultural activity in this quadrant, declining levels generally averaged 20 to 60 feet in the past twenty-five to thirty years, but it has run much higher in some localities.[9]

Water is unquestionably the major restrictive factor on New Mexico's economic well-being, and the state's future prosperity will depend on the degree of acuity demonstrated in shaping the direction for utilizing this meager resource. This is particularly applicable to underground sources, those which, in Mexico's economic well-being, and the state's future prosperity will depend how well it shapes the direction for using this meager resource. This statement is particularly applicable to underground sources—those which, in the absence of human intervention, remain reasonably durable. Success will depend on whether New Mexicans can be persuaded to recognize the problem and change some of their attitudes.

The problem stems from withdrawals above the rate of recharge, a condition that if continued will exhaust the entire supply within a comparatively short time. If that happens, New Mexico will be without an element necessary for survival.

New Mexico's historic policy has been one of profligate disposition of its water resources. The combined water rights of all appropriators of surface and underground waters should never grossly exceed the supply

available. This is far from the case in New Mexico. Waters drawing on a
common source have been fully appropriated at both levels. On the Pecos,
for example, the groundwaters which were distributed so generously in
the Roswell-Artesia area had earlier been appropriated downstream as
surface waters by the Carlsbad Irrigation District. This led to intrastate
conflict and depleted the river's flow, thus violating the conditions of the
Pecos River Compact with Texas. This error in judgment proved to be
very costly to New Mexicans both monetarily and in the loss of water
rights to that state.[11]

An answer to New Mexico's predicament must involve, among other
things, voluntary action on the part of the users of underground waters by
a reduction in their pumping and a corresponding limitation on their
operations. This can be accomplished only through mutual agreement,
cooperative planning, and belt tightening on the part of all. Whether this
solution is feasible remains to be seen. The alternative is continuation of
prevailing practices that ensure disaster.

NOTES

1.   Donald E. Green, *Land of the Underground Rain* (Austin: University of
Texas Press, 1973), is a standard account of the technological advances opened the
way for underground water use as well as of the early attempts at pumping water
for irrigation in New Mexico.

2.   Robert G. Dunbar's two articles, "Pioneering Groundwater Legislation
in the United States: Mortgages, Land Banks and Institution-Building in New
Mexico," *Pacific Historical Review,* 47 (1978): 565–84, and "The Adoption of
Groundwater Control Institutions in the Arid West," *Agricultural History* 51
(1977): 662–80, provide detailed accounts of this legislation and its impact.

3.   New Mexico Land Resources Assn., Land Resources of New Mexico
(n.p, n.d), 68; WQCC, *Water Quality and Water Pollution Control in New Mexico,
1990,* 29, 53.

4.   *Laws of 1949,* Ch. 178, 444–47.

5.   *City of Altus v. Carr,* 265 F. Supp., 828 (1966); *Sporhase v. Nebraska,* 458
U.S. 941 (1982) at 956, 958.

6.   Based on running accounts in the *El Paso Times* (New Mexico edition), *Las Cruces Sun-News,* and *Las Cruces Bulletin* through the course of the controversy.

7.   *Templeton v. Pecos Valley Artesian Conservancy Dist.,* 65 *N.M.* 59 (1958).

8.   *Laws of 1967,* Ch. 190, 1109–19; *Laws of 1970,* Ch. 64, 213–21; *Laws of 1971,* Ch. 277, 1048–93.

9.   NMEID, "Draft New Mexico Groundwater Protection Strategy, April 1988," 19, 30–32, 34, 36–37, and figures 11–2, 11–3, and 11–7. See also the following WQCC reports: *Water Quality in New Mexico, May, 1975; New Mexico Statewide Management Plan* (1978); *5 Year Strategy for Water Quality Management, 1982–87* (1982); *Water Quality and Water Pollution Control in New Mexico* (for years 1982, 1984, 1986, 1988, 1990).

10.   NMEID, "Draft New Mexico Ground Water Protection Strategy, April, 1988," 11–15, and figure 1–7.

THREE

COPPER MINING IN GRANT COUNTY, 1900–1945

Christopher J. Huggard

BY 1900 the Industrial Revolution was well under way, and copper was one of its main components. Electricity was the preferred source of energy, especially in the rapidly growing urban areas of the United States and Europe. Copper wire conducted energy for urban Americans from New York to San Francisco. As the twentieth century unfolded, the need for copper grew steadily. Armament industries during the first and second world wars demanded large tonnages of copper. In the 1920s the construction industry, stimulated by the population boom, required still more copper. The red metal was also needed to produce domestic luxuries, such as automobiles and household appliances. Rural electrification projects of the 1930s helped to sustain the copper mining industry even during the Great Depression.

For Grant County, New Mexico (see fig. 1), this need for electricity and other modern conveniences assured the steady development of the copper mining industry during the twentieth century. In 1909 copper mining in Grant County achieved regional and even national recognition in the mining world, when New York capitalists applied the open-cut (or open-pit) mining technique to the vast copper deposits of the Santa Rita Basin. Since the beginning of mill production in 1912, corporate management of this mineral resource has resulted in a sustained, though sometimes depressed, industry that continues even today.

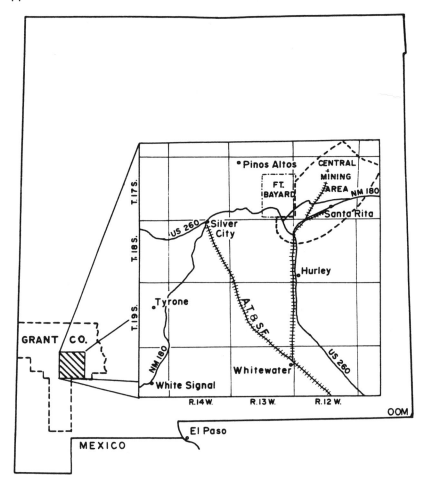

Fig. 1. Central mining area, Grant County, N.M., in 1941. From Eugene C. Anderson,
The Metal Resources of New Mexico and Their Economic Features Through 1954
(Socorro, N.M.: State Bureau of Mines and Mineral Resources, 1957), 49.

The Santa Rita deposits of Grant County have the distinction of being the first copper mines in the continental United States, attracting the Spanish as early as 1800. In 1804 Francisco Manuel Elguea won the Santa Rita del Cobre land grant and a contract to supply the Mexican government with copper for coinage. After Elguea's death in 1809, his heirs leased the mines to various entrepreneurs, including James "Ohio" Pattie in the 1820s. Pattie and later entrepreneurs struggled to mine in the Apache-dominated region from the 1810s to the 1870s. In 1873, Matthew D. Hayes, a Colorado investor, bought the grant from Elguea's heirs. Little was done with the mines until 1880, when J. P. Whitney acquired the mines from Hayes. Whitney organized the Santa Rita Mining Company, which became the dominant copper producer in the district until the Chino Copper Company arrived on the scene in 1909.[1]

After the depression of the 1890s, when the heyday of silver mining had come to an end in Grant County, mining companies were cautious in their plans to mine copper. Rather than taking risks in developing mines and incurring the mining costs themselves, owners leased their claims to others. These lessees paid 25 to 30 percent of profits as royalties to the mine owners. For example, the Santa Rita Mining Company, which by 1899 was owned by George Hearst and the Rockefellers, leased its mines to various companies until it sold out to the Chino Copper Company in 1909. Among the companies that leased Santa Rita's mines were the Hermosa Copper Company (a subsidiary of General Electric) and the Copper Queen Consolidated Copper Company (owned by the Phelps Dodge Company).[2] In the Burro Mountain District, the Burro Mountain Copper Company, the Chemung Copper Company, and the Copper Gulf Development Company (all newcomers to the area by 1902) produced from their own mines, although with limited production and inefficient technology.[3]

THE EARLY TWENTIETH CENTURY

In 1903 there were three mills in the county that concentrated copper ores: the 100-ton mill of the Santa Rita Mining Company, the 250-ton mill of the Burro Mountain Copper Company at Leopold, and the 400-ton mill of the Comanche Mining and Smelting Company at Silver City. The concentrates (the product from the milling of ores) were sent to be smelted at the Silver City Reduction Works until it burned down in 1902; the Comanche Company ran another smelter on the site until 1907. After 1907 the Santa Rita ores were reduced at the American Smelting & Refining Company (ASARCO) smelter in El Paso, Tesas, and the Burro Mountain ores went to the Copper Queen smelter in Douglas, Arizona. The blister, or 95.5 percent copper, was sent to refineries in the Connecticut Valley where impurities were burned off through electrolysis.[4]

At this stage in its development, the mining industry had hardly tapped the vast wealth of copper in Grant County. During the first decade of the century, in fact, copper production steadily declined in the county. At nearly 10 million pounds when copper reached 20 cents in 1901, production dropped to about 4 million pounds when copper fell to 12 cents in 1911. Increases in freighting and mining costs and the gradual reduction in the grade of copper ores hampered successful operations. In contrast, companies in neighboring southeastern Arizona combined to produce hundreds of millions of pounds of copper annually during this same period.[5]

The year 1912 marked an important turning point in the history of copper mining in Grant County. The price of copper jumped from 12 to 16 cents a pound in that year, and the Chino Copper Company began production at its mill in Hurley. Both of these events portended a dramatic increase in copper production from a twelve-year low of 4 million pounds in 1911 to nearly 34 million pounds in 1912. From then until 1945, the Chino Mine alone produced 90 percent or more of New Mexico's copper.[6]

John M. Sully, an MIT-educated mining engineer, realized the great potential of the vast low-grade copper deposits underlying the Santa Rita Basin. After three years of work, Sully was able to convince the New York investment firm of Hayden, Stone & Company to underwrite the venture in June 1909. The firm appointed Daniel C. Jackling as chairman of the board of directors for the newly created enterprise, the Chino Copper Company. The investors organized Chino with 750,000 shares at $5 each, giving the new company $3.5 million to begin development.[7]

After three years of developing the open pit, the Chino Company began producing concentrates at its mill in Hurley. In the first year the company produced 28 million pounds of copper. But that was just the beginning. From 1913 to 1920, Chino produced an average of 61 million pounds of copper a year, with a peak of 83 million pounds in 1917. The new company began operations at an opportune time: copper averaged 28 cents a pound in that same year.[8]

These same favorable market conditions enticed the Burro Mountain Copper Company to begin production at its operations in the county. Having ceased production since the economic downturn of 1907, the Burro Mountain Company had been developing its underground mines, mapping out the richest veins. It tested some of those ores to find the most efficient method of milling. Foreseeing a prosperous future, the home company, Phelps Dodge, decided to build a modernized company town at Tyrone. The company hired the famous New York architect E. G. Goodhue to plan and construct the town in southwestern style. Here the laborers lived and worked in a town that had shops and even a hospital. With town, mine, and mill in place and working, copper production climbed from just under 1.5 million pounds in 1915 to over 15 million pounds in 1918.[9]

The wartime economy also attracted smaller-scale investors into the county's mining industry. New companies emerged both in the Central (Santa Rita and Hanover, see fig. 2) and Burro Mountain districts to try their hands at making sustainable profits in copper mining. The exhilaration of 38-cent copper for a brief time in early 1916 resulted in rapid development. The federal government fixed the price at 23.5 cents a pound during World War I, but that was high enough to guarantee profits. Moreover the price continued to rise despite government attempts to control it. The need for tanks, planes, trucks, bullets, cannon, and communications equipment during the war required massive quantities

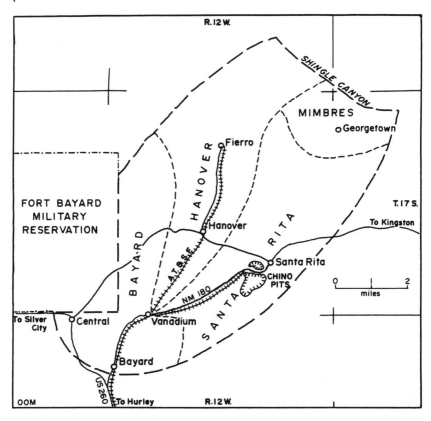

Fig. 2. Map of central mining area, Grant County, N.M., 1941. From Eugene C. Anderson,
The Metal Resources of New Mexico and Their Economic Features Through 1954
(Socorro, N.M.: State Bureau of Mines and Mineral Resources, 1957), 50.

of copper, making it strategically important. And it was America's duty (the copper companies and the government believed) to aid the Allies with supplies of copper and other strategic metal such as uranium.

But mining booms are often followed by busts. The war had elevated copper mining in Grant county to its greatest production levels ever. Yet when conditions settled down after the war, the copper industry throughout the country found itself in a precarious position. From 1919 to 1923, demand plummeted to less than one-third the wartime level. Surpluses that had been stockpiled in the United States to support both domestic and foreign needs had no market, resulting in a glut. The price of copper dropped from 24 cents in 1918 to 13 cents one year later. In addition, the wartime economy had inflated wages and mining and freighting costs to more than double the 1915 levels. Consequently, the county's copper production dipped from approximately 100 million pounds in 1918 to approximately 50 million pounds in 1919 and 1920. The final blow came in 1921 when production fell below 14 million pounds, the lowest amount since the Chino Copper Company had begun producing in 1912. Chino, in fact, closed down from April 1921 to April 1922. Phelps Dodge shut down Tyrone as well.[11]

By the end of 1923, the demand for copper was again soaring, but its price was not. As a consequence, market conditions favored companies with low operating costs and access to capital for investing in more efficient technology. Larger companies that had accumulated huge cash reserves during World War I were able to invest in research to improve their operations. The Chino Copper Company was Grant County's version of large-scale mining. This burgeoning corporation used its wartime profits to improve the efficiency of its operations. It lowered mining and milling costs in order to thrive during the 1920s despite the relatively low price of copper. Still more capital was available to Chino when in 1923 it was merged with the Ray Consolidated Copper Company of Arizona. This operation was in turn bought by the Nevada Consolidated Copper Company in 1926. Smaller producers were forced out of business because they depended on more costly technology and had limited capital.

During the second half of the 1920s, the accelerated expansion of electric power to homes and industries throughout the United States (which had grown in population by 17 million during the decade) created an unprecedented demand for copper. Electricity was both cheaper and cleaner than fuels such as coal. In addition, copper was one of the main ingredients in the mass production of household appliances and automobiles. The Ford Motor Company, for example, added five more pounds of copper to its new Model A in the 1920s. Grant County's copper production steadily rose with this demand, from 61 million pounds in 1923 to nearly 100 million pounds in 1929.[12]

The unprecedented economic growth of the 1920s, however, came to an abrupt end when the stock market crashed in October 1929, sending the nation into the Great Depression. Not surprisingly, the copper industry floundered along with the rest of the economy. By early 1931 the Chino Division of Nevada Consolidated, which had been producing over 95 percent of the state's copper, curtailed its operations to 30 percent of full production capacity. When the price of copper dropped to 6.5 cents a pound in 1932, production fell to 26 million pounds. In that same year, the Kennecott Copper Corporation bought the Nevada Consolidated's property and in October 1934 decided to close the Chino Division. The division did not reopen until January 1937. The county's production plummeted to 4.5 million pounds in 1935, with a slight rise to 6 million pounds in 1936.[13]

Although the copper market picked up in 1937, depressed conditions reemerged in 1938. Yet there was reason for optimism in the Grant County industry. In 1937 the Kennecott Copper Corporation, despite curtailing production, decided to construct a $3.5 million smelter at Hurley, next to the Chino Division mill. In part, Chino was benefiting from the great size of the Kennecott Corporation, which produced its own copper in Utah, Nevada, Arizona, and New Mexico while manufacturing the copper at the Chase Brass & Copper Company factories in Connecticut and Ohio. On the other hand, the rearmament of Europe (especially of Germany) and the rumors that there would be another war by late 1938 elevated the demand for copper.[14] Those rumors materialized when Germany attacked Poland in 1939, beginning World War II.

THE WORLD WAR II YEARS

Although the United States did not enter the war until 7 December 1941, the country began industrial mobilization in 1940. Copper was declared a strategic metal as it had been during World War I because most of the basic arms contained copper and brass (a copper and zinc alloy). The armed services ordered warships, tanks, fighter planes, and other military vehicles whose electrical systems depended on copper to operate properly and efficiently.

Having been unsuccessful in controlling inflation during World War I, the federal government in World War II took immediate steps to stabilize the economy. In the copper mining industry, two agencies played major roles during the war. The Office of Price Administration (OPA) set the price of many important commodities, including such metals as copper, iron, and zinc. The Metals Reserve Company (MRC) purchased the copper. The OPA established the price of copper at 12 cents in August 1941, and this price lasted through 1946. The MRC paid 5 cents more for every pound of copper in excess of the amount for which it contracted.[15]

By October 1940 Chino began operating on a twenty-four-hour basis, seven days a week, a schedule that continued throughout the war. The War Manpower Commission declared the Chino operations a "vital manpower area" to encourage production despite the labor shortage caused by the draft. At the same time idle and new mines contributed to Grant County's production. The Burro Mountain Copper Company, which had ceased production by the late 1920s, reopened and produced over 15 million pounds of copper during the war. As a result of the increase, Grant County averaged approximately 142 million pounds of copper annually from 1940 to 1945, peaking with an all-time high of over 160 million pounds in 1942.[16]

EMPLOYMENT AT CHINO, 1912–1945

The gradual increase in copper production in Grant County from 1912 to 1945 was largely due to the efforts of Chino's workers. From the outset of operations in 1909, the Chino Copper Company was one of the largest employers in New Mexico. By 1914 the company had hired 1,500 laborers to work at the mine at Santa Rita and in the mill at Hurley. Approximately 50 percent of the employees were Mexican and Mexican American and the other half Anglo American; generations of Bacas, Gonzales's, Humbles, and Dannelleys worked together at the Chino Mine.

During periods of curtailed production (30 percent to 50 percent below capacity), the company employed about half the maximum number of workers. During the shutdowns of 1921–22 and 1934–37, only those workers needed to maintain the grounds and equipment remained. Before 1950, the highest number of employees was 2,029 (in 1941 during the war-mobilization period and before the draft).[17]

Wages fluctuated with the price of copper: the higher the price of copper the higher the wages. Hence, wages rose during the late 1920s and the world wars and declined in the post World War I and Depression years. As was common throughout the mining industry of the Southwest, Mexican Americans and Mexicans received the lower paying unskilled jobs. Anglos were generally employed in the higher paying skilled and management positions.

A paternalistic system dominated employer-employee relations. Chino built company housing, ran a company store, and provided a company hospital with company doctors at Hurley and Santa Rita. Company police also ran the "bad men" and union sympathizers out of town. In addition, Hurley was segregated, the Anglos residing on the south side of the railroad tracks, the Hispanics on the north. "One pay scale applied to Anglos," noted longtime employee Barney Himes, "[and] a lesser one to Spanish-Americans." Furthermore, Kennecott virtually barred women from employment, hiring only two clerical workers before 1944; however, women were hired as truck drivers and general laborers at the pits due to the labor shortage during World War II.[18]

During both wars, Chino's management was forced to raise wages to keep workers from leaving their jobs. The military draft had siphoned off workers from industries throughout the country, opening positions that traditionally paid better than mining. Mine employees at Chino and other companies, therefore, expected and received pay increases.[19]

Wages declined after World War I but rose during and after World War II, due in large part to New Deal legislation, namely, section 7-A of the National Industrial Recovery Act of 1933. This section of the act gave workers the right to negotiate their labor contracts through collective bargaining and the right to strike. At Chino, these powers were limited prior to World War II because of company interference.

When Kennecott closed down the Chino Division from 1934 to 1937, the threat of strike loomed large in the decision to cease operations. In protest, the recently organized Union 63 of the International Union of Mine, Mill, and Smelter Workers charged the company with "interference, restraint, and coercion" when the employees voted down the union which was attempting to improve bargaining powers and mutual aid for the workers in 1935. Both the regional and national boards that reviewed the case decided in favor of the company later that year.[20]

This labor defeat was short-lived due to World War II. Because of the labor shortage, the federal government began strict enforcement of the New Deal labor laws. The first sign of improved conditions for workers came in June 1942 when the War Labor Board (WLB) forced Chino officials to sign a contract with the American Federation of Labor (A. F. of L.). The A. F. of L. represented the crafts or skilled laborers. First the WLB ordered a 50 cent raise, retroactive to January 16, which meant an extra $70 per worker in the next paycheck. The contract also awarded a week's vacation annually, three paid holidays at time and a half, and "straight seniority" based on length of employment. It created a neutral grievance committee to settle worker-management disputes, recognized A. F. of L. representation of the crafts, and called for an end to discrimination because of "race, creed, or color." A comparable contract was achieved for the unskilled workers of the Congress of Industrial Organizations.[21] Although changes had come slowly for workers, the World War II years dramatically changed employer-employee relations and led to greater equality, the hiring of women, and ultimately, to an end to corporate paternalism in the Grant County industry.

TECHNOLOGY AT CHINO, 1912–45

The operations at Chino were part of the technological revolution in copper mining that had begun at the Utah Mine in 1905. Instead of mining the higher grade (above 10 percent copper content) veins underground, companies chose to mine on the surface, extracting the low-grade ores (usually below 3 percent copper content) from open-pits. A large capital investment was required to pay for the costs of careful planning, efficient equipment, and technical know-how. Consolidation with other companies in the 1920s and early 1930s resulted in infusions of new capital. Thus, money was available to regularly upgrade the mining and milling, and after 1937 the smelting operations to maintain a profit margin.

At the mine the technological evolution of churn drills, shovels, and hauling equipment improved the efficiency and reduced the costs of mining from 1912 to 1945. The power source changed from steam to electricity, which meant that far greater tonnages of ore could be mined, while the cost per ton declined. For example, by 1927, electric shovels cost $55 less (an overall savings of 58 percent) to operate per eight-hour shift than those powered by steam. Shortly before World War II, the entire mine operation was converted to electric power. The savings were translated into higher wages and further technological experimentation in the postwar period.[22]

In the milling department, metallurgical innovations played the largest role in improvements during the study period. From 1912, when the first ores were milled, to 1915, the company used the gravity-separation method. This technique recovered about half the copper from the original ores, a disappointing return. Beginning in 1915, however, the company implemented froth flotation. Instead of separating copper from waste material through gravity, this technique separated the copper in chemical form and resulted in a higher recovery rate. By 1945 the mill had been converted to the flotation method. Chino's metallurgists had gradually improved the efficiency of the process, experimenting with different methods that resulted in nearly 90 percent of the copper being recovered from the original ores. In addition, regular improvements in machinery at the mill resulted in a steady production increase from 3,000 tons a day in 1912 to 8,000 tons in 1924, to 22,500 tons in 1945.[23]

The full processing of copper was not complete, however, until 1939 when the smelter began production at Hurley. Before that time the concentrates were shipped to ASARCO in El Paso for smelting. Now the mill was connected to the smelter, eliminating freighting costs, while also increasing the production capacity at the works; the smelter could produce each year as much as 500,000 tons of slab copper (95.5 percent pure). Implementation of the smelter resulted in an annual increase of 70 million pounds beginning in 1940. A year later the company further increased the efficiency of the smelter when it added fire-refining. This process produced pure copper that was sent directly to defense manufacturers in the West, saving the costs of shipping to the Atlantic Coast refineries.[24]

LAND USE AND NATURAL RESOURCES

To utilize new technology successfully required the acquisition and use of essential natural resources. Water, in particular, was needed for steam energy, wet milling, tailings transport, and other important operations. Similarly, the company had to acquire fuels such as coal and natural gas for powering the machinery of mining, milling, and smelting.

After the purchase of the mines and surrounding lands (which reached nearly 50,000 acres by 1945), the management of Chino had to secure a large supply of water. Originally, Chino's water came from four wells at Apache Tejo, the B Ranch, and Cameron and Whiskey creeks. As the need for water increased with the size of the operations, new wells were drilled in the vicinity to reach even deeper.

Overuse and the scarcity of water during droughts led to water conservation. As early as 1914 the Chino Copper Company was able to reuse about 83 percent (500 million gallons) of the water. By 1945, with the addition of Dorr thickeners (settling tanks that separated water and ores) at the mill, more than 92 percent of the water was reused. Still, 500 gallons a minute of new water was circulated into the system.[25]

Coal was another important resource at Chino. From the beginning the company depended on coal to fuel the steam boilers; after the transition to electricity, coal was needed to run the turbogenerators. To assure a ready coal supply after suffering shortages during national coal miners' strikes in 1913–14 and 1917, the Chino Company purchased the Victor-American Fuel Company in McKinley County. Chino officials sent Horace Moses to the newly named Gallup-American Coal Company (Gamerco) to break the union and set up an open shop, virtually securing the next twenty-five years' supply of coal, despite labor unrest.[26]

In part because of the labor problems at Gamerco, Chino officials began a transition to natural-gas fueling in the late 1930s. Natural gas was cheaper, cleaner burning, and easier to transport by pipe. Its major uses were to generate electricity and to heat the reverberatory furnaces at the smelter. The company made a permanent commitment to natural gas when in 1937 it contracted with the El Paso Gas Company for its supply. By 1945 the Gamerco operations had been sold, and natural gas had become the preferred fuel.[27]

CONCLUSION

By the end of World War II, the copper industry of Grant County had become integrated into the global economy. Copper, in fact, played an important role in the build-up of the military-industrial complex that maintained America's armed forces during the Cold War. Chino had elevated the county to industrial preeminence in the state, while faithfully serving as a component of the largest copper company in the world, the Kennecott Copper Corporation. The success of the industry, however, benefited more than just a powerful corporation. It paid wages to generations of workers, paid millions of dollars in taxes, and helped to sustain a thriving economy in Grant County. Indeed, copper was a major factor responsible for the affluent society of postwar America.

These rising demands for copper created favorable market and working conditions for the next three decades. With the profits, Kennecott regularly implemented new technology, such as the use of 170-ton diesel trucks to haul ores, and leaching to recover even lower grades of copper. The rest of Grant County also benefited, as auxiliary companies, such as Ingersoll-Rand and Caterpillar in Silver City, contracted to supply parts and equipment to the Chino operations. Phelps Dodge also began open-pit mining at its Burro Mountain properties at Tyrone in the late 1960s. Labor strikes in the late 1950s and mid-1960s helped to alleviate discrimination against Hispanics, who finally were promoted to managerial positions, even though the issue still worried labor.

The metals industry nearly collapsed in the early 1980s. Perhaps it was a sign of things to come because the copper industry is still threatened by the same problems: dwindling deposits, increasing foreign competition, emerging alternative technologies, and new costs for compliance to federal and state environmental regulations. Whether technological changes will be able to sustain the industry under these pressures remains an important question for the people of Grant County and the state of New Mexico as it enters the twenty first century.[28]

Notes

*I dedicate this chapter to O. Orland Maxfield, Emeritus Professor of Geography, University of Arkansas.

1. See Thomas A. Rickard, *The Chino Enterprise* (New York: Engineering and Mining Journal Press, 1923–24); and Billy D. Walker, "Copper Genesis: The

Early Years of Santa Rita Del Cobre," *New Mexico Historical Review* 54, no. 1 (January 1979): 5–20, for the early history of Santa Rita and the mining activities.

2.   Arthur B. Parsons, *The Porphyry Coppers* (New York: Arthur B. Parsons, 1933), 208; U.S. Geological Survey, *Mineral Resources of the United States* (Washington, D.C.: Government Printing Office, 1906), 280.

3.   Charles A. Dinsmore, "Mining in the Santa Rita District, New Mexico," *The Mining World* (20 November 1909): 1029; *Mineral Resources of the U.S.* (1907), 407.

4.   *Mineral Resources of the U.S.* (1906), 304; *Silver City Enterprise,* 14 February 1902; *Mineral Resources of the U.S.* (1910), 542–43.

5.   *Twelfth Census of the United States* (1900), "Mines and Quarries, 1902" (Washington, D.C.: Government Printing Office, 1905), 265; *Mineral Resources of the U.S.* (1900), 709; Rickard, *The Chino Enterprise,* 804. See James W. Byrkit, *Forging the Copper Collar: Arizona's Labor-Management War of 1901–1921* (Tucson: University of Arizona Press, 1982), for a history of early twentieth-century copper mining in Arizona.

6.   *Mineral Resources of the U.S.* (1929), 730; (1912), 828.

7.   Rickard, *The Chino Enterprise,* 807; *Engineering and Mining Journal* (12 June 1909): 1212.

8.   See the Chino Copper Company, *Annual Reports* (1913–20).

9.   Faris V. Bush, "Burro Mountain Porphyry Copper Development," *Mining Press* (6 February 1915): 222–23; *Silver City Enterprise,* 30 July 1915. See Phelps Dodge Corporation, "Burro Mountain Branch," *Annual Reports* (1915–18). For an extended discussion of Tyrone, see James B. Allen, *The Company Town in the American West* (Norman: University of Oklahoma Press, 1966), 33–49.

10.   *Silver City Enterprise,* 15 December 1916, 13 April 1917, 25 January 1918, 5 April 1918; Chino, *Annual Report* (1917), 8; Parsons, *Coppers,* 34.

11.   *Silver City Enterprise,* 25 July 1919, 21 February 1919; Parsons, *Coppers,* 34; Chino, *Annual Report* (1918), 13, and (1920), 6; *Mineral Resources of the U.S.,* 1922, 207; *Silver City Enterprise,* 18 March 1921.

12.   Parsons, *Coppers,* 13, 35, 40–41; *Census of the Population: 1950,* "Number of Inhabitants," (Washington, D.C.: United States Government Printing Office, 1952), 1–3; Ray Consolidated Copper Company, *Annual Report* (1923); 5; Nevada Consolidated Copper Company, *Annual Report* (1926), 5; *Mineral Resources of the U.S.* (1923), 597, and (1929), 733.

13. Nevada, *Annual Report* (1931), 3, and (1932), 2–3; Kennecott Copper Corporation, *Annual Report* (1933), 3; U.S. Bureau of Mines, *Minerals Yearbook, 1937* (Washington, D.C.: Government Printing Office, 1937), 461.

14. Kennecott, *Annual Report* (1937), 5, and (1938), 5–6; *Silver City Enterprise,* 3 June 1938, 7 October 1938, 16 July 1937; Arthur B. Parsons, *The Porphyry Coppers in 1956* (New York: American Institute of Mining, Metallurgical, and Petroleum Engineers, 1957), 131–32. See Leonard J. Arington and Gary B. Hansen, *"The Richest Hole on Earth": A History of the Bingham Copper Mine* (Logan: Utah State University Press, 1963), for the history of the open-pit operations in Utah; and Russell Elliott, *Nevada's Twentieth-Century Mining Boom: Tonopah-Goldfield-Ely* (Reno: University of Nevada Press, 1966), 173–307, for the history of the open-pit mine at Ely, Nevada.

15. Kennecott, *Annual Report (1940),* 5, 7, and (1941), 5, 7; *Minerals Yearbook* (1942), 439–40, and (1946), 150; Robert F. Campbell, *The History of Basic Metals, Price Control in World War II* (New York: Columbia University Press, 1948), 26–49. See Gerald D. Nash, *The American West Transformed* (Bloomington: Indiana University Press, 1985) and *World War II and the West* (Lincoln: University of Nebraska Press, 1990), for the broadest discussion of the impact of World War II on the social and economic life of the American West.

16. Kennecott, *Annual Report* (1941), 4, and (1943), 4; *Silver City Enterprise,* 2 May 1941; *Minerals Yearbook* (1945), 1497.

17. *Silver City Enterprise,* 7 August 1914; *New Mexico State Inspector of Mines, Annual Report, 1941* (Albuquerque: Valliant Printing Company, 1941), 15. Company housing was built for the workers at Hurley and Santa Rita; see Allen, *The Company Town,* 40–41.

18. "The Chino Copper Company," *The Mogollon Times,* (1913), 35; Barney Himes, *The Unions and the Chino Mine* (Laguna Niguel, California: Barney Himes, 1986), 6, 8.

19. Parsons, *Coppers in 1956,* 122; Chino, *Annual Report* (1917), 10–11; (1918), 9; (1921), 10. *Silver City Enterprise,* 14 February 1919; Nevada, *Annual Report* (1931), 9.

20. Gerald D. Nash, *The Great Depression and World War II* (New York: St. Martin's Press, 1979) 24, 32–33; *Enterprise,* 15 February 1935, 5 April 1935, 17 May 1935.

21. *Enterprise,* 11 June 1942, 16 July 1942.

22. H. A. Thorne, "Mining Methods at the Chino Copper Mines," *American Mining Congress* (July 1927): 61; Y. S. Leong, et al., *Technology, Employment, and Output per Man in Copper Mining,* Report No. E-12, Department of the Interior, Bureau of Mines (Philadelphia: Work Projects Administration, 1940), 43; John B. Huttl, "Chino Today," *Engineering and Mining Journal* (September 1939): 29; Kennecott, *Annual Report* (1940), 6. For a discussion of similar technological changes in the coal mining industry, see H. Lee Scamehorn, *Mill and Mine, The C. F. & I. in the Twentieth Century* (Lincoln: University of Nebraska Press, 1992), 128–30.

23. *Mineral Resources of the U.S.* (1910), 543, and (1915), 362; Chino, *Annual Report* (1912), 7; Ray, *Annual Report* (1923), 7, and (1925), 10; Parsons, *Coppers in 1956,* 125; Nevada, *Annual Report* (1927), 10; *Minerals Yearbook* (1941), 415, and (1948), 1573.

24. Parsons, *Coppers in 1956,* 131–32; *Silver City Enterprise,* 5 May 1939; *Minerals Yearbook* (1942), 455; Kennecott, *Annual Report* (1942), 4. Petroleum and natural gas had become important fuel alternatives for western industry as early as the World War I period; see Scamehorn, *Mill & Mine,* 127.

25. Parsons, *Coppers in 1956,* 130; Chino, *Annual Report* (1918), 16; *Silver City Enterprise,* 9 October 1914; J. T. Shimmin, "The Hurley Mill, Water Supply and Power Plant," *American Mining Congress* (July 1927): 4; Kennecott, *Annual Report* (1941), 6. In comparison, Silver City, with a population of more than 3,500, consumed about one-tenth as much water per month as did the Chino operations in 1914; see *Silver City Enterprise,* 19 June 1925. For a thorough discussion of groundwater issues in New Mexico, see Ira G. Clark, *Water in New Mexico: A History of Its Management and Use* (Albuquerque: University of New Mexico Press, 1987), 233–96.

26. *Silver City Enterprise,* 26 April 1912; Shimmin, "The Hurley," 4; Nevada, *Annual Report* (1928), 12; *Silver City Enterprise,* 29 June 1917; Chino, *Annual Report* (1917), 10. See Robert Kern, "Organized Labor: Race, Radicalism, and Retreat," elsewhere in this volume, for a discussion of labor relations in New Mexico after 1900.

27. *Silver City Enterprise,* 12 March 1937; Huttl, "Chino," 29, 32.

28. During the early 1980s, many of the multinational corporations in the metals industry nearly folded. Kennecott, in fact, sold Chino to Standard Oil of Ohio (SOHIO) in 1980. In turn, SOHIO sold the operations to Phelps Dodge and

Mitsubishi in 1984. Since the near collapse of the copper industry, Chino has resumed operations. Yet there has been a false sense of security, especially since Tyrone closed down in 1991. Gerald D. Nash, "Reshaping Arizona's Economy: A Century of Change," in Beth Luey and Noel J. Stowe, eds., *Arizona at Seventy-Five* (Tucson: Arizona State University Public History Program and the Arizona Historical Society, 1987), 123–47; Michael Malone, "The Collapse of Western Metal Mining: An Historical Epitaph," *Pacific Historical Review* 55 (August 1986): 455–64; "The Death of Mining," *Business Week,* 17 December 1984; "There's a Gleam in the Eye of Copper Producers," *Business Week,* 24 November 1986.

FOUR

NEW DEAL AT ZUNI:
Livestock Reduction and the
Range Management Program

Susan E. Perlman

LAND is the essence of the Pueblo economy. Since the arrival of the Spanish in the Southwest in the 1500s, through Mexican dominion and conflict with Navajo and Apache marauders, the Zuni Indians have managed to maintain their lands and to flourish in a harsh, semidesert environment. Foreign cultures did not succeed in greatly altering their lifestyle and economy. However, the Spaniards did leave an important legacy: they introduced sheep to the Zuni culture. These animals became a significant factor in the Zuni economy, culture, and religion.

Before the Spaniards' arrival, the Zunis used a territory stretching from the Grand Canyon in Arizona to the Rio Grande in New Mexico. Under Spanish and Mexican rule, they continued to use these aboriginal lands for religious and subsistence purposes. However, when the United States obtained the territories of present-day Arizona and New Mexico from Mexico in 1848, life changed dramatically for the Zuni people.

By the 1870s the lands that the Zunis had traditionally called their own had been settled by Anglo ranchers and homesteaders and Mexican herders. In 1877 the U.S. government established a reservation for the Zunis. This small tract of land proved to be inadequate for Zuni subsistence. Moreover, the influx of non-Zuni livestock and the loss of traditional grazing lands combined to cause serious environmental damage to lands in and surrounding the reservation.

By the first decades of the twentieth century, the Zuni people had begun to experience dramatic lifestyle changes. In addition to non-Zuni settlement of areas surrounding the reservation, tribal members witnessed depredations of their resources from such activities as clear-cut logging, dam building, livestock rustling, trespassing, and overgrazing. Officials of the U.S. government, which had a trust responsibility for the Pueblo of Zuni, first ignored Zuni pleas for protection from non-Zuni encroachment, then made limited efforts to protect them and their natural resources. By the 1930s the Zunis had to contend not only with resource degradation and loss of traditional grazing lands, but also with the effects of a nationwide economic depression.

Although traditional Zuni grazing land kept shrinking in the decades after Arizona and New Mexico came under U.S. control, the sheep population steadily increased. By the time it reached a peak of 65,000 head in 1913, Zuni stock raisers realized that their land base, coupled with competition from non-Zunis for area resources, was sorely inadequate for their large flocks.[1] Between 1913 and 1927 the sheep population dropped to 25,000, probably because the Zunis had begun to voluntarily reduce their livestock herds.[2] The Zunis have always been good livestock managers, and their own reduction of the sheep population can be seen as an effective method of improving their sheep industry.[3] In addition, the lack of adequate water supplies for stock, and the loss of range and good grasses from overgrazing, may have thinned flocks through disease and starvation.[4]

The common belief regarding government livestock reduction programs at Zuni is that the Indian Service, predecessor to the B.I.A., did not institute reduction until the late 1930s and early 1940s. But Indian Service officials became well aware of the range deterioration occurring at Zuni when the Blackrock Agency was established on the reservation in 1902. When the Indian Service employed a government stockman at Zuni in 1916, his goals included the reduction of the reservation livestock population.[5] But these early Indian Service reduction plans at Zuni are small scale compared to the programs of the 1930s and early 1940s.

After the establishment of the Blackrock Agency, Indian Service range conservationists initiated livestock-management programs in an attempt to improve the quality of the Zuni range and livestock herds. Zuni Agency officials, for instance, introduced a program to improve the reservation breeding stock. Other early programs offered government-reimbursable funds for livestock purchases, lectures on management techniques, and winter feeding of service rams and ewes.[6]

Although these various range-management programs produced some beneficial results by the eve of World War I, many Zuni stock raisers realized that more money could be made in wage-labor employment than in the livestock business. By the end of the 1920s many Zunis had begun to move away from the sheep industry for subsistence and toward a cash economy.[7] Even though the livestock industry remained economically important at Zuni, this trend away from agriculture had a major impact on the Zuni economic system. It caused a transformation from the traditional Zuni trade and barter system to a more wage-based economy typical of the U.S. capitalist system. For example, the introduction of wage-labor employment contributed to the change in the Zuni economic base. In addition to silversmithing as a cash labor, some Zunis began to hold wage-labor jobs for the government, railroad, and other off-reservation employers.

The New Deal era of the 1930s brought a series of programs designed to improve economic conditions on the reservation. Range management was an important aspect of these rehabilitation programs. The Indian Service, through range management, hoped to conserve what remained of the Zuni land base and rehabilitate land that had been damaged over several decades. Although based on sound scientific principles, the government's range-management program at Zuni resulted in severe economic hardship for many tribal members.

The election of President Franklin D. Roosevelt brought great changes to Native Americans, including the Zunis. Roosevelt's New Deal package included a vast program for Indians. Harold Ickes, Roosevelt's secretary of the interior, actively sought to apply New Deal programs to

Indian reservations. In 1933 Ickes appointed John Collier, who for years had been active in Indian-rights movements, as commissioner of Indian affairs. The appointment of Collier as commissioner proved to have a tremendous impact on federal government policies toward Indians.

Together Ickes and Collier worked to create the Indian New Deal, a program designed to institute emergency measures that would alleviate the devastating poverty among the nation's Indians. As a result of their efforts, many of the New Deal agencies allocated funds for various programs on the reservations. Programs such as the Civil Works Administration (CWA), Works Progress Administration (WPA), and Public Works Administration (PWA) employed Indians for work on tribal lands.[8] It was the Indian New Deal—its allocations, work programs, technical assistance, and manpower—that enabled Indian Service officials to institute a sweeping range-management program, including stock reduction, on the Zuni Reservation during the 1930s.

Soon after taking office, Collier asked Secretary Ickes to establish a separate Civilian Conservation Corps (CCC) program for Indians. In 1933 President Roosevelt approved a plan for the Indian Conservation Works program.[9] Thus the Emergency Conservation Works (ECW) program, a branch of the Civilian Conservation Corps-Indian Division, became a reality. Members of this program built reservation roads, storage dams, fences, wells, and erosion control structures. The ECW became one of the most important New Deal programs on the reservations of the Southwest.

This Indian New Deal had a great impact at Zuni because it initiated a variety of programs designed to improve both the Zuni land base and the tribal livestock industry. The ECW program offered employment to many Zunis. ECW laborers worked on conservation projects that included erosion control, gully plugging, and fence building.[10] This last project, completed in 1935, consisted of building a fence that surrounded the reservation. This fence prevented Zuni livestock from grazing off the reservation. What is more important, by concentrating the Zuni livestock herds on a small area, the fence accelerated the range degradation that had been building for decades.[11]

According to Graham D. Taylor, government officials in the 1920s encouraged the Pueblos and Navajos to increase their livestock herds. As a result the herds quickly surpassed the carrying capacity of the reservation ranges. Soil erosion, ever present in the Southwest, aggravated this condition.[12] The logical move for the government, from the Indian viewpoint, was to increase reservation lands. While New Deal programs did include land acquisition for the tribes, Commissioner Collier proposed livestock-reduction programs first for the Navajos and later for the Pueblos in the 1930s.[13]

These decades of constant overgrazing on the Zuni reservation resulted in serious soil erosion. Indian Service officials hoped to curb this erosion by reducing livestock herds to the carrying capacity of the range. The most intensive livestock-reduction programs at Zuni occurred during the 1930s and early 1940s. During this time, the Zuni sheep population fell from 21,581 head in 1937 to 18,665 head in 1947.[14] But the Zuni stock raiser considered reduction policies that affected his livelihood to be unacceptable.

Livestock reduction pitted scientific variables against Zuni beliefs and practices. From the standpoint of federal officials, the problem was not a complex one: the Zunis owned far more livestock than the reservation could support.[15] To the Zunis, however, sheep raising has traditionally been more than just a way to make a living—it is a way of life, whose roots have deep cultural meaning. Although government range experts based the reduction program on proven range-management techniques, these officials lacked understanding of or concern for the effects of large-scale livestock reduction on the native culture.

The reduction of the Zuni sheep herds also had some serious economic repercussions for the owners of these animals. Many sheep owners were left with flocks too small for subsistence. Other Zunis found themselves shut out of the livestock business when government officials set up grazing units and fee and permit systems.[16] Many stock raisers who experienced the government stock-reduction programs are still bitter toward the U.S. government for instituting a program that so disrupted their lives. They have passed these experiences on to their children and grandchildren. Sheep-owner Rita Lorenzo says that her aunt told her that there were drastic reductions at Zuni in the 1930s. For Lorenzo's family this was a traumatic experience: "from what my grandmother use to tell us it was just like losing a baby, losing a child. And she remembers crying and crying over that."[17]

Zuni stockwoman Ruby Wolf explains that her grandfather had 1,000 head of sheep in the early part of the twentieth century. Wolf's grandfather had to sell over 700 head to meet the limit set for his grazing area. Wolf said that these sheep sold for about $5 a head. This reduction proved "dramatic to the family, but my grandfather didn't want to give up."[18]

When Wolf questioned her father about why her grandfather had allowed the reductions, he replied that he did not think that his father had been given an option or that he had been allowed any input regarding the program.[19] Wolf recalls her father saying that at the time government officials instituted the reductions: "they [Wolf's family] just had to do what they were told to do. . . . Our family was hurt by it all, but we managed to survive. But I don't think my grandfather ever really re-covered from it. He just had it in his heart that the white men came in and just took away what he treasured the most."[20]

Many Zunis believe that government officials did not handle the reduction program well. Many maintain that the government illegally confiscated their stock with inadequate or no payment. Some charge that officials managing the program often failed to locate the true owners of the liquidated stock, paying stock owners for animals that did not belong to them.[21]

Many Zunis also felt that the method for deciding who had to reduce stock was inequitable. Barbara Holmes and Andrew Fowler describe an Indian Service reduction program in 1942 that the Tribal Council carried out.[22] At the outset the Zuni subagency determined the carrying capacity of the reservation and grazing units. Federal officials told those who grazed sheep in these units how many animals would have to be eliminated. Tribal officials decided apportionment according to the needs of each stock owner. Indian Service officials then issued permits to the stock owners, allowing them to graze a certain number of sheep.[23] According to T. J. Ferguson, the people within the unit would work out the reduction arrangements among themselves. Sometimes the reductions within a unit proved to be unequal. Often more than one band grazed within one unit. Among these different bands, some members probably had more power or influence than others. This power was used to manipulate reduction decisions in their favor.[24]

Another reason for inequitable reductions can be traced to the size of the different bands within a unit. If a unit contained bands of different sizes and the same number of sheep were cut out of each band, then the larger band would not suffer as drastically. But the smaller band, depending on the size of the cut and the number of sheep owned, would be severely damaged or even wiped out. Some band members ended up with a substantial amount of land and sheep, while others did not fare so well. Government officials later changed this policy, allowing each band its own grazing unit. The actual cuts were made when the Zunis' flocks were counted during dipping and lamb sales.[25]

Throughout the 1930s government officials conducted surveys on the reservation to determine range conditions. The information provided by these surveys guided resource managers in their range-management program. By 1937 two grazing surveys had been completed at Zuni, one conducted by the Soil Conservation Service (SCS) and the other by Indian Service forestry officials. The first survey reported a reservation carrying capacity of 22,000 sheep units; the second gave it only 12,000 sheep units. An SCS official requested a third survey, but this request was denied "on the grounds that it would bring forth a third figure."[26] In 1940 Zuni Agency officials examined the results of these past grazing surveys and devised a range management plan for the reservation. The United Pueblos Agency believed that the overstocking problem would end if the Zunis agreed to follow the new management plan. United Pueblo Agency superintendent Sophie D. Aberle wrote Collier on September 21 and informed him that the range management plan had been completed and "no more stock reduction at Zuni is necessary."[27]

It is interesting to note, however, that government officials did not label these range-management programs "stock reductions." Rather they were known as "livestock improvement programs." Aberle's letter to Collier stated that Zuni officials had "eliminated" all goats, cull horses, wether lambs, and excess scrub bulls and rams from the reservation.[28] Maybe this language made it appear that government actions had been less harsh than they actually were.

The new management plan consisted of five components. First, it called for separate ranges for sheep and cattle, with the cattle range fenced. Second, it recommended that additional water sources be developed on the reservation. Third, federal officials suggested new grazing methods, such as moving sheep camps more frequently, continuing the improved breeding program, and enhancing the lambing program. Fourth, the plan called for the continuation of the program of acquiring and consolidating alienated lands around the reservation boundaries. Fifth, it stressed dividing the range into units to facilitate proper range management.[29] This last recommendation met with Zuni displeasure and resistance. The Zunis traditionally had vested rights to their grazing lands and did not understand how they had lost them.

The livestock-reduction program at Zuni proved to be a double-edged sword. If the stock of the reservation had not been reduced to the carrying capacity or near-capacity of the range, the Zuni livestock industry would have been unable to subsist because of the resulting serious range degradation. The government objective was to halt range destruction and begin a program of rehabilitation. Indian Service range conservationists could not right past wrongs, so they tried to prevent further range destruction. On the other hand, the reduction program resulted in great hardship to the Zunis, both economically and culturally. Unlike the obvious economic consequences, the cultural impact of the stock-reduction program cannot be measured in numbers. There is still bitterness on the reservation today that can be traced to these range programs of the 1930s and 1940s. This bitterness is felt by those who experienced the reduction and those whose elders passed on their painful experiences to them.

Yet the Indian Service range-management program at Zuni did have several positive effects on the reservation livestock industry. For example, Indian Service range conservationists instituted many changes in the marketing of Zuni livestock. In 1938 all Zuni lambs and cattle, for the first time, were sold by weight instead of by the head. Range conservationists believed this method brought a better price for the animals.[30] Zuni Agency officials also developed several beneficial range-management plans for the reservation. One such plan instituted separate sheep and cattle ranges, a water development program, and land consolidation and acquisition plans. These measures improved the existing reservation grazing lands and added new pasturage to the land base. In addition, the establishment of range-management codes and livestock associations today ensures that the livestock industry at Zuni is regulated and that the reservation is not overstocked.[31]

Yet many Zunis specifically criticized the methods employed by Indian Service officials in carrying out the New Deal livestock-reduction programs. Government administrators exhibited a lack of understanding of Zuni culture and a lack of consideration for the consequences of these projects. Although range experts deemed these actions necessary for the survival of the livestock industry on the reservation, they did not take into consideration the economic hardships they would inflict upon Zunis who depended on stock raising for subsistence. Government livestock-reduction programs plunged many Zunis into a poverty from which the government offered no relief. At Zuni, as on the other pueblos and the Navajo Reservation, the people suffered greatly from these programs. For many tribal members, sheep were their only source of income and an important food source as well. After spring shearing, livestock owners sold their wool to the traders to clear off debts. In the fall, lamb sales to these same traders served the same purpose again.[32]

Sheep hold an important role in the Zuni culture and are valued for their religious as well as economic significance.[33] The involuntary removal of sheep, especially by outsiders, is a serious matter. The livestock-reduction program forever tarnished John Collier in the eyes of many Pueblos and Navajos, and is remembered as the low spot of the Indian New Deal. It is an event in history that will never be forgotten or forgiven by the tribes so dramatically affected by it.

NOTES

1. E. Richard Hart, "Boundaries of Zuni Land: With Emphasis on Details Relating to Incidents Occurring 1846–1946," expert testimony submitted to the U.S. Claims Court as Docket 327-81L, appendix I.

2. Ibid., appendix I; T. J. Ferguson, "Patterns of Land Use and Environmental Change on the Zuni Indian Reservation, 1846–1985: Ethnohistorical and Archaeological Evidence," expert testimony submitted to the U.S. Claims Court as evidence in the case *Zuni Indian Tribe v. United States,* Docket 327-81L, 1981, (Institute of the North American West, Albuquerque), 137.

3. Ibid., 141–42.

4. Barbara E. Holmes and Andrew P. Fowler, "The Alternate Dams Survey: An Archaeological Sample and Evaluation of the Burned Timber and Coalmine Dams, Zuni Indian Reservation, McKinley County, New Mexico," Zuni Archaeology Program, Pueblo of Zuni (Pine Hill, NM: Tsa' Aszi' Graphics Center, 1980), 245.

5. Ibid., 246–47.

6. Ibid., 248–49.

7. Susan E. Perlman, "Livestock Policy of the Zuni Indian Tribe: 1900–1945" (Master's thesis, New Mexico State University, 1989), 67, 77.

8. Kenneth R. Philp, *John Collier's Crusade for Indian Reform, 1920–1954* (Tucson: University of Arizona Press, 1977), 123–25.

9. Ibid., 120.

10. Arrell M. Gibson, *The American Indian: Prehistory to the Present* (Lexington, MA: D.C. Heath & Co., 1980), 538.

11. Perlman, 112–13.

12. Graham D. Taylor, *The New Deal and American Indian Tribalism* (Lincoln: University of Nebraska Press, 1980), 120.

13.   Although the Navajo livestock-reduction program is the most widely known, the Collier administration introduced stock reduction among the western Pueblos in the mid-1930s. Apparently, federal officials did not learn from the tragic Navajo program, and the Pueblos complained of the economic hardships that reduction imposed on their tribal members.

14.   Hart, "Boundaries," appendix I.

15.   Brian W. Dippie, *The Vanishing American: White Attitudes and U.S. Indian Policy* (Middletown, CT: Wesleyan University Press, 1982), 333–34.

16.   Perlman, 141–42.

17.   Rita Lorenzo, interview by author, Zuni, 11 August 1988.

18.   Ruby Wolf, interview by author, Zuni, 12 August 1988.

19.   Ibid.

20.   Ibid.

21.   E. Richard Hart, "Damage to Zuni Trust Lands: 1900–1946, Part III," expert testimony submitted to the U.S. Claims Court as evidence in the case *Zuni Indian Tribe v. United States,* Docket 327-81L, 1981 (Institute of the North American West, Albuquerque), 465–66. The official in charge of the program denied these allegations.

22.   According to a 1940 letter from United Pueblos Agency superintendent Sophie D. Aberle to Commissioner John Collier (see note 27 below), the stock-reduction program at Zuni was completed by 1940. According to Dorothea Leighton and John Adair, *People of the Middle Place: A Study of the Zuni Indians* (New Haven, CT: Human Relations Area Files, Inc., 1966), the government instituted a stock reduction program at Zuni in 1942. This may have been an additional program instituted to further reduce the grazing pressures on the reservation.

23.   Holmes and Fowler, 254.

24.   T. J. Ferguson, interview by author, Albuquerque, 20 January 1989.

25.   Ibid.

26.   Melvin Helander, acting superintendent, Zuni Subagency, to Sophie D. Aberle, general superintendent, United Pueblos Agency, 31 December 1939 (Zuni Tribal Archives, Blackrock).

27.   Sophie D. Aberle to John Collier, U.S. Department of the Interior, Office of Indian Affairs, 21 September 1940 (Zuni Tribal Archives, Blackrock).

28.   Ibid.

29.   Memorandum from Charles H. Schram, junior range examiner, to L. Stevens, 6 November 1940 (Zuni Tribal Archives, Blackrock).

30.   "Program for Zuni Pueblo, Fiscal Year, 1938" (Zuni Tribal Archives, Blackrock), 5–6.

31.   Memorandum from Charles H. Schram, junior range examiner, to L. Stevens, 6 November 1940 (Zuni Tribal Archives, Blackrock).

32.   Ruth Roessel and Broderick H. Johnson, eds., *Navajo Livestock Reduction: A National Disgrace* (Chinle, AZ: Navajo Community College Press, 1974), 41.

33.   Barbara E. Holmes, interview by the author, Zuni, 22 July 1988.

Mammie Harris (right) in doorway at her homestead near Ft. Sumner, New Mexico, c. 1918. Courtesy of John W. Grassham.

Midwife ready to depart for a delivery. Courtesy of HSSD Collection, State Records Center and Archives.

Southwestern New Mexico cowboy Sidney Smith, c. 1920. Henry Schmidt, photographer. Courtesy of Center for Southwest Research, General Library, University of New Mexico, negative number 000–179–0699.

*Group of miners and mill boys, "Bridal Chamber Mine," at Lake Valley, New Mexico,
c. 1890. Henry Schmidt, photographer. Courtesy of Museum of New Mexico, negative number 56218.*

*Alianza Hispano Americana banquet in Albuquerque. Brooks Studio Collection, 78.51.669.
Courtesy of Albuquerque Museum Photoarchives.*

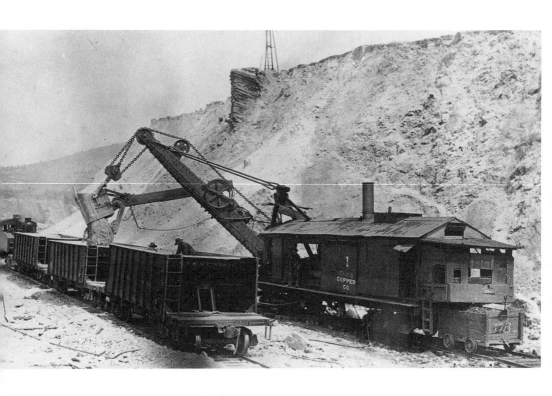

Steam shovel and train in the Hearst Pit at the Chino Mine, located near Silver City, New Mexico, in 1915. Courtesy of Silver City Museum.

La Bajada road constructed with penitentiary labor, c. 1925. Courtesy of Center for Southwest Research, General Library, University of New Mexico, negative number 991–031–0038.

Pueblo of Taos. J. R. Willis Postcard, c. 1925. Courtesy of Center for Southwest Research, General Library, University of New Mexico, negative number 987–002–0074.

Methodist Deaconess Sanitarium located in Albuquerque at 1621 East Central Ave., c. 1940.
Brooks Studio Collection, 78.51.669. Courtesy of Albuquerque Museum Photoarchives.

Camp Funston, located on the campus of the University of New Mexico, c. 1918. Milner Studio Collection, 92.005.587. Courtesy of Albuquerque Museum Photoarchives.

Rattlesnake Oil Field looking toward Shiprock in northwestern New Mexico, 1941. Courtesy of DOD Collection, #7747, State Records Center and Archives.

Pueblo of Zuni, c. 1920. Courtesy of Center for Southwest Research, General Library, University of New Mexico, negative number 000–099–0789.

Groundwater irrigation in Roosevelt County, c. 1920. Courtesy of Special Collections, Eastern New Mexico University.

FIVE

RANCH CULTURE IN THE TWENTIETH CENTURY

STEVE CORMIER

IN the twentieth century New Mexico ranching has experienced many changes. The railroads, selective breeding of livestock, telephones, computers, the pickup truck, and improved veterinary medicines have all helped to modernize ranching. Census information from 1900 to 1960 suggests that the number of large ranches increased.[1] This trend reflects both the increase in mechanization and the loss of thousands of homesteads with insufficient water to make New Mexico ranching profitable. Among the many large ranches was the Moise Livestock Company, which grew from zero to approximately 72,000 acres by 1947.[2]

As ranches grew in size and dwindled in number, homesteaders lost their crops and thus their land to adverse weather. Eventually almost all either turned their land over to merchants as debt payment or sold outright to ranchers.[3] Some homesteaders returned to where they came from, others perhaps became ranch hands on large ranches. Census reports indicate that the number of ranch employees reached a high in the 1920s, probably because of homesteaders losing their land and taking up ranch employment.[4]

There were, however, exceptions to the consolidation of ranches. Many of the largest ranches of the nineteenth century were broken into smaller units in the twentieth century. For example, the 440,000-acre Bell

Ranch was broken into six pieces in 1947 (although it was later increased to approximately 300,000 acres). Other large ranches, such as the Flying A (managed by Captain Burton Mossman) and the CA Bar (owned by James Hinkle), both headquartered out of Roswell, were broken up and eventually sold as smaller pieces.[5]

New Mexico ranchers embraced modern methods of raising cattle as soon as these ways proved profitable. Rarely if ever was sentiment for the "cowboy ways" of the past allowed to interfere with profit. By 1950, for example, pickup trucks rather than horses were the norm on ranches.[6] From the single Longhorn cattle breed of the mid-nineteenth century, ranchers progressed to the Hereford and Durham imports of the late nineteenth century and finally to the dozens of exotic and crossbred breeds of the present.

In the nineteenth century the spring roundup basically consisted of "working" the calves by branding them with the owner's brand and castrating the male calves. By the mid-twentieth century, "working" the calves consisted of branding, castrating, dehorning, vaccinating for various diseases, and implanting the calves with a growth hormone to increase weight by as much as 10 percent. Roping calves and dragging them to the work crews are activities that have generally been replaced by chutes that close around the animals and restrain them while they are being worked.

None of this is to suggest that ranch work has somehow become easier. Quite the contrary. There are still long hours of fencing, fixing water gaps, doctoring sick animals, feeding during the winter, and covering many thousands of miles hunting for problems on the ranch.[6]

Among the trends of twentieth-century ranching were changes in the ethnic and gender makeup of ranch employees. European immigrants such as the Moise and Ilfeld families from Germany became involved in New Mexico ranching. Census figures for 1900 through 1960 indicate that "stock herders, drovers, and feeders" increased in number until 1930 and then steadily declined until 1960.[7] Roughly the same percentage of men and women were employed on cattle and sheep ranches in all types of labor in 1960 as in 1900. The decline in the percentage of men employed is largely due to mechanization. In 1900, 4.2 percent of the total number of ranch hands were women.[8] This figure varies from census to census. In 1910, it was 2.4 percent, in 1920 2.9 percent, in 1930 1.4 percent, in 1940 .06 percent, 1950 2.5 percent, and in 1960 3.7 percent.[9] The number of women ranch employees reflected the unemployment trends in the nation as a whole during the decades of the 1930s and 1940s. Obviously the Great Depression was equally hard on men and women.

What of the racial makeup of ranch employees? Official census reports did not delineate racial composition until 1970. Census reports before then grouped Hispanics and Anglos together as white. "Non-white" people were understood to be either Native American or African American. However, the Census Bureau has recently issued racial break-downs for the years 1900, 1910, and 1920. Researchers such as Mo Palmer of the Albuquerque Museum have made invaluable inquiries into these and subsequent years. Palmer's research points to the ever greater real-ization that the New Mexico "cowboy" of story, myth, and history book is in fact as much a vaquero as a cowboy. Her research in Mora County and around the town of Santa Rosa for the years 1900, 1910, and 1950 indicates that a majority of "agricultural workers" (which in this area would have been mostly ranch workers) were Hispanic.[10] This should not be surprising. Although by 1890 Hispanics had lost 80 percent of their land guaranteed by the 1848 Treaty of Guadalupe Hidalgo[11] through fraud and lawyers' fees, they remained on the land and worked for the predominantly Anglo ranchers.[12] Even in Little Texas (Southeast New Mexico) there were many vaqueros working on sheep ranches (much to the disgust of the incoming cattle-raising Texans, who be-lieved Mexicans and sheep raising to be inferior to Texans and cattle raising).[12]

A common theme in works on New Mexico is the blending of three cultures: Anglo, Hispanic, and Native American.[13] Social, economic, and political progress are portrayed as ever upward, and the three cultures as successfully blending to form a unique individual—the New Mexican. But there has been little melding of Hispanic and Anglo ranch culture. Disputes over land have occurred periodically throughout the twentieth century and continue to the present day. From clashes in Little Texas to legal battles involving all three major cultural groups in northern New Mexico during the 1930s[14] to the Tijerina-led disputes of the 1960s, Anglos and Mexican Americans (and sometimes Native Americans) have been defining and redefining their relationships.

Frank Brito recalls that in Torrance County during the 1920s,

> newcomers moved in from nearby communities. Homesteaders arriving by wagon trains from Texas and Oklahoma brought much unrest and demanded services and land from the native Spanish. Fight, bloodshed and horse-dragging settled disputes. Eugenio [his brother] and I were always in midst of these fights.[15]

Ralph E. Fresquez writes about friction between the two cultures, and he claims that "two societies" existed in and around Roswell between the world wars.[16]

Anglos and Hispanics have not always been at odds, but cultural differences remain. Hispanic ranch culture has its own rhythm. Amado Chavez, in his family history, describes some of this society:

> We had many neighbors—the Jose Giron family, the Sernas, the Candelarias and the Lovatos. Dances were held at the ranches. They included "Valse de la Silla" and "Quadrillas." People were of a very happy nature. At New Years, the men banded together and serenaded all homes. They started at 12:00 at night. They had wonderful times. At each home the women and children welcomed them with "pastelitos" and "mula" (white mule) brewed at home. The women baked in outside ovens.[17]

Also from a family history come these comments by Teodocio Herrera:

Life was hard but everyone helped and things were good until, in 1961, disaster struck. While everyone was in church for Good Friday services the house burned to the ground. It was a sad time in our lives but with the help of family and people from Torreon the new house was built and we started over one more time.

During these years there was not much money for entertainment but people could always drive by and hear the playing of guitars as we'd gather on our front porch to sing songs of past and present. Or, I remember how the girls used to try and get ready by kerosene lamp for the Saturday night dance. It was fun to watch them fuss and bother to make sure their only pair of bobby sox were the whitest they could be.[18]

To these reminiscences can be added the *corridos* (story songs) and border songs that have been sung for years by vaqueros and rural Hispanics. The relation of these *cantas* (songs) to vaquero culture has been studied by such scholars as Enrique Lamadrid, Adrian Trevino, and John Robb.[19]

Although both cowboy and vaquero cultures have their traditional music, much of the old story-oriented work songs have been replaced by Nashville style country and western music. With the coming of the record player, radio, movie theater, and television, ranch workers have been exposed to music that sings the praises of open spaces, beautiful sunsets, and idyllic ranch settings. It is common for a New Mexico ranch hand to be driving the pickup and checking the condition of fences with the radio or cassette player blaring the latest George Strait, Tanya Tucker, or Hank Williams song. This music has become the cowboy music of the twentieth century.

There is currently a revival of cowboy poetry at annual gatherings, such as those at Elko, Nevada; Lubbock, Texas; and Lincoln and Ruidoso, New Mexico. Much of this poetry reflects the working ranch culture. The poems are both nostalgic (horses and the open range) and contemporary (fencing in the winter, opening gates for the pickup truck).[20] The media has descended upon these poetry gatherings, and several working cowboys, including Waddie Mitchell of Nevada and Nyle Henderson of Colorado, have found secondary careers reciting poetry, often for as much money in one night as they would make in one month as a ranch hand.

Where is the vaquero culture in music and media? Aside from an occasional beer and cigarette commercial in Spanish, the image of the ranch hand that emerges is primarily Anglo. In the hundreds of movies and television shows since the making of the first western, *The Great Train Robbery,* by Thomas Edison in 1903,[21] Hispanics have been portrayed mostly as villains and sidekicks. An exception was the "Cisco Kid," which aired on television in the 1950s. "Zorro," though the story of an upper class Spaniard in colonial California righting the wrongs of a corrupt governor, had an Anglo in the leading role. In Walt Disney's *The Nine Lives of Elfego Baca,* the lead was also played by a non-Hispanic actor. When Mexicans such as actress Katy Jurado, or Mexican Americans have had prominent roles, they have often played easily excitable, overly emotional characters. More than eighty movies have been made about Billy the Kid. Yet during his time a far more important conflict was occurring in Lincoln County between indigenous Hispanic ranchers, vaqueros, and farmers on one side and incoming Texans on the other. And the story of the conflict in Little Texas has yet to reach the screen. The significance of Hispanics in ranching and cultural conflict has not yet received a balanced treatment.

This bias is reflected in other aspects of ranch culture as well. Hispanics developed many of the ranching practices that were brought into the twentieth century, practices such as the roundup, the roping of animals to treat them, large-acreage grazing, and, of course, the use of the horse to herd animals. A very good case could also be made that the sport of rodeo is Hispanic in origin. Yet very few rodeos in the first half of the century had Hispanic participants. A review of the national rodeo champions during the period reveals that the names are all non-Hispanic.[22] Yet in 1899 the great New Mexico bronc rider, Jose Gonzalez, gave an exhibition of his skill in front of Theodore Roosevelt at the 1899 Rough Riders Reunion in Las Vegas, New Mexico.[23]

Women also have not received their due in the study of ranch culture. Traditional western historians or folklorists such as J. Frank Dobie, C. L. Sonnichsen, and David Dary have viewed the role of women as secondary partners who helped with ranch work but who were primarily confined to the home.[24] More balanced and thorough treatments of ranch women have been given by Teresa Jordan, Joan Jensen, Stan Steiner, and Sharon Niederman.[25] It must be emphasized that ranch women in New Mexico were and are an integral part of the culture. They should not be confined to parenthetical mention in historical accounts. The primary literature is simply too rich with stories of women as employees or full-fledged partners. Because a woman was married to a rancher did not mean that the husband did all the outside work and the wife, all the inside work. Work was often shared, and the wife was often as much a ranch hand as the husband. Several county histories and personal reminiscences used for this study bear this out.

In writing of her life around 1904, Jessie Del Prado Farrington recalls, "Tommy and I joined all the nearby roundups, and I learned to 'herd a bronc'. . . . I became quite a cowhand as far as roundup, or cutting out cattle went, but I never became a roper or 'bronco buster.' "[26] The Chavez County Historical Society records that Nettie Lusk Amonett worked cattle at an early age on the family ranch, Portia Jones ran the family ranch by herself from 1943 to 1970 after her husband's death, and Beryl Kimball and daughter Genevieve did the same with their sheep ranch from 1955 until 1970.[27]

From the *History of Torrance County* comes this account by Ruth Elliott of her years on her father's ranch:

> Dad was going to top the hills to see if he could see me ever so often. He did that several times and didn't see me. When I got to the northeast corner there was a dirt tank of water with cattle all around it. Dad was getting aggravated. Well it took some hard riding to get all those cattle away from that tank and started toward the house. In a little while he saw me driving that long

string of cattle so he knew what had happened. He had a few
head of cattle. I had 100 or more.[28]

Also from the *History of Torrance County* is this account of Maud
(Hawk) Medders: "Will [Maud's husband] passed away in 1965. Maud
kept on ranching till a broken hip confined her to a walker, but she still
goes to the mesa to check cattle with her son, Bill."[29] And from the same
volume comes the account of Virginia O'Neal: "Both Virginia and Lewis
were equally equipped to deal with digging post holes by hand, feeding
cattle by sleds in the winter, breaking ice, breaking horses, branding
cattle, growing gardens, hauling water, living on gravy and red beans and
all the other things that make up routine living on a ranch."[30]

In addition to their work as ranch owners and ranch hands, from the
turn of the century until World War II, women were an integral part of
rodeo in New Mexico and throughout the West. Research by historians
James Hoy and Michael Allen suggests that women were removed from
rough stock-riding and roping events because of financial troubles, such
as the need to cut costs and the desire to make rodeo look "more
professional."[31] The contributions to rodeo by such greats as Fern Sawyer
of Nogal and Goldy Smith of Raton have been overlooked. Fern Sawyer
has received credit for her ability from Teresa Jordan,[32] but Goldy Smith,
a pre–World War I rodeo athlete, has remained unknown until recently.
The recollections of E. L. "Steve" Stephens include the following anec-
dote on Smith:

> Went through Raton and into Colorado and delivered the cattle.
> Was a big wild West rodeo going on in Trinidad, Colo. We stayed
> there three days and taken the rodeo in. Some of us punchers en-
> tered all the bronc riding show. We drew every day. The second
> day was four of us drew. Was two prizes. The first prize was $500.
> The second prize was $250. They was three boys and one girl and
> then we drawed who we was going to ride against, so it fell my
> way to ride against the girl.
>
> Her name was Goldy Smith. So we drawed to see who rode

first. She rode first so she came out of the chute on a bay pony. He
was a good pony. They drove a buckskin pony in the chute and I
buckled my saddle on him and crawled on him and said let him
out. He done everything but chin the moon. I could see his head.
The girl beat me on points. She got the money, so I went over
where she was and thanked her and patted her on the back.[33]

Since World War II, women have been allowed to participate profes-
sionally only in barrel racing. Since the 1960s, in New Mexico and
throughout the West, they have struggled for equal prize money and to
overcome their image as a "cheap contract act." Women have improved
their image in the rodeo, and thanks to efforts by such athletes as Peggy Jo
Koll, professional women contestants enjoy money that is comparable to
that of the men.[34] Women have also formed their own association, the
Girls Rodeo Association, in which they ride bucking horses and bulls, and
rope competitively.[35]

This essay has discussed the trends of New Mexico ranch culture in
the first six decades of the twentieth century. In that time ranches decreased in number and increased in size (to between 50,000 and 100,000
acres). The immense nineteenth-century ranches were either broken up
into more manageable sizes or sold to major corporations. Though a small
segment, women have been an integral part of ranch culture. Ranch
culture divides between Anglo cowboy culture and Hispanic vaquero
culture, although European immigrant families were also involved in
New Mexico ranching. The stereotypes for ranch culture in general have
been set by Hollywood. However New Mexico ranch culture has a diverse
past not reflected in these stereotypes, and the accurate story of New
Mexico ranching has yet to be told on the screen.

NOTES

1.   U.S. Department of Commerce, Bureau of the Census, 18th Census of
the United States, 1960, Agriculture, vol. 3, General Report, Statistics by Subjects
(Washington, D.C.: U.S. Government Printing Office, 1963), 116.

2. Author's conversation with the foreman of the Moise Livestock Company, 1987.

3. See Agnes Morley Cleveland, *No Life for a Lady* (Lincoln, University of Nebraska Press, 1977), 331–33, reprint of 1941 edition; Fabiola Cabeza De Vaca, *We Fed Them Cactus* (Albuquerque: University of New Mexico Press, 1954), 149–53; and Mae Price Mosely, *Little Texas Beginnings* (Roswell, NM: Hall-Poorbaugh Press, 1973), 48–49.

4. U.S. Census Reports, Agriculture, 1920, 1930, 1940, 1950, 1960.

5. See David Remley, *The Bell Ranch* (Albuquerque: University of New Mexico Press, 1992), 3; and Elvis E. Fleming and Minor S. Huffman, eds., *Roundup on the Pecos* (Roswell, NM: Chaves County Historical Society, 1978), 241.

6. C. L. Sonnichsen, *Cowboys and Cattle Kings* (Norman: University of Oklahoma Press, 1950).

7. U.S. Census, Occupations, Female, 1900, table 41.

8. U.S. Census, Occupations, Female, 1900, table 41, 341.

9. Ibid., 1910, table 7, 493; 1920, table 1, 979; 1930, table 16, 1078; 1970, table 13, 319; 1950, table 74, 31–103; 1960, table 120, 33–219.

10. Manuscript Census, Precinct 8, Guadalupe County, 1900, 1910, and 1950, microfilm (New Mexico State Historic Preservation Survey for Mora County). Researched by Mo Palmer.

11. Victor Westphall, *The Public Domain in New Mexico: 1854–1891* (Albuquerque: University of New Mexico Press, 1965), 49.

12. Mosely, *Little Texas Beginnings,* 19.

13. See Erna Fergusson, *A Pageant of Three Peoples* (Albuquerque: University of New Mexico Press, 1964); and Susan A. and Calvin A. Roberts, *New Mexico* (Albuquerque: University of New Mexico Press, 1988). See also any of the tourist information from the official state tourist information services.

14. See David H. Dinwoodie, "Indians, Hispanos, and Land Reform: A New Deal Struggle in New Mexico," *Western Historical Quarterly,* 17, no. 3 (1986): 291–323.

15. "Frank Brito Family," *History of Torrance County,* 108. Coronado Room, Zimmerman Library, University of New Mexico.

16. Fleming and Huffman, *Roundup,* 212–16.

17. "Amado Chavez Family," *History of Torrance County,* 120–21.

18. "Teodocio Herrera," *History of Torrance County,* 181.

19. "Directory of Trevino Archives–Southwest Music," Hispanic Student Services, University of New Mexico; and John Robb, *Hispanic Folk Music of New Mexico and the Southwest* (Norman: University of Oklahoma Press, 1980).

20. See Hal Cannon, ed., *Cowboy Poetry: A Gathering* (Salt Lake City: G. M. Smith, 1985).

21. Ironically, *The Great Train Robbery* was filmed in New Jersey.

22. Robert D. Hanesworth, *Daddy of 'Em All: The Story of the Cheyenne Frontier Days* (Cheyenne, WY: Flintlock Publishing Co., 1967), 162–66; and Max Kegley, *Rodeo, the Sport of the Cow Country* (New York: Hastings House, 1942).

23. Cabeza De Vaca, *We Fed Them Cactus,* 129.

24. See, for example J. Frank Dobie, *Afield with J. Frank Dobie: Tales of Critters, Campfires, and the Hunting Trail* (Silver City, NM: High Lonesome Books, 1992) and *Cowpeople* (Austin: University of Texas Press, 1981); CL. Sonnichsen, *Cowboys and Cattle Kings: Life on the Range Today* (Westport, CT: Greenwood Press, 1980), *The Southwest in Life and Literature: A Pageant in Seven Parts* (New York: Knopf, 1981) and *True Tales of Old Time Kansas* (Lawrence: University Press of Kansas, 1984).

25. See Teresa Jordan, *Cowgirls: Women of the American West* (Garden City, NY: Doubleday, 1984); Joan Jensen, *Promise to the Land: Essays on Rural Women* (Albuquerque: University of New Mexico Press, 1991); Stan Steiner, *The Ranchers: A Book of Generations* (Norman: University of Oklahoma Press, 1985); and Sharon Niederman, ed., *A Quilt of Words: Women's Diaries, Letters, and Original Accounts of Life in the Southwest, 1860–1960* (Boulder, CO: Johnson Books, 1988), 181–211.

26. Jessie Del Prado Farrington, "From Rocking Horse to Cow Pony," *New Mexico Historical Review* 26 (1956): 43.

27. Fleming and Huffman, *Roundup,* 271, 438.

28. "Ruth Elliott," *History of Torrance County,* 1979, 149.

29. "Maud (Hawk) Medders," *History of Torrance County,* 223.

30. "Lewis O'Neal Family," *History of Torrance County,* 234.

31. At the Western Historical Association meeting in Austin in 1992, Hoy delivered a paper titled "Marge Roberts: National Cowgirl Hall of Fame." Another paper, titled "Mabel Strickland: National Cowboy Hall of Fame," was given by Allen.

32. Jordan, *Cowgirls,* 227–35.

33. E. L. "Steve" Stephens, "West of the Pecos," *New Mexico Historical Review* 35, no. 2 (April 1960): 98.

34. Author's conversations with Peggy Jo Koll, 1989 and 1992.

35. Jordan, *Cowgirls,* 237–75.

SIX

FROM WESTERN FRONTIER TO THE SPACE FRONTIER:
The Military in New Mexico, 1900–1940

Barron Oder

THE first four decades of the twentieth century, in the eyes of some military historians, shaped the military as we know it today. From the end of the Frontier Wars to the outbreak of World War II the military defined its place in American society. New Mexico, at that time one of the republic's newest states, contributed to and benefited from the transition from the traditional militia system to today's professional standing army.

War was not unknown in the Southwest when the Spanish arrived in the late 1530s and early 1540s in search of the fabled Seven Cities of Gold. These Spaniards found nothing resembling the Aztec and Inca empires. It was not until 1598–99 that Spain's first colonies on the middle Rio Grande took hold. New Mexico's Pueblo Indians, descendants of the Anasazi peoples, consisted of several autonomous groups. While they shared a common sedentary (as opposed to nomadic) tradition, the Pueblo Indians represented diverse cultural and linguistic groups. Pueblo Indians occasionally resisted the Spanish intrusions by taking up arms. Most resistance met with limited success. The Pueblo Revolt of 1680, however, temporarily drove the Spanish out of New Mexico. Under Don Diego de Vargas, soldiers of the Spanish Crown reclaimed New Mexico in 1692–93.[1]

Relations with Pueblo Indians stabilized during the eighteenth century, but raids by Apaches from the north and Comanches from the east

99

punctuated frontier life in New Mexico well into the nineteenth century, long after Spain had yielded control of the Southwest to Mexico in 1821 and Mexico had ceded the area to the United States in 1848.

In August 1846, during the Mexican-American War, U.S. soldiers under Colonel Stephen W. Kearny arrived from Fort Leavenworth, Kansas, and occupied Santa Fe. After installing a government under the U.S. flag, Kearny and 300 of his original force of 1,700 men departed for California to assist John C. Fremont's army. At the same time, Colonel Alexander Doniphan led a regiment of cavalry overland from Santa Fe to Chihuahua. After a pause in Chihuahua, Doniphan proceeded to Monterrey in Nuevo Leon to join General Zachary Taylor's army. This division of units violated the military maxim of concentration of forces and invited defeat in detail. The animosities aroused by the U.S. invasion of Mexico erupted into violence known as the Taos Rebellion in which Governor Charles Bent (appointed by Kearny) and several other Americans died. With so few American soldiers in the area, and aware that no reinforcements were readily available, the uprising was well-timed and enjoyed a brief success. In February 1847, however, an expedition led by Colonel Sterling Price stormed Taos Pueblo and ended the revolt.[2]

Fifteen years later, in 1862, Confederate forces from Texas invaded New Mexico. A force of 3,000 men under Brigadier General Henry Sibley had formed in El Paso from April 1861 to February 1862. Optimistic Confederate plans called for this army to conquer New Mexico, capture Colorado's gold mines, and then march to California to capitalize on pro-South sentiments while securing ports that were free of the Union blockade.

Major General Edward R. S. Canby, commander of 3,800 Union men, occupied Fort Craig (about twenty miles south of Socorro and near the Rio Grande) to halt Sibley's invasion. Sibley won the ensuing battle of Valverde. While Canby's men fell back on Fort Craig, the Confederates marched to Santa Fe.

In Santa Fe, Sibley faced a shortage of supplies for his men and animals. To replenish his stores, Sibley moved his army, now depleted to about 1,700 men, farther north and east in hopes of capturing Fort Union, about seventy-five miles away. However, on March 27–28, 1862, Sibley encountered another Union force at Glorieta Pass. The Confederates were close to winning on the battle's second day when word reached Sibley that Union troops had slipped into the Confederate rear and had destroyed his camp and supplies. Sibley erroneously assumed these were Canby's men. Although Canby's men had actually remained at Fort Craig, Sibley now feared he had encountered a much larger Union force than he had anticipated and faced imminent defeat. His own lack of supplies compounded his plight. Sibley therefore broke off the fight. Short on provisions, wagons, and draft animals, Sibley called off the campaign and the rebels returned to Texas.[3]

The regular army resumed responsibility for New Mexico after the Civil War. From the early 1870s until Geronimo's capture in 1886 (when the army decided New Mexico's Indian Wars had ended), the army was occupied with sporadic expeditions against Apache war bands. Between 1846 and 1880, the army established more than sixty posts in New Mexico. By 1886, however, only forts Stanton and Bayard (near Lincoln and Silver City, respectively) had sizable garrisons.[4]

As the century ended the United States was moving toward war with Spain. Unrest in Cuba and American interest in the outcome of Cuban internal affairs led to the dispatch of the USS *Maine* to Havana. On February 15, 1898, an explosion of uncertain origin destroyed the ship and killed or wounded many of its crew. American pride, inflamed by a jingoistic press, demanded war.[5] Theodore Roosevelt in the First U.S. Volunteer Cavalry's charge at San Juan Hill and Commodore George Dewey in the naval action at Manila Bay seemed to vindicate U.S. reliance upon the citizen-soldier. However, this "splendid little war" set in motion many reforms and political battles over the continued professionalization of a standing army in the United States.

Each period in the brief military history described so far has one thing in common: the militia. Whether it was a part of Spain, Mexico, or the United States, New Mexico had some form of militia. The citizen-soldier formed the backbone of each militia. Except under the Americans, large bodies of professional soldiers did not operate regularly in New Mexico.

Most states and territories of the United States disbanded their militias and established National Guard units in the period 1877 to 1900. New Mexico followed this trend in 1897.[6] Citizens of New Mexico Territory, though long familiar with the military traditions of three nations, entered the twentieth century unaware of the many changes the shift from the militia to the National Guard would bring to their lifestyle and region.

At first New Mexicans could not tell the difference between the militia and the National Guard. Until 1904 the guard was essentially a renamed militia. Guard members remained citizen-soldiers. The federal government paid no money to support individual state and territorial guard units. The National Guard could still serve active duty outside the state or territory for limited periods. The territory provided arms, ammunition, supplies, uniforms, and other standard provisions. The guard did not have a place in the regular army's table of equipment and organization. The guard would enter federal service not as a unit, but rather as individuals who volunteered en masse to join an outfit in the U.S. Volunteers, just as they had done as members of the militia.[7]

The timing of the territorial legislature's establishment of a National Guard during the buildup to the Spanish-American War showed that while New Mexico was a relatively poor, sparsely populated, and isolated region, its citizens recognized the importance of international events. With the declaration of war against Spain on April 25, 1898, the territory needed to organize, arm, and transport a large body of soldiers to fill the quota for active military duty levied by Washington. This first call to arms required 340 men from New Mexico. On May 6 and 7, 1898, the entire First New Mexico Cavalry (14 officers and 342 enlisted men organized as a squadron) mustered into military service for the United States.[8]

The squadron lost its identity as a New Mexico unit when it became part of the First U.S. Volunteer Cavalry Regiment. Led by Colonel Leonard Wood and Lieutenant Colonel Theodore Roosevelt, the unit captured popular attention under its nickname—the Rough Riders. Rough Riders from New Mexico distinguished themselves in combat, especially at the battles of El Caney and San Juan Hill.[9]

Although it is impossible to trace the career of each New Mexican who returned to the territory after the war, some stand out. Captain George Curry served as governor of New Mexico. Lieutenant David Leahy and Corporal Numa Frenger became district judges. Captain Maximiliano Luna accepted a commission in the regular army. From a distinguished family in New Mexico's history, Luna served in the Philippines during the Philippine Insurrection. He died while on active duty during the insurrection.[10]

The National Guard represented the largest military presence in the territory at the turn of the twentieth century. The regular army established many posts during its active campaigns in the area between 1846 and 1880, but by 1900 its presence had all but disappeared from New Mexico. On January 12, 1900, the army turned over one of its finest posts, Fort Bayard, to the medical corps for use as a hospital.[11] The medical corps eventually turned the hospital over to the territory. The hospital at Fort Bayard became renowned for its service to victims of tuberculosis. This work foreshadowed the days when tuberculosis patients, moving to New Mexico in search of "the cure," would play a prominent role in New Mexico's economy.

The only other military reservation on the active lists in 1900 was Fort Wingate Ordnance Depot. Located near Gallup in McKinley County, Fort Wingate played a leading role in efforts to develop the northwestern part of the state. Gallup's first mayor had served at Fort Wingate for some time before his resignation from the army. Many New Mexicans know that General Douglas MacArthur of World War II and Korean War fame lived at Fort Selden from ages four through seven while his father was posted there. Few people know, however, that MacArthur's father served at Fort Wingate in 1881–82 and lived there with his infant son.[12]

The garrison at Fort Wingate numbered 88 officers and troops in July 1901. Soldiers at the post had few regular duties other than law enforcement. Such limited duty did not, however, prevent the post from boosting the local economy. For example, in 1905 the road from the railroad station to the fort was paved, and over $50,000 was spent in the area on remodeling and upgrading the buildings at the post. The U.S. Forest Service in 1908 used Fort Wingate as one of four installations for woodlands management. Part conservation, part entrepreneurship, this work included the sale of millions of feet of western lumber at market prices.[13]

In the period 1900–1914, the New Mexico National Guard did not turn out for military duty except for summer camps. Although funding for the guard had improved over haphazard territorial appropriations for the militia, some members feared that long periods of inactivity might jeopardize future budgets. To increase public awareness and participation in its work, the guard in 1906 began a push for construction of arsenals around New Mexico. Lacking construction funds in its annual appropriations, the guard cooperated with local businesses across the territory for financial support. In asking for donations, guard members pointed out that the legislature had granted permission to build arsenals but had failed to earmark construction funds. As a result of the guard's efforts, armories appeared over the next few years at Albuquerque, Las Cruces, Santa Fe, Las Vegas, Roswell, Silver City, Deming, and Carlsbad. Local money paid for construction of most arsenals on sites donated by local business.[14]

In the midst of this construction boom, relations between the United States and Mexico deteriorated. The Mexican Revolution brought a series of governments to the Mexican republic between 1910 and 1916. Violence along the U.S.–Mexican border became commonplace.

Among the revolutionary generals was Francisco "Pancho" Villa, who fought the forces of the President Venustiano Carranza. As Villa raided northern Mexico to protest Carranza's policies, many Mexican soldiers and civilians fled to the United States. The unexpected appearance of Mexican soldiers forced the temporary reopening of Fort

Wingate. In May 1914 about 4,000 Mexican soldiers, as well as women and children from the families of several senior officers, arrived at the fort from assembly areas in Texas. Many internees resented the barbed wire and the armed sentries, who had orders to shoot to kill anyone attempting to escape. Three internees tried to break out; guards shot one dead, and Apache scouts helped track down the other two, who had managed to escape unharmed.[15]

Violence, real or rumored, increased tension along the border. The U.S. Army deployed troops in a series of camps guarding the international border. The number of soldiers at each post was small, and posts depended upon the support offered by nearby garrisons. Nevertheless, the presence of these few American troops further inflamed already ruffled sensibilities. Mexico and the United States each resented the presence of the other nation's armed forces on the border, but neither could or would demobilize its troops.

In the early hours of March 9, 1916, Villa raided Columbus, New Mexico. The raid ended within hours, but eighteen Americans died and seven others suffered from a variety of wounds. An army garrison at Columbus had received information indicating Villa was in the vicinity, but the garrison commanders had not believed that Columbus was Villa's target. The apparent incompetence of the army commander reinforced New Mexicans' belief that President Woodrow Wilson had bungled relations with Mexico from the start. New Mexicans wanted Villa punished for his raid. While the state seemed split as to what course of action should be taken, most agreed that Wilson's stand ("We are too proud to fight.") had been misunderstood by Mexicans as U.S. weakness. New Mexicans resolved to clarify any misconceptions arising from the president's official policy.[16]

General John J. Pershing led a punitive expedition into Mexico March 15, 1916 to February 5, 1917 in retaliation for Villa's raid. On May 11, 1916, President Wilson activated all National Guard units across the nation. The First New Mexico Infantry was one of two non–regular army outfits attached to Pershing's command. Only regular troops entered Mexico, however. New Mexico's guard troops, anxious to see action at the front, had some trouble adjusting to their support role. Consequently, many guard members on border duty did not take an oath of federal service as stipulated by the National Defense Act of 1916.[17]

The punitive expedition brought several changes to New Mexico. Federal spending on supplies, transport, and other necessities for Pershing's soldiers and the guard in garrison along the Mexican border helped many local economies. Of equal importance over time, New Mexico began its long association with military air power. Several aircraft were attached to Pershing's command during the expedition. Primitive airframes, these winged wonders nonetheless captured the fancy of many New Mexicans. Brigadier General Harry T. Herring, adjutant general of the New Mexico National Guard, appreciated the potential of air power. He recommended to the governor that New Mexico make concerted efforts to train pilots for the guard and urged him to fund the purchase of an airplane for combat training. General Herring's vision ultimately became reality on July 7, 1947, when the federal government formally recognized the 188th Fighter-Bomber Squadron as the New Mexico Air National Guard.[18]

New Mexico guard members were among the first deployed along the border and the last to stand down after the punitive expedition. The first Guard troops to report to Columbus following the raid showed up in the forenoon on the day of the attack. When about thirty members of the guard who lived in Deming heard of the raid, they assembled, gathered arms, and on their own initiative proceeded to Columbus—a model of efficiency for the citizen-soldier. New Mexico guard troops served on active duty from May 1916 until April 5, 1917.[19]

The irony of the guard's stand-down date lies in the fact that it was one day before Congress declared war on Germany. As the United States entered World War I, citizen-soldiers helped define national participation in the "war to end all wars."

World War I contradicted most maxims of American political and military history. The United States tried to remain politically free from events overseas while capitalizing on European strengths and weaknesses. Never before had the nation deployed a large army overseas to help determine the course of European events. Because the nation had never before engaged in such foreign adventures, many Americans did not realize that the traditional reliance upon coastal defenses against an amphibious invasion had no place in this war. Although the United States still enjoyed a comfortable cushion of time to call up and train citizen-soldiers, these soldiers required arms, food, ammunition, medical supplies, and transport to Europe. World War I not only tested the ability of U.S. military planners, it also mobilized the economic and demographic resources of the nation.

When the New Mexico National Guard received notice on April 21, 1917, to activate for World War I, it mustered thirty-nine officers and forty-nine enlisted men. The federal government assumed responsibility for recruitment for the guard and federal ranks. Some of the armories constructed in the previous decade served as mustering points. Recruiting offices opened in post offices. Camp Funston, located in Albuquerque east of Yale Avenue on the north side of Central Avenue (now covered by parking lots, Johnson Gymnasium, and Mesa Vista Hall on the University of New Mexico campus), became the concentration point for units from around the state. The legislature authorized New Mexico State University and the New Mexico Military Institute to teach the mechanical arts needed for modern war. These two institutions, as well as the University of New Mexico, received funds for the construction of new facilities to meet war needs.[20]

The entire state mobilized for victory. Councils and boards for war work sprang up throughout New Mexico. Given the rural nature of New Mexico, the response was noteworthy. Farmers planted more food crops, such as pinto beans, corn, and wheat. Women's auxiliaries and councils suggested effective ways to employ women in New Mexico's fields and its few factories. New Mexico took the lead in developing medical care for injured soldiers before the federal government had an effective system in place.[21]

New Mexico mobilized human resources reflecting a cross-section of the state. Railroad engineers, representing the major industry then based in the state, were in demand by the army. Students from throughout the state—including those who had joined the recently (December 13, 1916) organized Reserve Officers' Training Corps at New Mexico Military Institute—showed up at recruiting offices in large numbers. It was said that the whole football team at the state university went into service. Speaker's bureaus trained Four Minute Men, a cadre of orators who roused sentiments through short, patriotic addresses in English and Spanish to many small and isolated groups throughout the state. The *New Mexico War News* newspaper circulated propaganda for home consumption. Although the state did not recruit on reservations, almost one hundred American Indians from New Mexico entered federal armed services.[22]

New Mexicans who volunteered for service lost any territorial affiliation with New Mexico: they were now soldiers of the United States. New Mexicans joined dozens of regiments and divisions in the army as well as at least sixty-five air squadrons. In all, at least 17,251 soldiers came from New Mexico's population of about 354,000.[23]

The end of World War I came in phases. The Armistice, in effect as of 11 A.M. on November 11, 1918, did not end the war. Allied forces occupied Germany until the Treaty of Versailles, which was signed by European belligerents on June 28, 1919, to take effect on January 10, 1920. Although the United States never ratified the treaty, it nevertheless withdrew its forces from Germany.[24]

As this gradual demobilization sent New Mexicans home, news of the horror of the war spread throughout the nation. Disillusionment over the carnage of the war, coupled with a realization that this might not have been the last war after all, spawned a peace movement in the 1920s and 1930s. However, New Mexicans were not overly sympathetic to this peace movement. Like most of the nation, they merely looked forward to a return to normal.

Normal for much of New Mexico meant the slower pace of a rural society. Industry had not taken root in New Mexico during the war, and the situation did not change much during the 1920s. Tourism and health care remained centerpieces of the state's economy. Cities such as Albuquerque grew slowly. New Mexico began a slight shift toward prosperity in 1925, but the stock market crash of 1929 quickly ended this trend.[25]

At the close of the war, New Mexico drew little federal funding for payrolls or internal improvements. Nevertheless there was some federal presence. For example, the army reactivated Fort Wingate in 1918 as an ordnance depot. With a minimal military staff (sometimes a single active-duty soldier), the depot employed civilian mounted guards and explosives handlers. Normally, there were between fifteen and twenty-five civilians on the payroll. In 1921 an ammunition plant was located just outside the fort to facilitate the manufacture of several million cartridges each year.[26] Although the exact number of employees at this plant is not recorded, it is evident that the money introduced into the local economy eased the poverty of the area.

In 1925 Congress authorized use of abandoned post buildings at Fort Wingate as schools for Navajo and Zuni children. Congress also set aside half a million dollars for new construction and renovation of the area for the schools. The parade ground became a baseball field and barracks were remodeled into dormitories. The army turned over more than eight thousand acres of the outpost to the Department of the Interior for inclusion in the Navajo Reservation in 1928. Despite such major changes to much of its area, Fort Wingate remained operational with minimal changes to its mission as an Ordnance Depot.[27]

Another source of federal money and internal improvements came to New Mexico slowly. The U.S. Army Corps of Engineers—responsible for harbors, dams, and waterways—pulled out of New Mexico in 1875. The subsequent political chicanery and personal greed of some early territorial officials, collectively known as the Santa Fe Ring, had made personal fortunes but failed to improve the lifestyles of other New Mexicans. The Santa Fe ring never called on the corps of engineers for internal improvements. Only when Miguel A. Otero, Jr., became territorial governor in 1897 did New Mexico begin to break the stranglehold of the ring. Even after the ring had lost much of its power and New Mexico had attained statehood, the stigma of the ring's actions remained. This, coupled with the average New Mexican's desire to be left alone by the federal government, further hindered those seeking help from the Corps of Engineers.[28]

As the size of the army shrank during the 1920s and Americans became obsessed with the good life, the military in New Mexico assumed a low profile. There were, however, occasions for prominence. For example, after World War I the government decided, in light of events such as the Villa raid, to establish an air patrol over the U.S.–Mexico border. As late as 1935, Lordsburg had a contingent of enlisted men from the Army Air Corps operating the only government-owned airfield in New Mexico.[29]

The New Mexico National Guard reorganized and served in a variety of capacities during the 1920s and 1930s. After the war, the guard consolidated its units into the 111th Cavalry Regiment; the 120th Engineers; and Battery A, 158th Field Artillery. The 111th was deployed to enforce martial law in San Miguel County in 1937. In 1935, proving that the military had a role in civilian life, the regiment fought a grasshopper infestation in Union County. Along with other New Mexico guard troops, the members of the 111th posed as British soldiers for thirty days in 1939 during the filming of the motion picture *The Light That Failed,* based on a Rudyard Kipling novel. The guard served during two floods. It searched for and provided medical care to lost hunters or campers. It served as a search and rescue team when two Illinois families disappeared in New Mexico in 1934.[30]

The general meeting of the National Guard Association was held in Santa Fe in 1935. The highlight of the event was the display of aircraft flown by air national guards from several states. Over seventy airplanes— a veritable armada for those days of the Depression—flew into Santa Fe's airport.[31]

The first two administrations of Franklin D. Roosevelt helped yank

New Mexico out of its protective shell as more and more federal projects came to the state. A warm friendship grew between the president and New Mexico governor Clyde Tingley. Federal relief dollars flowed into the state. The Army Corps of Engineers undertook its first massive effort in New Mexico, the Conchas Dam project. (There had been earlier water projects carried out in the state under the aegis of the Bureau of Reclamations in the 1920s—most notably on the Pecos, with the Avalon and McMillan dams, and on the Rio Grande at Elephant Butte. New Mexico leaders demonstrated political savvy in overcoming initial reluctance at various levels in the bureaucratic maze of Washington, D.C.[32]

By 1939 with Europe on the verge of war, New Mexico remained unindustrialized. Tourism and the health industry had gone into eclipse. High unemployment rates across the nation meant that most National Guard units, as well as the federal armed services, could enroll enough men to fill authorized positions. The only change in the National Guard at the end of the 1930s was the conversion of the 111th Cavalry to the 200th Coast Artillery (Anti-Aircraft).[33] The state adjutant general received permission in early 1939 from the War Department to begin conversion of the 111th. War Department officials agreed but stipulated that New Mexico had to provide the improved facilities required for an artillery unit. The state had no funds available for conversion of the unit. Governor John Miles exercised his power as chief executive and commander-in-chief of the National Guard by declaring a limited state of emergency. His action allowed mobilization of the guard and forced the state treasurer to find monies to cover the costs of mobilization. As the 111th activated, the governor also sought funds for construction of facilities around the state for the proposed artillery regiment.[34]

Although the governor had received a favorable decision from the state attorney general, the state treasurer challenged it. The case went before the state supreme court, which upheld the governor's action. As soon as the court announced its decision, the adjutant general undertook the conversion.[35] This case helped define the constitutional authority of all governors over their National Guard units in times of peace.

The conversion of the 111th Cavalry to the 200th Coast Artillery proceeded without further incident. The New Mexico School of Mines (now the New Mexico Institute of Mining and Technology) at Socorro offered a training class for officers and noncommissioned officers of the new unit. Those long accustomed to horses now had to learn about ranges and trajectories. By August 1940 they had completed training, and almost all equipment had arrived at the unit's armories. Summer encampment at Camp Luna near Las Vegas marked the first time the 200th took the field, and in early January 1941 the unit activated for federal service. Its performance during the next few months earned it the distinction of being the premier anti-aircraft outfit in the U.S. Army. In August 1941 the unit received orders commensurate with its status: to report to the Philippines. There during the Japanese invasion of 1941–42, the unit distinguished itself in the Bataan and Corregidor campaigns. The 200th earned a reputation as "the unit first to fire and the last to lay down arms." The rigors of the Bataan Death March and years as prisoners of war in Japanese camps brought out the honor and valor of the 200th Coast Artillery.[36]

Construction of the Albuquerque Army Air Depot in 1941, arguably the most significant event in the period 1900–1942, foreshadowed the future relationship between New Mexico and the military. A small base with a few buildings, its growth accelerated during World War II. New Mexico participated in the national growth of military installations with several Air Corps bases.[37]

The Albuquerque Army Air Depot eventually joined with two other bases to form Kirtland Air Force Base. Named after Roy C. Kirtland, a pioneer in the Army Air Corps, Kirtland today dominates the southeastern quadrant of Albuquerque. The base serves as host to a variety of defense-related agencies, including Sandia National Laboratories; Field Command, Defense Nuclear Agency; the Naval Weapons Engineering Facility; and the Air Force's Phillips Laboratory.[38]

Holloman Air Force Base near Alamogordo and Cannon Air Force Base at Clovis were established in 1942.[39] Holloman and Cannon both began as training bases for bombing and gunnery missions. Holloman eventually became an early center for air force research and development in rocket and missile technology. Cannon Air Force Base became associated with the Air Force Tactical Command after World War II. During the 1990s the Cannon and Holloman bases were home to the F-111 and F-117A (Stealth Fighter) fleets, respectively.[40]

A fourth major installation set up during World War II was White Sands Missile Range. Opened in February 1945, it served as a base for experiments on captured German V-2 "buzz bombs." The first atomic bomb was tested at Trinity Site on White Sands Missile Range on July 16, 1945, as part of the Manhattan Project. White Sands also served as a test range for tactical missiles developed by the army and the air force. In the 1980s the range became the home of some of the most advanced laser technologies in the Department of Defense.[41]

During the first four decades of the twentieth century, New Mexico gradually became enmeshed in national defense. New Mexico began the century as an isolated territory of the United States with a newly formed National Guard. The guard had deep roots in the militia of New Mexico—back to 1606 according to one historian—and the future held out profound promise.[42] Slow to realize the potential of federal spending, New Mexico did not come to the attention of federal budget authorities until the depression. Then the military, in the guise of the Army Corps of Engineers, the National Guard, and the army, helped develop the economy of the state. The Corps of Engineers constructed dams that increased agricultural prosperity while reducing damage caused by floods. The guard helped provide money and mechanical training to New Mexicans. The guard also served its community by assisting after floods and fires and searching for lost families, hunters, campers, and children. It garrisoned the United States–Mexico border before and during the Punitive Expedition to Mexico. Along with private citizens, the guard mobilized to fight the Spanish–American War, World War I, and World War II. The army contributed many local political leaders to New Mexico during the late territorial period. As the army mobilized and expanded in size for

World War II it, brought tremendous changes to New Mexico's economy. At the end of World War II, when the army embarked upon atomic, space, and missile technology research, the groundwork laid by the military in New Mexico from 1900 to 1940 served the interests of the nation while marking a new era in New Mexico's history.

NOTES

1.   Myra Ellen Jenkins and Albert H. Schroeder, *A Brief History of New Mexico* (Albuquerque: University of New Mexico Press, 1974), 13–24.

2.   Ibid., 47–50; Allan R. Millett and Peter Maslowski, *For the Common Defense: A Military History of the United States of America* (New York: Free Press, 1984), 145.

3.   Martin Hardwick Hall, *Sibley's New Mexico Campaign* (Austin: University of Texas Press, 1960).

4.   Dale F. Giese, *Echoes of the Drum: Forts of New Mexico* (Tyrone, NM: The Phelps Dodge Corporation, 1976), 16–17, 28–29. For details on the size and unit designations of garrisons, see S. C. Agnew, *Garrisons of the Regular U.S. Army: New Mexico, 1846–1899* (Santa Fe: Press of the Territorian, 1970).

5.   Millett and Maslowski, *For the Common Defense*, 267–69.

6.   John Pershing Jolly, *History [of the] New Mexico National Guard, 1606–1963* (n.l., n.p., 1964), 12.

7.   John K. Mahon, *History of the Militia and the National Guard* (New York: Macmillan, 1983), 108–24.

8.   Jolly, *History*, 13.

9.   Ralph Emerson Twitchell, *Leading Facts of New Mexican History,* 5 vols. (Cedar Rapids, IA: Torch Press, 1911–17), vol. 2, 536–39 gives a fiery contemporary account from a New Mexican perspective. Compare this with Theodore Roosevelt's *The Rough Riders* (many editions). For a look at artifacts from New Mexico's Rough Riders, visit the Rough Rider Museum in Las Vegas, New Mexico.

10.   Jolly, *History*, 71. The text goes on to say that Captain Luna was "honored by the State Legislature and a bronze plaque has . . . been placed in . . . the House Chamber at the State Capitol. Camp Luna, Las Vegas, New Mexico,

for many years the annual training site for the New Mexico National Guard, was named in his honor."

11.   Giese, *Echoes*, 16–17.

12.   Elaine W. Higgins, et al., *The Bear Springs Story, 1850–1960: A History of Fort Wingate, McKinley County, New Mexico* (typescript prepared by the Fort Wingate Centennial Commission, Historical Committee, 1960), 22.

13.   Ibid., 22–23.

14.   Twitchell, *Leading Facts*, vol. 5, 372–73.

15.   Higgins, *Bear Springs Story*, 24; pages 24–27 recount an assortment of incidents—some poignant, some quaint—at Fort Wingate while these Mexican soldiers were present at the post. The loyalty of these troops is not recorded. There is a possibility that they were loyal to former general Victoriano Huerta, who had seized power in February 1913 just before the assassination of President Francisco Madero. This might explain why some soldiers feared reprisals should they return to Mexico. On the other hand, this might have been merely an excuse to remain in the United States. There is also the fact of the Mexican government's negotiations for the return of the soldiers: given the volatility of events in Mexico, would Carranza's government have wanted the return of men loyal to Huerta, even though Huerta had died? Given this factor, it seems likely that these soldiers were loyal to Carranza; however, further research is needed before a definitive statement can be made.

16.   This account of the raid was summarized from Haldeen Braddy, *Pancho Villa at Columbus: The Raid of 1916 Restudied* (El Paso: Texas Western College Press, 1965). Twitchell, *Leading Facts*, vol. 5, 379–80.

17.   Jolly, *History*, 17. Guard troops from all over the nation reflected a similar desire for active duty, and all were disappointed with border garrison duty. For details, see Mahon, *History of the Militia*, 151–52. The other guard unit attached to Pershing's forces was the second Massachusetts Infantry.

18.   Twitchell, *Leading Facts*, vol. 5, 400, quotes extensively from Herring's report. Interview by Barron K. Oder with Cheryl Tuttle, New Mexico Air National Guard Recruiting Office, May 4, 1992. For a brief account of the origins of U.S. air power and the limited role of aircraft in support of the punitive expedition, see John F. Shiner, "Benjamin D. Foulois: In the Beginning," in John L. Frisbee, ed., *Makers of the United States Air Force* (Washington, D.C.: Office of Air Force History, U.S. Air Force, 1987), 11–41. For a first-hand account

of these operations, see the three-part article by Benjamin D. Foulois, "Early Flying Experiences," in *Air Power Historian* (April 1955, July 1955, and April 1956).

19.   Jolly, *History,* 15.

20.   Lansing B. Bloom et al., "New Mexico in the Great War," *New Mexico Historical Review* (April 1926): 115–16; (October 1926): 419. Jolly, *History,* 19, gives the location of Camp Funston. A second site for training New Mexico volunteers was Camp Cody in Deming.

21.   Bloom et al., "New Mexico in the Great War," *New Mexico Historical Review* (April 1926): 109–14, 116.

22.   Ibid., 110–12; Bloom et al., "New Mexico in the Great War," *New Mexico Historical Review* (October 1926): 425–26; J. R. Kelly, *A History of New Mexico Military Institute, 1891–1941* (Albuquerque: University of New Mexico Press, 1953), 129–30.

23.   Bloom et al., "New Mexico in the Great War," *New Mexico Historical Review* (October 1926): 425–28. This figure does not include those who enlisted in the armed forces of the Allied nations before U.S. entry into the war, or several hundred New Mexicans accepted into service by local draft boards but returned home for medical reasons after they had reported for duty. Thus, the number of New Mexicans who served is slightly higher than the figure provided in the text.

24.   Michael Martin and Leonard Gelber, *Dictionary of American History* (Totowa, NJ: Littlefield, Adams, 1978), 659–60.

25.   Jenkins and Shroeder, *Brief History,* 76.

26.   Higgins, *Bear Springs Story,* 28.

27.   Ibid., 29.

28.   Michael E. Welsh, *A Mission in the Desert: Albuquerque District, 1935–1985* (Washington, D.C.: U.S. Army Corps of Engineers, 1985), 19–21.

29.   Charles J. Sullivan, *Army Posts and Towns: The Baedeker of the Army* (Burlington, VT: Free Press Interstate Printing, 1935), 198.

30.   Albuquerque, *Journal,* June–September, 1934; Jolly, *History,* 23–24.

31.   Jolly, *History,* 24–25.

32.   Welsh, *Mission,* 20–25.

33.   Jolly, *History,* 21–26, 29.

34.   Ibid., 29.

35.   Ibid., 29–30, cites this case as *Charlton v. French.*

36. Ibid., 30, 32–39.

37. Don E. Alberts and Allan E. Putnam, *A History of Kirtland Air Force Base, 1928–1982* (n.l., n.p., 1985), 20–31. In 1943, RKO filmed the motion picture *Bombardier* at Kirtland. This movie offers sporadic views of the airfield, practice bombing ranges, and the city of Albuquerque.

38. Information brochure published by 1606th Air Base Wing Public Affairs Office, "Kirtland Air Force Base," (n.p., n.l., n.d.).

39. Daniel F. Harrington, "A Brief Military History of New Mexico," unpublished typescript. United States Air Force Phillips Laboratory History Office, Kirtland Air Force Base, Albuquerque, NM.

40. Ibid.; Interview, Barron K. Oder with TSGT Scott P. Berry (historian for 27th Tactical Fighter Wing, stationed at Cannon Air Force Base), May 6, 1992. George F. Meeter, *The Holloman Story: Eyewitness Accounts of Space Age Research* (Albuquerque: University of New Mexico Press, 1967), 185.

41. Harrington, "Brief Military History"; Jenkins and Schroeder, *Brief History,* 77.

42. Jolly, *History.*

ANNOTATED BIBLIOGRAPHY

Many sources contributed to this brief discussion of the military in New Mexico, 1898–1940. Some, however, played a more prominent role than others. The works contributing the most to this essay were: Alan R. Millett and Peter Maslowski, *For the Common Defense: A Military History of the United States of America,* (New York: Free Press, 1984); Russell F. Weigley, *The American Way of War: A History of United States Military Strategy and Policy,* (New York: Macmillan, 1973; also in paperback edition: Bloomington: Indiana University Press, 1977); Russell F. Weigley, *The History of the United States Army,* (New York: Macmillan, 1967); Marvin Fletcher, *The Peacetime Army, 1900–1941: A Research Guide* (New York: Greenwood Press, 1988); John K. Mahon, *History of the Militia and the National Guard* (New York: Macmillan, 1983); John Pershing Jolly, *History [of the] National Guard of New Mexico, 1606–1963,* (n.l., n.p., 1964); Charles J. Sullivan, *Army Posts & Towns: The Baedeker of the Army* (Burlington, VT: Free Press Interstate Corporation, 1926 [1st ed.], 1935 [2d ed.], 1942 [3d ed.]); and Elaine W. Higgins et al, *The Bear Springs Story, 1850–1960: A History of Fort*

Wingate, McKinley County, New Mexico (typescript prepared by the Fort Wingate Centennial Commission, Historical Committee, 1960). Millett and Maslowski, Weigley's works, and Mahon's book each provided a general framework for perspective on national affairs and how New Mexico reflected or refuted national military trends. Fletcher's bibliography—an essential reference for students of the military in this period—is a well-organized and comprehensive annotated bibliography. Fletcher concentrated on assembling a list of English-language publications appearing, for the most part, after World War II that addressed Army history. Fletcher excluded publications that dealt mainly with the Navy or the evolution and development of air power. Each of the book's two chapters (the Army from 1900 to 1917, and the Army from 1919–1941) is divided into sixteen topics ranging from general studies to education in the Army to developments in technology and strategy. J. P. Jolly, former Adjutant-General of the New Mexico National Guard, provided a single source for most significant activities of the New Mexico National Guard. Jolly's work is most useful as a fact-book—there is little analysis of events. Despite the author's close association with his subject, Jolly tends to gloss over problems (the pace of enlistments by New Mexicans for World War I, reasons the legislature might have limited funds for the militia, quality of officers, and the like). Higgins et al present a readable popular history of Fort Wingate. This typescript is based on interviews with individuals who lived at the post as well as documents in the Fort's historical files. Anecdotal in some areas, *The Bear Springs Story* tells the tale of the military in human terms. Finally, Sullivan produced a series of handbooks for Army personnel to familiarize them with an area prior to transfer for service. Like Karl Baedeker's guidebooks for Europe, Sullivan presented local weather conditions, transportation lines, descriptions of local communities, and similar useful information. *Army Posts & Towns* puts New Mexico into a national perspective, and allows quick comparison with the Army's presence in other states.

SEVEN

A MIGHTY FORTRESS IS THE PEN:
DEVELOPMENT OF THE NEW MEXICO
PENITENTIARY

JUDITH R. JOHNSON

PRISONS created a measure of stability in the western territories of the United States. As part of the overall system of law and order, these institutions reflected and incorporated society's values, traditions, and controls. In order to develop secure and, if possible, profitable penitentiaries, officials in the territories turned to Washington, D.C., and to eastern models. Although the circumstances for each territory differed, external and internal forces in each influenced the growth of penal institutions. In many ways, these prisons mirrored contemporary issues and trends in other areas of the country. The problem of overcrowding and the need to provide work for inmates dominated the concerns of prison authorities in the West just as they did those in the East and the South.[1] The development of the territorial penitentiary in New Mexico for adult male inmates clearly demonstrated that pattern.

In 1853 Congress authorized $20,000 for New Mexico to build a prison, but construction was complicated and delayed for over three decades by conflicts within the territory over the site and objections to the prison's distance from Washington and to the unrealistic congressional stipulation that New Mexico complete the facility in two years.[2] In the interim convicts sentenced to hard labor served their time in nearby state prisons, and local jails housed those sentenced for shorter periods. Factors such as the cost of sending prisoners outside the territory; the arrival of the railroad, which increased the population of the territory; and the potential for using convict labor eventually motivated the territorial government to put aside conflicts and build a prison.

Concerned U.S. citizens and prison administrators organized the National Prison Association (NPA) in 1870 to improve conditions within penitentiaries with an emphasis on reform of inmates rather than punishment. However, officials in New Mexico postponed joining that group until after the turn of the century. Legislators concentrated less on reform and more on the establishment of a punitive, regulated, and secure institution. At the same time those lawmakers hoped to make the prison self-sufficient, even profitable, by contracting inmate labor to private enterprises or to the government for use on public projects. An appropriate beginning of the convicts' labor, the legislators reasoned, was in the construction of the prison itself.

Finally, in 1885 New Mexico officials completed a stone structure outside the city of Santa Fe. Although the legislature had not designated the capital city for the location, it had empowered the board of penitentiary commissioners to choose an appropriate site. The commissioners examined plans used in the construction of the Utah State Prison, but they adopted instead a design patterned after that used for the penitentiaries at Joliet, Illinois, and Sing Sing, New York.[3]

After completion of the penitentiary, the convicts worked on the capitol grounds in Santa Fe or as contract labor for private citizens. Within a year, inmates also began a brick-making business, using materials from the prison site. With inmate labor and prison-made bricks, the territory again saved money in 1892 when the legislature voted to increase the size of the prison.[4]

Work, officials believed, offered one way for prisoners to escape the drudgery of incarceration. However, there were never enough projects to keep all the prisoners busy. The administration tried to remedy this situation with the establishment of a library and religious services, but the problem of unoccupied inmates remained a constant source of concern.

Aware of the potential for disciplinary problems, Superintendent Edward Bergman stressed in his annual report in 1899 that employment not only produced material benefits but also improved the moral and physical health of inmates. Reform became possible, he added, with "habits of industry" that did not conflict "with honest men's work." Therefore, the superintendent pursued work activities and supported the practice of teaching inmates a trade. During Bergman's tenure as superintendent, the convicts acquired useful skills as stone cutters, masons, and carpenters laboring on building projects for the territory.[5]

The quest to find profitable and rehabilitative employment for all inmates was a focus of prison administrators throughout the early years of the twentieth century. In 1903 officials in New Mexico created a scheme to use prisoners in building highways for the territory. In an act approved by the legislature, the members voted "to authorize and require use of penitentiary labor to construct a public road from Santa Fe to Las Vegas, New Mexico." The lawmakers noted that road work served as healthful employment for the inmates, provided a policy for controlling the prison labor problem, and avoided competition with free labor. The territory included a "good time" allowance for inmates who worked on the road. The allowance offered a decrease in sentence commensurate with the amount and quality of work performed.[6] Because of the program's success in New Mexico, other states in the West eventually adopted a road-building program for their prisoners.

Road construction for inmates attracted the support of Progressive reformers active throughout the United States in the first two decades of the twentieth century. The Progressive Era added a decisive element to prison reform and, through a variety of programs, aimed to create social justice and control. Probation, parole, and the indeterminate sentence were characteristic Progressive innovations in the field of criminal justice. These were programs that emphasized the treatment of each criminal as an individual.[7]

Progressives, including Theodore Roosevelt, also believed that constructive labor led to the reform of the criminal. In identifying work as a rehabilitative tool, reformers recognized that interesting, productive, and meaningful work is a necessity for all, whether free or imprisoned.[8] The New Mexico road-building plan appealed to Progressives because it involved individualized treatment and reform through labor. Completed roads, of course, also benefited the people of the state or territory by improving the transportation system.

Encouraged by the Good Roads Commission's statewide campaign demanding better highways, New Mexico in 1912 increased the number of convicts engaged in road work and expanded the area served. For example, inmates worked at La Bajada, a steep, tortuous mountain pass between Santa Fe and Albuquerque, the two principal cities of the state.[9] Moreover, in response to a request by the Retailers' Association of Raton for improvements on the highway near their city, the penitentiary sent forty convicts to work there. The businesses had supported their petition with a claim that the road was the main highway from Texas and Oklahoma along the scenic route. It brought tourists to New Mexico, they claimed, and helped local farmers and ranchers transport their goods.[10] For this work, the state highway department paid the prison one dollar per day for each man who worked eight hours. By 1917 the inmates earned 15 cents a day and forty days of "good time" for every thirty days they worked.[11]

Besides providing employment, New Mexico officials initiated reforms to improve discipline and to modernize custody. The prison board eliminated the striped suit except as a form of punishment and substituted blue uniforms. Prisoners had to participate in formal exercises in the yard, and after working they played baseball, handball, and quoits.[12]

The most significant reform of this era for New Mexico, and one endorsed by the Progressives, was the opening of a prison school in November 1914. This effort represented the first attempt by the state to educate inmates, and although it was small, the program was a beginning and a recognition of education as a reformatory tool. An educated inmate taught reading and writing in English and Spanish to the forty men who enrolled in the school. The students attended class one hour each weekday and studied in their cells in the evening.[13] The inmates also had access to a small prison library that circulated books in both languages.[14]

New Mexico officials earlier explored the concept of education to include vocational components. For this purpose, the prison board urged the legislature in 1912 to purchase 250 to 300 acres of irrigable land near the prison for farming. There, the board suggested, the inmates could learn scientific agriculture and husbandry under hired specialists.[15] This is another example of New Mexico's use of Progressive principles.

When the United States entered World War I, convicts in New Mexico used their farming skills to aid the war effort. Throughout the war inmates cultivated 640 acres in the northern part of the state held by the local Council of Defense. For this effort the penitentiary received compensation from a war-fund appropriation, and the state earned credit toward its account for agricultural production.[16] Other contributions from inmates during the war included the purchase of Liberty Bonds and the manufacture of socks for the Red Cross using a knitting machine the organization installed in the prison.[17]

Although the prison population decreased during World War I, officials in New Mexico continued to view parole as a means of alleviating overcrowding as well as a reform agent. Earlier, at the request of Warden John B. McManus, the legislature had adjusted policy to pay the parole officer out of an appropriation in the budget rather than from the convicts' earnings.[18] This change gave credence to the decisions of the parole division and facilitated financial transactions. By 1916 the prison board reported that 93.2 percent of the parolees "made good" and that this record "was probably equaled by few if any other state in the Union."[19]

After the war and despite the success of parole, education, and work projects for inmates, more conservative elements in society became disenchanted with what they saw as a trend away from individual responsibility. They rejected reforms that were intended to improve inmates as well as their living conditions. New Mexico society during the 1920s returned to the principle that criminals should pay for their crimes while incarcerated. An editorial in the Albuquerque *Evening Herald* argued against the "molly coddling" of prisoners. While opposing a return to brutal treatment of prisoners, the writer urged the adoption of a system that emphasized cleanliness, proper food, and adequate shelter under the close supervision of guards. All the same, the editor concluded, prisoners should have to work at jobs that earned money for the operation of the penitentiary.[20]

While inmates continued to labor on road projects and to manufacture bricks and tiles, there was never enough work for all the prisoners. Consequently, disciplinary problems increased. Overcrowding four hundred inmates serving time in a structure designed for about two hundred contributed to the problems.

A clear example of the destructive behavior of idle inmates occurred in the evening of July 19, 1922, when convicts staged a revolt against prison conditions. Under the leadership of J. W. Stocking (alias Joseph McMasters), who was serving six to seven years for robbery, the inmates demanded more food, a greater variety in the meals served, and the elimination of beans from their diet. When the convicts resisted an order to return to their cells, the guards in the towers fired, killing one inmate and wounding five others.[21]

An investigation by the penitentiary commission followed that incident and stimulated a debate over the quality of prison management and the use of excessive force to maintain discipline. Ruling that the revolt stemmed from a lack of control, the penitentiary commission censured the staff of the prison, particularly Warden Placido Jaramillo, for shooting at the convicts. The root of the problem, according to the report, was the appointment of unqualified and inexperienced political appointees to positions of authority at the prison. In a practice not unique to New Mexico, newly elected governors throughout the early decades of the twentieth century routinely selected as wardens friends and supporters from their own political party. Instead, New Mexico needed a trained expert to administer the penitentiary and to control inmates without resorting to brutal force.[22]

Another investigation by the state attorney general's office after the riot revealed that inmates who spoke against the warden suffered beatings and solitary confinement. As a result of this finding investigators urged the penitentiary board to examine conditions related to poor management, slack discipline, and cruel treatment.[23]

The board of prison commissions held a second inquiry, but the focus shifted as the investigation became absorbed in political turmoil. Some board members who opposed Warden Jaramillo on partisan grounds attempted to remove him from office with a charge of malfeasance. Taking the issue to the public forum, other board members tried to justify the actions of the warden and the guards. They reminded citizens that the prisoners involved in the revolt were not the "Sunday School" type but hardened criminals with records of violence and attempted escapes.[24] The opponents of Jaramillo won when the new governor, James J. Hinkle, convinced John McManus to return as warden.

The new warden in his 1923 report to the board of penitentiary commissioners described the deplorable physical condition of the prison, the ineffective disciplinary measures, and the poor quality of food and clothing for the inmates. McManus also protested that the cell houses were dirty, cluttered, and overrun with vermin. Prisoners wore civilian clothing rather than the prescribed uniform. As a final indictment of the distressful conditions in the penitentiary, McManus complained that of 179 blood samples taken from prisoners on admission, 28 tested positive for syphilis.[25]

The uprising in 1922 and the dispute over the prison administration attracted the public attention, but the question of pardons by the governor stimulated an even livelier debate. Wardens had previously complained that the indeterminate sentence limited their power. Administrators throughout the United States believed in the 1920s that the politically inspired pardons by governors weakened their positions of authority and diluted their control. The prerogative of the governor, immediately after the costly process of arrest and trial, to release or pardon the criminal caused a loss of respect for the court system.[26]

While the state disputed the value and propriety of pardons, Warden

McManus concentrated his efforts on increasing the efficiency of penitentiary management and ended his first fiscal year in 1924 with all bills paid.[27] A short time later, controversy again disrupted the prison administration. In 1925 Governor A. T. Hannett forced the resignation of Bronson Cutting from the penitentiary board. As a Progressive, Cutting opposed machine politics and corruption in government. When Cutting challenged the governor on other state appointments and refused to follow party lines, Hannett removed him from the board. The governor's political enemies then leaped to the defense of Cutting, precipitating a debate that lasted for almost a year. In the meantime Warden McManus managed to remove himself from the dispute and brought a brief period of stability to the penitentiary.[28]

Before the end of the decade another problem developed at the prison. In 1929 the state legislature passed a bill that required the enforcement of capital punishment by electrocution instead of by hanging. The act also specified that executions take place at the penitentiary rather than in the county of sentence. The new law required the warden to supervise the construction of the death-cell house. At that time no one in the state knew how to build an electric chair, so the new warden, Pat Dugan, sought outside assistance. Dugan also began a search for an expert who knew how to carry out the electrocution. By July the warden reported that he had corresponded with someone who had performed "executions of this character" in other state institutions and who believed satisfactory arrangements could be made. By the middle of 1930 the warden reported that the death house had been completed and that inmates had constructed a workable electric chair.[29]

The advent of the Great Depression brought additional problems to the prison. Particularly troubling were federal restrictions on the interstate sale of prison-made goods. The limitation decreased income for the penitentiary and work for the prisoners. New Mexico partially solved the problem in 1933 with the establishment of a license-plate factory.[30] The factory helped relieve unemployment in the prison, but the governor, state senators, and the warden all remained concerned about the future of prison industries in the state.

Prison officials were troubled by serious problems throughout the Great Depression, but the entry of the United States into World War II brought relief, particularly in employment for the inmates. Early release through expanded probation and parole programs helped reduce overcrowding, and inmates enthusiastically embraced both plans.

An element of patriotism permeated the penitentiary during the war. As early as 1940 more than 100 inmates petitioned Governor John E. Miles to help them enter the military. In requesting the governor's support, the inmates pointed out that during World War I special consideration had been given to prisoners who wanted to serve their country. In an outburst of patriotism and flowery prose, the inmates wrote that they considered "it an honor to offer our Services with our blood and our lives on the altar of Sacrifice for the preservation of principles laid down by our forefathers."[31]

By 1944 some inmates had left the prison on a conditional release that allowed them to work in war industries. During the year, 282 inmates left, though approximately 30 of them failed to fulfill the requirements of the program. Nineteen former inmates who had gained early release, however, performed exceptionally well and earned a suspension of custody so that they could join the army.[32]

The inmates who remained incarcerated helped the war effort, too. Production remained constant at the brick and tile factory during the war, except for a short time in 1944 when a nationwide coal strike forced the plant to close so that fuel could be conserved for heating. The prison-made bricks were used in the construction of military projects in the state.[33]

Despite a decrease in population, the physical condition of the prison continued to deteriorate during the war. Warden Morris A. Abram reported to Governor Edwin L. Mechem that the facility, built in 1885, had become obsolete. Even though repairs and improvements were made over the years, the prison's limited space and design faults prevented officials from initiating advanced practices for the care and treatment of convicts. Because of these constraints, the warden could not segregate hardened criminals from younger ones or implement any other type of classification system. The warden and the board of penitentiary commissioners agreed that a larger and more modern prison was critical to the success of new programs to shift the focus of incarceration from punishment to rehabilitation. Although members of the legislature agreed in principle with the need for a new prison, appropriations in the budget failed to match their expressions of enthusiasm.[34]

Not surprisingly, the situation inside the prison continued to deteriorate during the postwar period as overcrowding led to increased tensions. The problem became clear to outside observers when on June 15, 1953, inmates staged a riot that lasted over eight hours. The convicts held hostage Deputy Warden Ralph Tahash and twelve guards. Claiming that Tahash, a veteran federal prison official, was "too tough," the inmates demanded his removal. Then "slowly swinging a long butcher knife past his ear," the convicts forced Tahash to write his resignation. The inmates had no guns, but some had armed themselves with homemade weapons and kitchen utensils. Homer Gossett, one of the ringleaders, carried two tear-gas bombs. When he accidentally dropped one, Tahash grabbed it and threw it at the rebelling inmates. At that point, a state policeman near a window passed a gun to the deputy warden, who began shooting. Other law enforcement agents entered the prison from another door. During the shoot-out two prisoners were killed: Gosset, who was a convicted murderer, and Adolph Benavidez, serving time for armed robbery.[35]

As a result of the riot, officials made some changes at the penitentiary, although Tahash continued as deputy warden. Among the innovations was a classification system. Commissioners designated funds and staff for a classification board. Members of the board wrote summaries after interviewing new prisoners. Administrators used these reports to determine the appropriate level of security for inmates and the services available to them. The recommendations of the classification board also determined whether new prisoners could participate in educational and work programs.[36]

Prison administrators also supported the construction of a new penitentiary to relieve overcrowding and to facilitate control. Finally, in

1956 New Mexico built a new facility with a capacity of 1,022 inmates at a site eleven miles from Santa Fe. On 320 acres, with an enclosed area of 37 acres, the new facility was surrounded by two fences, a twelve-foot-high outer fence and a ten-foot-high inner fence. A twenty-two-foot-wide space separated the two enclosures. Inside the building, planners provided for individual cells for 422 inmates and dormitory arrangements for 600 more. The individual cells were ten feet long, six feet wide, and seven feet high, and each contained a toilet, wash basin, locker, table with a drawer, mirror, and clothes hook. When locked up in the cell at night, prisoners were given earphones so that they could listen to radio programs from a central control station.[37]

Inmates moved to the new facility in groups during August 1956. Before the move the administration, recognizing the importance of public opinion, held an open house so that citizens of the state could tour the completed structure. Interest ran high: more than 10,000 people visited the new site in July. To reinforce understanding of the need for the change, administrators held an open house at the old prison after the convicts had left. This event, which attracted almost as many visitors as had visited the new facility, allowed the public to compare the two prisons and view the "inhumane hole, the rattletrap isolation quarters, the vice-breeding club, and other features of the 72 year old penitentiary."[38]

With the physical changes of 1956 came other important innovations in treatment and attitude. For example, an admission or reception unit housed new prisoners for the first four weeks of their stay. During this time the inmates underwent a complete medical examination and a battery of psychological tests. Staff members from both the security and service units questioned each convict before the classification board met. The results of those tests and interviews as well as the severity of the inmate's crime played a crucial role in determining the degree of custody. In keeping with the program devised after the riots in 1953, the board wrote a plan for each prisoner that included an education program, medical and psychological treatment, and vocational training.

Placement in a residential unit of the penitentiary was, however, still determined by race. Separate areas were designated for blacks, Hispanics, and Anglo whites.[39] That policy remained in effect until the 1960s, when the nationwide Civil Rights Movement reached prisons and forced a readjustment in policy to address racial and ethnic inequality. Eventually civil rights advocates widened the scope of their quest to include the rights of prisoners to adequate living conditions, treatment, and appropriate duration of sentence.

External as well as internal forces continued to disrupt the New Mexico Penitentiary in the following decades. Federal courts heard and ruled on cases concerning prisoners' rights that challenged the structure and process of incarceration. Riots, particularly one in February 1980, revealed a lack of control brought on by overcrowding, limited rehabilitation programs, and growing tensions. Frequent warden changes in a system that still often relied on political appointees thwarted attempts to establish orderly and effective management.

At the same time New Mexico society, faced with increasing prison costs, expressed doubts about the purpose of incarceration. Over the years, public opinion had swung from the conservative to the liberal and then back again to the conservative position on the treatment of criminals. Sadly, the debate over punishment versus rehabilitation remains unsettled. And until that question is answered, the penitentiary in New Mexico and those in other states seem doomed to constant struggle, disruption, and despair.

Notes

1.   Blake McKelvey, "Penology in the Westward Movement," *Pacific Historical Review,* 2 (December 1933): 419–20; James A. Wilson, "Frontier in the Shadows: Prisons in the Far Southwest, 1850–1917," *Arizona and the West* 22 (Winter 1980): 323, 332.

2.   Lee Hilley, "The New Mexico Territorial Penitentiary: A Political and Penal History to 1899" (M.A. thesis, University of New Mexico, 1985), 5, 32.

3.   Ibid., 33–37.

4. Ibid., 114.

5. *Message of Miguel A. Otero to the 33rd Legislative Assembly of New Mexico* (Santa Fe: New Mexico Printing Company, 1899), 11–14.

6. *1903–1905 Acts of Legislative Assembly of the Territory of New Mexico, 35th and 36th Sessions* (1909), 56, 113.

7. Arthur S. Link and Richard L. McCormick, *Progressivism* (Arlington Heights, IL: Harlan Davidson, Inc., 1983), 93.

8. Eugene N. Foss, "Reform Through Labor," *Annals of the American Academy of Political and Social Sciences* 46 (March 1913): 38; Theodore Roosevelt, "The New Penology," *Annals of the American Academy of Political and Social Sciences* 46 (March 1913): 5.

9. *Report of Good Roads Commission to Governor, January 1912* (New Mexico, 1912).

10. Petition by Retailers' Association of Raton to Governor William C. McDonald (1913), McDonald papers, New Mexico State Records Center and Archives (hereafter cited as NMSRCA), Santa Fe.

11. *Report to Governor, State Penitentiary 1917–18,* (W. Lindsey Papers, NMSRCA), 10.

12. *Report of Board of Penitentiary Commissioners for 63rd Fiscal Year Ending November 30, 1912* (1913); *Report to Governor, Report of the New Mexico State Penitentiary December 1, 1913* (McDonald Papers, NMSRCA), 3.

13. *Report of Board of Prison Commissioners and Superintendent to the Governor of New Mexico for the 2nd Fiscal Year Ending November 30, 1914* (1915), 6.

14. *Report to Governor, New Mexico Board of Penitentiary Commissioners 1912* (McDonald Papers, NMSRCA).

15. Ibid.

16. *The [Albuquerque] Evening Herald,* 16 May 1917.

17. *Report to Governor, State Penitentiary Report 1917* (W. Lindsey Papers, NMSRCA), 12.

18. John B. McManus to Governor W. C. McDonald, 1 March 1912 (McDonald Papers, NMSRCA).

19. *The Evening Herald,* 28 December 1916.

20. Ibid., 1 June 1920.

21. *Albuquerque Herald,* 19 and 20 July 1922.

22. Ibid., 25 July 1911; Wilson, "Frontier in the Shadows," 328.

23. *Albuquerque Herald,* 26 August 1922.

24. Ibid., 29 August 1922.

25. Report to the Governor, *Annual Report of the Board of Penitentiary Commissioners for the 11th Fiscal Year 1923* (1924), 1–2.

26. *Albuquerque Herald,* 24 November 1922.

27. Ibid., 2 January 1925.

28. Ibid., 15 July 1925; Robert Larson, "The Profile of a New Mexico Progressive," *New Mexico Historical Review* 45 (July 1970): 239; Frank D. Reeve, *History of New Mexico,* vol. 2 (New York: Lewis Historical Publishing Company, 1961), 358.

29. *Report of the Superintendent of the New Mexico State Penitentiary to the Governor, July 1, 1929* (Dillon Papers, NMSRCA); *Report to the Board of Commissioners and Superintendent of the State Penitentiary to the Governor of New Mexico for the 18th Fiscal Year Ending June 30, 1930* (1930), 6.

30. *Albuquerque Journal,* 24 January 1933.

31. Petition to Governor John E. Miles, June 1940 (Miles Papers, NMSRCA).

32. *New Mexico Penitentiary Annual Report, 1944, to Governor John J. Dempsey* (Dempsey Papers, NMSRCA).

33. Penitentiary of New Mexico, *Report of the Board of Commissioners and Superintendent to the Governor of New Mexico for the 34th Fiscal Year Ending June 30, 1946,* 2.

34. Penitentiary of New Mexico, *Report of Board of Commissioners and Superintendent to the Governor of New Mexico for the Fortieth Fiscal Year Ending June 30, 1952* (1952), n.p.

35. *Albuquerque Journal,* 16 June 1953.

36. Penitentiary of New Mexico, *Report of the Board of Commissioners and Warden to the Governor of New Mexico for the Forty-First Fiscal Year Ending June 30, 1953* (1953), 2.

37. *The New State Penitentiary, New Mexico, Governor John F. Sims, June 1956* (1956), 7.

38. *The Enchanted News* (New Mexico Penitentiary newspaper), 25 September 1956.

39. Blake McKelvey, *American Prisons: A History of Good Intentions* (Montclair, NJ: Patterson Smith, 1977), 330.

EIGHT

URBAN IMPERIALISM IN THE MODERN WEST:
FARMINGTON, NEW MEXICO, VS. DURANGO, COLORADO, 1945–65

ARTHUR R. GÓMEZ

IN 1940 Arthur M. Schlesinger, Sr., published a seminal essay, "The City in American History." In this provocative paper, Schlesinger challenged the time-honored theories of Frederick Jackson Turner on the evolution of American history, particularly as it applied to the West. Arguing that urban development was as significant a factor in national growth as the existence of a vast frontier, Schlesinger offered a theoretical model with which to reevaluate American history from an urban point of view. In his analysis, Schlesinger coined the term urban imperialism to describe the phenomenon that resulted in the spectacular growth of the United States after independence. The competition between America's leading cities to establish regional preeminence, he contended, facilitated the nation's westward thrust.[1]

Some scholars applied Schlesinger's concepts to their own interpretation of American history. Most notably, Richard Wade, in his classic examination of the five leading trans-Allegheny cities, asserted that towns—not merely rugged individuals—were spearheads of the western frontier. "One of the most striking characteristics of western urban development," Wade asserted, "was the emergence of urban imperialism— the scramble and competition between new cities to establish power and influence over the entire country." Others argued that western cities, hungry for acceptance into the national mainstream, offered seemingly inexhaustible natural resources as an incentive for capital investment and political recognition. Thus throughout the nineteenth century Omaha, Denver, San Francisco, Los Angeles, Portland, Seattle, and Houston—in imitation of eastern cities—dominated western development.[2]

Exploitation of resources was significant in the growth of the West before 1900, and even more important after World War II, with one notable difference: aided by the tremendous federal subsidies of the New Deal, the West cast aside its traditional role as a resource colony of the industrial East to forge a distinct regional economy. The scientific and technological advances of the postwar period—another by-product of unprecedented government expenditure—accelerated the pace of urban imperialism among leading cities in the West. As settlement extended and population grew, the demand for energy resources, abundant in the hinterland communities, also increased.[3]

In 1945 competition for regional primacy, which some writers cited as the inspiration for progress, intensified among western cities. A close examination of the postwar period reveals a startling relationship between the metropolitan areas of the West and the hinterland communities surrounding them. Colonialism was still clearly discernible, but in a new form. The exigencies of post–World War II growth forced expanding cities in the West to exploit their own regional resources as never before. Western capitalists assumed the characteristics of their eastern counterparts, adopting the mythical belief that western resources were limitless.[4]

The transition from interregional to intraregional rivalry was most evident between metropolitan giants such as Dallas, Houston, Los Angeles, San Francisco, Portland, Seattle, Denver, Omaha, and their outlying communities. Contrary to rural Populists of an earlier frontier era, who protested the West's status as a resource colony of the East, hinterland communities of the modern West viewed economic ties to urban America as vital to future expansion. Thus it was not uncommon during the 1950s and 1960s for small western cities to champion the exploitation of their natural resources by larger cities. In their quest to promote subregional development, rural communities exercised their own version of urban imperialism. The resulting competition between Farmington, New Mexico, and Durango, Colorado—two small cities nestled in the energy-rich mountains surrounding the San Juan Basin—presents an excellent case study with which to examine western small-city urban imperialism.

The town of Farmington was first settled in 1876 by William and Simeon Hendrickson, two gold seekers from Animas City, Colorado. Durango, about fifty miles northwest, was founded five years later. Originally an agricultural supply center for the Rocky Mountain mining camps of the San Juan Basin, Farmington had a small but steadily growing population that thrived on fruit and cereal production. The arrival of William Jackson Palmer's Denver and Rio Grande Western railroad at Durango in the 1880s prompted Farmington residents to assess the potential of local energy resources. The presence of generous reserves of coal in northwestern New Mexico stimulated an intense rivalry between General Palmer and Edward Henry Harriman, president of the Southern Pacific Railroad: both men sought to establish a link between Farmington and the transcontinental lines that intersected at Gallup. Harriman envisioned the transportation of coal from Farmington to the port city of Guymas, Mexico, for shipment and sale overseas. After two years of litigation, Harriman secured a contract and the right to begin his survey. His untimely death in 1909, followed by the outbreak of the Mexican Revolution one year later, halted the project. As a result, Farmington was left without a major railroad link to the West. Its only rail transportation was Palmer's short-line, narrow-gauge connection to Durango.

The succeeding decades witnessed strenuous efforts in the San Juan Basin to produce alternative sources of energy for a growing America. With the advent of motor travel in the 1920s, oil replaced coal as the nation's leading fuel. Farmington made an early contribution in 1926 with a major petroleum strike just southwest of Shiprock on the Navajo Reservation. The find stimulated Farmington's first population boom, as geologists and roughnecks converged upon the tranquil agricultural community. Most newcomers found work in the oil fields or at the newly built Continental Oil gasoline refinery.

More significant to Farmington's transformation from rural com-

munity to energy boom town was the 1932 discovery of natural gas by the
Southern Union Gas Company of Dallas.[5] Relatively insignificant as a fuel
source before 1945, natural gas—a byproduct of petroleum—grew mea-
surably in the postwar market. Advanced technology aided in natural gas
production, while demand for it as a heating fuel tripled from 1945 to
1960 throughout the Midwest and the Far West. This unprecedented
demand had a long-range impact on the growth of the two San Juan Basin
communities.[6]

Curiously, it was the production of neither oil nor natural gas that
first called national attention to Durango. Rather, postwar demands for
uranium, needed to develop the U.S. atomic-weapons arsenal, focused
government interest on the Four Corners. In response to the Cold War,
the United States placed its highest priority on national security. Central
to this policy were the scientific research laboratories scattered throughout
the West. These were designed to meet U.S. defense needs through
nuclear weapons production. In anticipation of a nuclear confrontation,
the Atomic Energy Commission (AEC) undertook the task of increasing
the nation's stockpile of uranium.

Based on preliminary findings released in January 1948, the AEC
estimated that southeast Utah and southwest Colorado held most of the
world's uranium reserves. Later that year the AEC announced plans to
reactivate the Durango smelter, which had been closed after the silver-
mining days of the 1880s. The plan called for conversion of the facility
into a mill to process carnotite ore. Locals were quick to envision Durango
as the nation's leading producer of uranium concentrate. One enthusiast
saw the project as not only economically beneficial to the community, but
also "a lasting service to mankind for generations to come."[7]

In his State of the Union address in January 1952, President Harry S
Truman proposed a record-breaking defense budget appropriately titled
"The Road to Security." The president stressed production of small
atomic weapons and nuclear submarines as crucial to the security of the
United States. Alarmed by the sudden Communist aggression in Korea,
Truman underscored the need to increase uranium production in the

Mountain West. The AEC would in turn use the processed uranium to supply weapons production plants such as those located in Los Alamos and in Albuquerque. The proposed budget set aside $2.75 million for construction of a fully modernized processing plant in Shiprock.

In 1953 the government announced the sale of its Durango operation to the Vanadium Corporation of America (VCA), a subsidiary of Union Carbide with holdings in South Africa and Latin America. VCA reported that the Durango mill, listed as one of the world's largest producers, was responsible for most of the estimated $75 million worth of uranium ore processed during 1954.[8] It appeared to local residents, at least, that the southwest Colorado mountain town was well on its way to becoming the resource capital of the Four Corners.

Farmington held firm in the belief that its future lay in oil and gas production. In October 1946, Southern Union Gas encouraged these hopes with a significant find in the Barker Dome area, fifteen miles northwest of town. Meanwhile, the Byrd-Frost Company of Dallas, an independent producer, announced its recovery of oil in Kutz Canyon near Bloomfield, New Mexico. These discoveries combined to stimulate serious interest in Four Corners oil and gas exploration among the nation's top petroleum producers—Gulf Oil, Standard Oil of California, Sinclair Oil, Shell, Phillips Petroleum, and Atlantic-Richfield.

So enthusiastic were New Mexicans about the find that one *Albuquerque Journal* reporter proclaimed Farmington "one of the last great undeveloped oil fields in the nation," predicting that drains on national reserves since World War II would result in an inexhaustible market for New Mexico petroleum products. Others were elated over Farmington's potential to become a leading energy producer. A second reporter prophesied, "There is every reason for optimism, indications are that 1949 will be one of the most active years in the history of San Juan Basin."[9]

In that year El Paso Natural Gas announced an ambitious undertaking, a multimillion-dollar pipeline from San Juan Basin gas fields to Toprock, Arizona. At Toprock, the pipeline would link with that of Pacific Gas and Electric to supply San Francisco's sprawling coastal population with gas for heating. In an agreement between the two giant utility companies, El Paso Natural Gas promised to supply the Pacific slope with New Mexico gas at the rate of 205 million cubic feet (mcf) per day beginning October 1, 1949, and ending November 1, 1977. Furthermore, El Paso promised delivery of 17 mcf daily to Gallup, New Mexico, as well as to Holbrook, Winslow, Flagstaff, and other Arizona towns en route to the California border.

Concurrent with these public notices of expansion, Colonel Harold Byrd and Jack Frost, co-owners of the most important wildcat operation in the Four Corners, outlined plans for a second major pipeline. This transmission line, through which the Byrd-Frost Company promised to deliver 450 mcf per day, would link with the Utah Natural Gas Company—chief supplier for the Salt Lake City region. The pipeline would then proceed westward to San Francisco and, company officials hoped, eventually to the Pacific Northwest cities of Portland and Seattle. Byrd-Frost officials stressed the importance of their project to national defense, suggesting that the pipeline could easily be converted to transport crude oil and aviation fuel to the coastal military installations "in the event of a war in Asia."[10]

Farmington's satisfaction with the proposed exploitation of San Juan Basin petroleum resources is clearly evident in the following editorial comment: "Neither oil lease hounds nor newspaper writers can make a boom. We just do our part and wait for someone to bring in the grease." A special feature publication in the *Albuquerque Tribune* noted that the town's population had doubled to an estimated 5,000 inhabitants just two years after the first petroleum strikes. Three hundred new housing starts and a $50,000 office-hotel complex were attributed to increased oil and gas activity in the basin. The arrival of Frontier Airlines' first commercial flight to Farmington validated the city's emergence as a regional energy center. Finally, the enlargement of the corporate city limits from 630 acres to more than three times that size anticipated growth projections of 20,000 inhabitants by 1960.[11]

Not all New Mexicans, however, were eager to go along with the whims of the major producers. Foremost among the dissenters was Senator Dennis Chavez, New Mexico's outspoken senior member of congress. Chavez called for regulatory safeguards to ensure the reservation of enough New Mexico gas for state consumption before shipment to California and Arizona. While Chavez's reasons to limit gas export made sense, stronger arguments were made in favor of supplying gas for national defense. Meanwhile, a battle raged in Washington between the Navy Department and the AEC over who should have greater access to New Mexico's petroleum reserves. The navy regarded its proposed transmission lines as "more essential to national security than the Arabian oil pipelines." Conversely, the AEC, with support from senators Chavez and Clinton P. Anderson, argued in favor of local usage, citing the importance of these resources to atomic weapons research at Los Alamos and Sandia Laboratories.[12]

With the new decade, two momentous events occurred to end the bickering over natural resource exportation. First, the outbreak of the Korean War rallied support in New Mexico for the national defense argument. In his inaugural address of January 1951, governor-elect Edwin L. Mechem pledged the state's oil and gas reserves to the war effort. "We must be in a position to take the fullest advantage of our resources," Mechem said, "particularly those that are important to the maintenance of our independence and our system of government." Equally important, the Byrd-Frost Company announced an enormous gas discovery in southeast Utah, that brought the estimated reserves of the Four Corners to a staggering three trillion cubic feet—enough gas to supply consumers with 100 mcf per day for the next twenty years.[13] This find, combined with the decision to give priority to national security, ensured New Mexico's preeminence among the nation's chief suppliers of oil and gas. Moreover, the state's commitment to supplying the nation assured local residents that Farmington was destined to become a bona fide boom town.

Thus by the 1950s Durango could no longer proclaim itself the unchallenged energy producer in the San Juan Basin. Quite the contrary, Farmington boasted in 1952 that it was the fastest growing city (in terms of percentage) in New Mexico and that housing construction had doubled since the beginning of oil and gas recovery. Seemingly unimpressed, the *Durango Herald News* countered with a special booster publication depicting the southwest Colorado community as the nation's foremost "region of wealth."[14] These claims of regional superiority set the stage for urban imperialism between Farmington and Durango, a development intensified by still another transmission pipeline proposal.

In June 1952 the Pacific Northwest Pipeline Corporation of Houston announced its decision to abort plans to acquire natural gas from Canada to sell in the Pacific Northwest. Instead, the firm opted to build a 1,400-mile pipeline from New Mexico to the Pacific slope states of Oregon and Washington. En route to the West Coast, the company planned to supply natural gas to Green River, Utah; Denver, Colorado; and much of Wyoming.[15] The news touched off a heated court battle between the Houston firm and El Paso Natural Gas Company, which opposed the proposal on the grounds that it infringed upon gas reserves earmarked for California. New Mexico's Oil and Gas Conservation Commission supported El Paso's protest, arguing that a second project of such magnitude would result in a serious depletion of state gas reserves.

Residents of southwest Colorado, on the other hand, were delighted at the prospect of the new pipeline because Pacific Northwest, after its discovery of a natural-gas pool near Ignacio, Colorado, had promised to headquarter the entire operation in Durango. More persuasive was the estimated $60 million the company anticipated spending in southwest Colorado to make the project operational. For this reason, a Durango Chamber of Commerce spokesperson advocated construction of the proposed pipeline in an appearance before the Federal Power Commission.

In light of Durango's support of the new pipeline, R. R. Spurrier, executive director of the New Mexico Oil and Gas Conservation Commission, withdrew earlier objections and testified in favor of Pacific Northwest's proposal before the FPC hearings in Washington, D.C. Spurrier concluded that the San Juan Basin held adequate reserves to meet the demands of both the El Paso and the Pacific Northwest pipelines. In addition, ample supplies remained for Southern Union Gas to satisfy its Santa Fe and Albuquerque consumers. Arguing that Pacific Northwest would create an entirely new market for New Mexico's chief export, Spurrier anticipated an increase of 500 to 800 new wells in the Farmington area alone.

Pacific Northwest won its fight the summer of 1954 when the FPC ruled in favor of the pipeline construction. The Canadian government issued a strong protest against the ruling, however, because it hoped to remain the sole supplier of natural gas to Oregon and Washington. Upon receiving news of the decision, Durango civic leaders boarded a plane for Houston in an attempt to persuade Pacific Northwest to place its offices in southwest Colorado as promised. Most residents believed that the new pipeline represented "the closest thing to a (petroleum) boom that Durango was likely to experience."[16]

Durango boosters failed in their bid to host the east Texas firm: Pacific Northwest instead selected Albuquerque as its project headquarters. As the citizens of Durango watched their dreams of regional supremacy fade, Farmington residents observed in the spring of 1955 the completion of El Paso Gas Company's pipeline to California. El Paso's completion of the pipeline caused gas production in the Farmington area to quadruple. Later that summer, the firm made a major petroleum discovery, which promised to make Farmington one of New Mexico's leading oil producers as well.[17] With these developments, the former agricultural community was nearer to fulfilling its desire of becoming the preeminent energy producer in the Four Corners region.

By 1956 Farmington boasted a population of more than 15,000, four times the number of residents listed in the 1950 federal census. City officials anticipated becoming New Mexico's second largest city by the start of the next decade. Observers cited a multifaceted economy that combined energy resource development, irrigated agriculture, and manufacturing as the reason for the city's meteoric rise. Also noteworthy was the proposed Navajo Dam, which promised to further stimulate community expansion as construction workers sought housing in Farmington.[18]

Meanwhile, nuclear arms reduction during the Kennedy years caused the market for processed uranium to decline sharply. In 1962 the AEC terminated its contract with the Vanadium Corporation of America, forcing its transfer from Durango to Shiprock, closer to the handful of mines still in operation on the Navajo reservation. Because of a collapsing mineral-resource economy and the prospect of only marginal success in the energy field, civic leaders turned to tourism as their economic salvation. Local boosters capitalized on a growing nostalgia for the Old West. The re-creation of a frontier town in modern America, they suspected, would lure thousands of would-be cowboys to southwest Colorado. From the mid-1960s on, it can be argued that Durango no longer challenged Farmington as a regional energy capital.[19]

Although Farmington's position as the dominant energy producer remained uncontested, rivalry between the two communities by no means ceased. In the late 1950s and early 1960s, Farmington and Durango were embroiled in controversy over the region's most precious and irreplaceable commodity—water. The controversy centered upon the Upper Colorado River Reclamation and Storage Project. In 1950 the federal government authorized construction of the Navajo Dam on the San Juan River, a tributary of the Colorado, in conjunction with the San Juan–Chama Diversion and Navajo Indian Irrigation Projects. The debate, however, dated back to the 1922 signing of the Colorado River Compact, when Secretary of Commerce Herbert Hoover proposed dividing the waters of the Colorado River among seven western states. On October 11, 1948, the Upper Colorado Basin states—Nex Mexico, Colorado, Arizona, Utah, and Wyoming—signed a second agreement in which they apportioned their share of the Colorado River among themselves.[20]

Farmington residents were uneasy over the proposal that Albuquerque divert its portion of the New Mexico allocation of the San Juan River, thus depriving local farmers of irrigation water. The Navajo Tribe, dependent on the San Juan as its principal source of irrigation for reservation farmlands near Shiprock, expressed similar discontent. The Navajo Tribal Council appealed to the Bureau of Reclamation, claiming prior appropriation rights to 600,000 of the allotted 838,000 acre-feet. The request forced a federal government compromise.

In January 1953 the Bureau of Reclamation proposed a solution calling for three distinct undertakings on the San Juan: the Shiprock Project, an irrigation program for exclusive use by the Navajo Tribe; the South San Juan Project, a second irrigation plan for the non-Indian water users; and the San Juan–Chama Diversion Project, a reclamation proposal authorizing the transmountain diversion of water from the San Juan to the Chama River, a tributary of the Rio Grande, for municipal and industrial use in Albuquerque. The combined irrigation programs called for construction of a storage unit of 1.2 million acre-feet thirty miles east of Farmington.[21]

The Colorado River Storage Project seemed a workable compromise to satisfy all of New Mexico's water needs. Nevertheless, Senator Anderson, chair of the Senate Committee on Interior and Insular Affairs, warned Farmington constituents that passage of the proposal was no certainty. As predicted, the bill met with formidable opposition when it reached the floor of Congress in June 1954. Texas senator Price Daniels objected to the diversion for fear it would take water away from northwest Texas. Two-thirds of El Paso's water supply, Daniels claimed, was derived from the Chama River. Even stronger objections were made by Representative John P. Saylor of Pennsylvania who, like others from coal-producing states, opposed any plan including hydroelectric power in the West. Saylor, a senior member of the powerful House Appropriations Committee, cited the Upper Colorado project as "one of the big battles of the 84th Congress."

Supporters of the proposal included Chairman Clyde Tingley of the Albuquerque City Commission, who argued that the San Juan–Chama project would alleviate serious water shortages in Albuquerque, one of the Southwest's fastest growing municipalities. Mayor Tom Bolack of Farmington underscored the construction of Navajo Dam as vital to industrial growth in the San Juan Basin. The most intriguing testimony in support of the diversion plan was that of Senator Anderson. First, he stressed the importance of San Juan water to New Mexico's principal defense facilities: Los Alamos, Sandia Laboratories, and Kirtland Air Force Base. Next, the senator linked the San Juan project to future reclamation and hydroelectric programs, saying, "If this project is stopped now, a great deal of all reclamation work in the West will stop."[22]

The defense argument for the storage plan had particular appeal in the mid-1950s. Civil Defense Administrator Val Peterson applauded the project on the grounds that in the event of a nuclear attack, West Coast residents would presumably evacuate to the mountain states. It was imperative, therefore, that the region have adequate water and power facilities to accommodate them.[23]

President Eisenhower's endorsement of the project in his State of the Union message in January 1955 virtually assured passage of the bill. On April 11, 1956, Congress authorized construction of four storage units: Glen Canyon on the Colorado River in Arizona, Flaming Gorge on the Green River in Utah, Curecanti on the Gunnison River in western Colorado, and Navajo Dam on the San Juan in northern New Mexico. Although construction on Glen Canyon and Flaming Gorge began the same year, the $10 million in appropriations for Navajo Dam was not budgeted until January 1959.[24] The four-year lapse between authorization of the dam and its construction suggests that opposition to the San Juan diversion project still lingered.

Durango citizens became the strongest opponents of the controversial proposal. Their complaints stemmed from Farmington's claims to water from the Las Animas River—a San Juan tributary that bisects Durango—in addition to its use of the San Juan. Coloradans argued that upon completion of Navajo Dam, Farmington would have more than enough water for municipal use; therefore, the city should relinquish prior claims to any additional water. Durango's strident protest, it appears, was economically self-serving. Southwest Colorado had plans of its own for a reclamation project on the Animas and La Plata rivers. Citizens of Durango believed the proposed Animas–La Plata reservoir would rival Navajo Dam as the basin's premier recreational site. Accordingly, southwest Colorado residents voiced opposition to the San Juan reclamation project before the House Committee on Interior and Insular Affairs in May 1960, citing the San Juan plan as a Farmington "water grab."[25]

The interurban controversy was easily resolved, although perhaps not to the satisfaction of Durango residents. Colorado's senator John Carroll and governor Steve McNichols proposed a compromise to senators Chavez and Anderson of New Mexico. If the New Mexico senators agreed not to oppose construction of the Curecanti Dam on the Gunnison River and to a less-important storage unit on the Florida River near Durango, McNichols and Carroll would ameliorate any "misunderstandings" over the diversion proposal.[26] With last-minute opposition overcome, the long-awaited Navajo Dam, heralded by New Mexicans as "the most significant development since statehood," was dedicated in September 1962.

The mid-1960s marked a turning point in the competitive relationship between Farmington and Durango. No longer energy conscious, Durango turned its full attention to its natural amenities in hope of converting the city to a year-round vacationland. Central to this goal was the announcement in January 1965 of plans to build a multimillion-dollar ski facility north of town.

Farmington, on the other hand, rested its hopes for the future on the time-tested oil and natural gas industry. In 1965 El Paso Natural Gas, with assistance from the AEC, detonated an underground nuclear device to release millions of cubic feet of gas reserves inaccessible through conventional means of production.[27]

Farmington emerged as the dominant energy producer in the Four Corners, and Durango became the undisputed champion of outdoor recreation. Still to come, however, was a bitter feud over the designation of a regional airport; friendly competition for recognition as the area's cultural and educational mecca; and a spirited rivalry to attract an ever-growing national and international tourism market. By 1965 the future of the San Juan Basin looked brighter than ever before. In exploiting the Four Corners' potential in energy production as well as in tourism and recreation, Durango and Farmington readied themselves for renewed urban competition.

NOTES

*This essay is an excerpt from my forthcoming book *In Search of the Golden Circle: The Four Corners and the Metropolitan West, 1945–1970*.

1.   Arthur M. Schlesinger, Sr., "The City of American History," *Mississippi Valley Historical Review* 27 (June 1940): 48–50.

2.   Richard C. Wade, *The Urban Frontier: The Rise of the Western Cities, 1790–1830* (Cambridge: Harvard University Press, 1959), 321–22; Robert R. Dykstra, *The Cattle Towns* (New York: Alfred A. Knopf, 1968); Lawrence H. Larsen, *The Urban West at the End of the Frontier* (Lawrence: University of Kansas Press, 1978), 121–24; Gene M. Gressley, *Bankers and Cattlemen: Politics, Investors, Operators from 1870 to 1900* (New York: Alfred A. Knopf, 1966).

3.   Earl Pomeroy, *The Pacific Slope: A History of California, Oregon, Washington, Idaho, Utah, and Nevada* (Seattle: University of Washington Press, 1965); Gerald D. Nash, *The American West in the Twentieth Century: A Short History of an Urban Oasis* (Albuquerque: University of New Mexico Press, 1973).

4.   For views on the vastness of western natural resources see Carey McWilliams, introductory notes, in Ray B. West, ed., *Rocky Mountain Cities* (New York: W. W. Norton, 1949), 7–28; and especially Bernard DeVoto, "The West Against Itself," *Harper's* 194 (January 1947): 1–13. For an opposing view, see Morris E. Garnsey, *America's New Frontier: The Mountain West* (New York: Alfred A. Knopf, 1950).

5.   Eleanor Davenport MacDonald and John Brown Arrington, *The San Juan Basin: My Kingdom was a County* (Denver: Green Mountain Press, 1970), 73–91; Jerry L. Williams and Paul E. McAllister, ed., *New Mexico in Maps* (Albuquerque: University of New Mexico Press, 1979), 102.

6.   Gerald Nash describes how the population of the West grew at a rate four times that of the remainder of the nation during these years. Increases ranged from 83 percent in Los Angeles to 600 percent in Las Vegas between 1945 and 1960: *Twentieth Century West*, 213–15. Also, Gerald D. Nash, *World War II & The West: Reshaping the Economy* (Lincoln: University of Nebraska Press, 1990).

7. *Durango Herald Democrat,* 25 January 1948 (Durango Public Library Microfilm Collection); Duane A. Smith, *Rocky Mountain Boom Town: A History of Durango* (Albuquerque: University of New Mexico Press, 1980), 161.

8. *Albuquerque Journal,* 21 January 1952 (University of New Mexico, Zimmerman Library Microfilm Collection); *Durango Herald News,* 25 April 1954 (Durango Public Library Microfilm Collection).

9. *Farmington Times Hustler,* 4 October, 1 November 1946 (University of New Mexico, Zimmerman Library Microfilm Collection); Bill Hesch, *Albuquerque Journal,* editorial, reprinted in *Farmington Times Hustler,* 18, 21 February 1947; quote cited in, Vicente T. Ximenes, "The Economic Significance of the Natural Gas Industry in New Mexico," (Master's thesis, University of New Mexico, 1953), 10.

10. *Durango Herald Democrat,* 14 July and 5 December 1948, 4 January 1950; *Farmington Times Hustler,* 16 July and 22 October 1948, 13 May 1949, 28 December 1950, 5 January 1951; Ximenes, "Natural Gas Industry," 30–31.

11. *Farmington Times Hustler,* 3 June 1949 (quote), 20 June 1947, 23 July 1948; projections on Farmington's growth taken from *Albuquerque Tribune,* 17 December 1948 (University of New Mexico, Zimmerman Library Microfilm Collection).

12. *Albuquerque Tribune,* 14 February 1951; Ximenes, "Natural Gas Industry," 22; *Farmington Times Hustler,* 17 December 1948; *San Juan Valley Sun,* 14 December 1950 (University of New Mexico, Zimmerman Library Microfilm Collection).

13. Excerpts from Governor Mechem's inaugural speech cited in *Albuquerque Journal,* 2 January 1951. Estimates of Four Corners gas reserves ranged from 2.2 trillion to 3 trillion cubic feet; see *Durango Herald Democrat,* 4 January 1950; *Farmington Times Hustler,* 22 October 1948.

14. *Albuquerque Tribune,* 31 December 1952. Building permits increased from $891,622 in 1950 to $2,473,544 in 1955. Meanwhile, a special census taken in 1955 indicated Farmington's population had increased to 12,500, three times the 1950 figure of 3,572; see "Fabulous Farmington, New Mexico: The Energy Capital of the West," Chamber of Commerce Report, 1961, 2; *Durango Herald News,* 12 May 1953.

15. *Albuquerque Journal,* 17 June 1952; *Durango Herald News,* 3 February 1953.

16. *Durango Herald News,* 3, 6 February 1953, 18 June 1954; *Albuquerque Tribune,* 18 June 1954.

17. *Albuquerque Tribune,* 21 March and 25 July 1955.

18. *Albuquerque Tribune,* 10 October 1956. A second special census taken in 1956 showed that Farmington's population had tripled since 1950 to 15,115 inhabitants; see "Fabulous Farmington New Mexico," 2.

19. *Durango Herald News,* 4 December, 24 January 1965; *Farmington Daily Times,* 31 January 1967.

20. For a detailed summary of the Colorado River Compact, see Norris Hundley, Jr., *Dividing the Waters: A Century of Controversy between the United States and Mexico* (Berkeley: University of California Press, 1966), 41–136. For coverage of the agreement signed in Santa Fe, see *Farmington Times Hustler,* 15 October 1948.

21. *Albuquerque Journal,* 24 June 1950; *Gallup Independent* editorial, reprinted in *Farmington Daily Times,* 1 March 1951; U.S. Bureau of Reclamation, *Navajo Dam and Reservoir* (Denver: Government Printing Office, 1966), 5–8; *Albuquerque Tribune,* 3 January 1953.

22. U.S. Congress, House Committee on Interior and Insular Affairs, *Colorado River Storage Project: Hearings before a Subcommittee of the House Committee on Interior and Insular Affairs on H.R. 1445,* 83d Cong., 2d sess., 1954. Senator Anderson's quote cited from testimony, 244, 250–55, 526–28, 669.

23. *Albuquerque Tribune,* 2 March 1955.

24. *Albuquerque Journal,* 21 July 1955; *Albuquerque Tribune,* 6 January 1955, 15 October 1956, 19 January 1959; U.S. Congress, House, *An Act to Authorize Construction of Dams on the Upper Colorado River,* P. L. 485, 84th Cong., 2d sess., 1956, H.R. 1445.

25. U.S. Congress, House Committee on Interior and Insular Affairs, *San Juan-Chama Diversion Project: Hearings before a Subcommittee of the House Committee on Interior and Insular Affairs on H. R. 1818,* 86th Cong., 1st sess., 1960; *Durango Herald News,* 7 April 1960; *Albuquerque Journal,* 8, 13 April 1960.

26. *Durango Herald News,* 20 May 1960; *Albuquerque Journal,* 13 April 1960.

27. *Durango Herald News,* 4 December, 24 January 1965; *Farmington Daily Times,* 31 January 1967.

NINE

ORGANIZED LABOR:
Race, Radicalism, and Gender

Robert Kern

IN broad perspective, New Mexico began the twentieth century with a small proportion of its labor force in industry. It has remained rural and nonindustrial, dominated by agriculture, ranching, and service jobs. Only after 1920 did a few areas of employment reach a size that allowed penetration by unions and the spread of a labor consciousness in the work force. In the first half of the century, ethnic lines divided worker affiliation and permitted one group to be used against the other. At times of economic catastrophe radical politics flourished and led to violence and public reaction. After midcentury, however, prosperity and anticommunism bred by the Cold War caused a decline in domestic radicalism and separated gender and ethnic questions into independent issues. But now the state's recent brief and modest period of prosperity may be at an end, and deindustrialization raises serious questions about the future of organized labor in New Mexico.

Starting out in the 1880s, miners and railway workers were the first groups large enough to attract the attention of organized labor. The first local in the state was created by miners in the Black Range south of Socorro, probably around 1884.[1] Soon after, rail workers on the Atchison, Topeka, & Santa Fe joined Knights of Labor chapters in Raton and Las Vegas. The national organization of the Knights of Labor, however, was short-lived. Local ethnic nationalism and the Hispanic *mutualista* tradition soon led workers in other directions.[2] The Mexican mutual groups offered the opportunity for a local social life, and some also provided burial policies and survivor benefits. They were "friendly societies," the first stage in the evolution of unionism.

The Pullman strike of 1894 in Chicago attracted new members and led to minor strike activity in Raton, Las Vegas, and Albuquerque, but New Mexican rail workers generally remained nonunion until 1905 or 1906.[3] Mutualista organizations could not combat the labor policies of powerful eastern companies, but they prepared Hispanic workers for greater collective action.[4]

This was most noticeable among Hispanic northern New Mexican miners, who set a notable example of labor organization by aggressively participating in the militant Western Federation of Miners (WFM), which fought the Rocky Mountain labor war (1892–1918) in southern Colorado.[5] After 1905 other Hispanic miners joined the Industrial Workers of the World (IWW), an anarcho-syndicalist federation with an industrial union philosophy.[6] Both the WFM and the IWW occasionally propagandized mining camps in Dawson, Madrid, and Gallup, although neither the WFM nor the IWW organized coal miners extensively. In the end, the WFM and IWW fought so much over tactics and members that the IWW did not survive the 1920s as a union, and the WFM (which changed its name in 1916 to the International Union of Mine, Mill, and Smelter Workers) fared poorly.[7]

The basic reason for this failure was that miners in these camps had a propensity to strike characteristic of "isolated mass" workers. Wildcat strikes and violence were common.[8] The radicalism of the two unions created an antilabor backlash, and in 1919 the New Mexico legislature passed a criminal syndicalism act aimed at the two groups.[9] This conflict continued spasmodically until the 1950s.

The reemergence of railway employee militancy after a long delay due to the failure of the Pullman strike in 1894 revived union growth. The Rail Brotherhoods gave their support to the Socialist presidential candidate, Eugene V. Debs, an ally of the WFM and later the IWW.[10] The scant records of Albuquerque locals indicate major membership gains and lively activity during Debs's frequent campaigns. Militancy rose to a high point in 1922, when shop workers went on a brief nationwide strike.

During this early period, there was more substantial growth in the American Federation of Labor craft unions than in the industrial unions. The AFL was nearly thirty years old in 1910. The United Brotherhood of Carpenters and Joiners was its largest affiliate in the state and operated locals in Albuquerque, Santa Fe, Roswell, Alamogordo, Tucumcari, Clovis, Carlsbad, and Las Vegas. Other sizable craft unions included machinists, painters, and electricians, most of whom trained young craftsmen through apprenticeship programs and handled the major aspects of labor locally. Many contractors were former union members whose rapport with business agents facilitated cooperation on bids and other work. Union headquarters served as an employment service, a role not assumed by state government until the 1940s. Craft unions quickly became full-fledged American institutions. They assumed a central position in local economic life and contributed to new and growing states like New Mexico by recruiting out-of-state labor.

The railroads brought Anglo workers west. A carpenter, for example, might learn his craft by migrating from job to job, building wooden elevators along rail lines in Iowa, Nebraska, Kansas, Oklahoma, or Texas before arriving in New Mexico. The mines needed skilled woodworkers, Albuquerque was in the process of erecting warehouses to store wool, and other towns showed signs of growth. In general, there were enough projects in the early part of the century to attract a small but steadily growing labor supply.

Job creation jumped throughout the state with the outbreak of World War I and led to a large increase of Hispanic workers. New military camps, increasing mining and forestry activity, and a shortage of railway workers especially attracted Mexican workers from across the border. They were culturally naïve and restless, and more militant than local workers, having experienced the Mexican Revolution. Bosses hired them, but they viewed the Mexicans with suspicion. Harsh treatment of labor became common. The Ludlow massacre in southern Colorado on Easter evening 1914 of striking miners and their families by the Colorado militia, on orders of the governor and the business community, demonstrated this attitude and set a standard for ruthlessness. Ludlow intensified militant labor consciousness as well, and the deportation in 1917 of striking miners and their families from Bisbee, Arizona, to southern New Mexico, typical of similar acts that followed, created even greater uncertainty and anger in the Hispanic community.[11]

Volatility increased within the ranks of labor as larger numbers of Mexican American and Mexican workers entered mining and railway work. Anglo workers got the better paid, semitechnical positions, while minority workers filled the less skilled, often backbreaking jobs. One union official in the 1950s recalled his early days as a miner in 1922 as follows:

> [Minority] groups [were] relegated to the hard and dangerous work of stripping and tunneling [in the mines], but they . . . received about half the wages paid to Anglo workers . . . Mining managers readily admitted that they encouraged and exploited ethnic divisions in their labor force to frustrate unionization. Separate payroll lines, washrooms, toilet facilities, and housing for Mexican-Americans were . . . commonplace.[12]

The National War Labor Board struggled to calm tempers in the Southwest, but the war's end only brought new discontent as wages fell and production dropped.[13] Miners in McKinley County remained particularly obstreperous. There the United Mine Workers of America (UMWA) struggled to organize Gallup American Co. (Gamerco), the largest coal mine in the state, and the union continued its organizing efforts after 1918. The UMWA had used the war years to organize the western bituminous coal industry, but lost the Gamerco contract in 1917 when the mine was sold. Gamerco took part in the UMWA's national strike of November 1919 which affected western mining, even though the federal judiciary aggressively used injunctions to prevent an interruption of production.[14]

Gamerco's troubles typified the turbulence of the postwar era. Economic bad times in the Southwest were especially severe in New Mexico because a drought bankrupted farmers of the Estancia Valley and ranchers throughout eastern New Mexico, thus increasing unemployment just as servicemen returned home.[15] To protect craft unions, the New Mexico Federation of Labor (NMFL) was formed, with offices in Albuquerque and, in 1920, in Gallup. Among NMFL officials, M. J. Lynch, C. P. Fisher, and W. P. Seyfred sided with the UMW and, to a degree, at least, aligned the NMFL with the union. Seyfred, in fact, was arraigned in 1922 for conspiring to bomb the Raton Pass tunnel on the Santa Fe Railway in a vague conspiracy against mine owners.[16] Arthur Hannett, a future governor, successfully defended Seyfred, but labor-union anger remained high and reached a zenith in 1922 when Gamerco miners went on strike in Gallup.[17] Work stoppage lasted for several weeks and led to violence on the strike lines and in town, partly in response to the presence of the state militia and the vigilante activities of the McKinley County Council of Defense.[18] A statement by the sheriff during this period nicely mingled frontier jargon with patriotism: "Anyone who objects to having soldiers about in time of . . . need is either an outlaw, or not an American citizen, or in sympathy with outlaws, or against our government."[19]

The strikes in 1922 shook New Mexico's small population. One state official warned that "we are sitting on a powder keg."[20] Labor issues had already intruded into New Mexico politics during Washington E. Lindsey's term as governor in 1917–18, and the subsequent administration of Octaviano Larrazolo so feared the Railway Brotherhoods that it had them watched.[21] Only Arthur Hannett's administration in 1925–26 took a prolabor stand, but Hannett roused such great controversy over election reform and from the Ku Klux Klan that he was defeated for reelection.[22] The cause of labor-law reform, an important plank in Hannett's program, suffered from his loss.[23]

Racial tension grew worse after intervention by the Harding administration in the railway strike of 1922. U.S. Attorney General Harry M. Daugherty requested an inquiry into the Santa Fe strike to determine whether the work stoppage, by stranding passengers, mail, and perishables in the desert, was a criminal conspiracy created by the thousands of Mexican American and Mexican workers involved in the strike.[24] His investigation got nowhere, but as the surplus of labor increased in the mining industry, companies went to extraordinary lengths to dismiss Mexican miners recruited during World War I. Often no distinction was made between Mexicans and Mexican Americans, and union officials sometimes cooperated in purging all Spanish-speaking workers.

The situation was ready-made for exploitation. The National Mine Union (NMU), founded in 1928 in affiliation with the Communist Party USA (CPUSA) and composed of former IWW and WFM activists, opposed the UMWA for having discriminated against Hispanics in the Gamerco workforce during the strike of 1922.[25] During the next seven years, the NMU used the issue of ethnicity to make slight inroads among western miners and often exploited strikes as major revolutionary crises.

The impact of this tactic was devastating. Jesús Pallares, a native of Chihuahua, Mexico, provides a good example of the emotional complexities caused by ethnicity and radicalism. He had come to the United States during World War I and worked as a miner in Gallup, where he became a member of the NMU. He was fired in 1930 for criticizing Gamerco, found work in Madrid, and became a UMWA representative there, where the coal mining company paid in scrip and made unnecessary paycheck charges and deductions.[26] After a 1934 strike, Pallares was accused of being a communist agitator (even though he was no longer a NMU member), evicted from his house, fired, and blacklisted. He later helped found and organize *La Liga Obrera de Habla Española,* a radical pro-Hispanic pressure group that by 1935 claimed a membership of 8,000.[27] The legislature in 1935 had La Liga and NMU in mind when it unsuccessfully attempted to amend the antisyndicalist law to add, as a felony punishable by fourteen years imprisonment, possession of literature advocating communism. Pallares became a target, and on April 25, 1936, he was jailed by immigration officials pending a deportation hearing as an undesirable alien. Convicted of being a communist, his deportation on June 30, 1936—one of many ordered by the Immigration and Naturalization Service (INS) against Mexicans active in U.S. labor during this period—proved to be a serious blow for La Liga.[28]

The Great Depression only worsened the situation of minority workers. On June 16, 1932, for instance, Gamerco cut wages after its sales dropped by half.[29] Walkouts became frequent as the NMU and UMWA jockeyed to represent miners. Finally, in 1933, when Section 7A of the National Industrial Recovery Act first guaranteed labor's right to organize, the NMU won the struggle to represent Gamerco workers. When the company refused to bargain, the union declared a strike that lasted from August 29 to November 22, and informally much longer.[30] The arrests of principal NMU leader Eusebio Navarro and NMU organizers Bill and Martha Roberts crippled the walkout, but some miners still refused to return and others, many of them Hispanic, were fired. The state militia was sent in and remained in place even after work resumed. Gamerco began hiring nonunion replacements over the protests of NMU officials, who attempted to maintain morale by organizing unemployed or discharged miners into an unemployed council, a tactic frequently used by the CPUSA in the early 1930s.[31]

The climax of this duel came in April 1935 after the sale of company-owned housing to a state senator, who began evicting delinquent renters in the Chihuahuaita district where many of the Mexican miners lived. Navarro, first to be evicted, was arrested and jailed. On April 4 protestors gathered in front of the McKinley County courthouse and jail to challenge his incarceration. Sheriff Mack F. Carmichael took Navarro out the back door for safekeeping elsewhere, but the crowd caught sight of them, and in the melee that followed the sheriff and three protestors were killed and eight others were hospitalized with gunshot wounds.[32] In the next few days, fifty-five miners (the majority Mexican or Mexican American) were arraigned for conspiracy to murder a peace officer, "possibly the largest collective body ever to face criminal charges for a single homicide in the nation's recent history."[33]

Before the trial could be held, another episode dramatically underscored the tension in Gallup. In May a representative of the CPUSA and an International Labor Defense League lawyer were kidnapped by hooded vigilantes and dumped, unharmed but badly frightened, on the Zuni reservation south of the town of Gallup.[34] The CPUSA widely circulated a pamphlet, *Nightriders of Gallup,* and Governor Clyde Tingley was inundated with mail protesting antilabor discrimination in Gallup. Tingley gave the mail to the Federal Bureau of Investigation.[35]

Judicial proceedings were moved from Gallup to Aztec, New Mexico, and ultimately limited to ten defendants. In October 1935, after two weeks of testimony, seven were found guilty of second-degree murder. Following Supreme Court appeals, five were deported, and the two American citizens were ordered out of the state.[36] The NMU was later abolished by the CPUSA as a part of Popular Front strategy that deemphasized frontline communist organizations for broader social protest groups like La Liga, and in 1939, only a few years before the Gamerco mine was shut down, the UMWA finally won the right to represent the miners of Gallup.

By the end of the 1930s the New Deal's labor legislation and collective bargaining provisions had eased the labor crisis. After 1941 World War II boosted the economy by vastly increasing availability of jobs at the many new federal facilities in New Mexico, At the war's end, however, conservatives reacted to the New Deal stress on labor peace through collective bargaining with a concerted effort to weaken the unions. The elections of 1948 included a right-to-work amendment to the state constitution. The measure failed by a wide margin, however, due to opposition from organized labor and the Catholic archdiocese. The archdiocese in particular feared that the initiative, coming so soon after the Depression, would harm its parishioners.[37] Even though the amendment was an important part of the conservative renaissance accompanying the Cold

War, the measure had suspicious origins in at least one very reactionary, racist group, the Christian Knights, a Dallas-based organization.[38] They sought to weaken organized labor by allowing workers to refuse union membership in shops where collective bargaining contracts existed. Although New Mexico has never become a right-to-work state, the idea continued to be reintroduced in the legislature every year or two, and Democratic governors have had difficulty with the issue.

Radicalism did not immediately disappear at the end of the decade, and ethnic awareness increased. Ethnic awareness grew with the integration of the military by President Harry S Truman in 1947, efforts to secure a fair employment practices bill within the state in 1949, and Senator Dennis Chávez's influential role in Truman's executive order establishing a Fair Employment Practices Committee at the federal level in 1951.

One strike during the postwar period fused both radicalism and ethnicity. From October 1950 to January 1952 a strike at Empire Zinc in Hurley, New Mexico, again raised questions about labor and race relations in the Southwest.[39] The preponderantly Hispanic miners (only twelve of the ninety-two strikers were Anglo), represented by the allegedly procommunist International Union of Mine, Mill, and Smelter Workers' (IUMMSW) Local 890, struck over unmet wage and hour demands.[40] St. Joseph Lead Co., Empire's owner, was accused by the IUMMSW of "foster[ing] division between Mexican Americans and other workers to break labor unity." For the first time in its history the IUMMSW took a pro-Hispanic position. It took this position largely because charges of communist infiltration made against it by the federal government had brought the union near to collapse.[41] Once again the fifteen-month-long strike witnessed all of the confrontations and threats, fanned by participation of a suspect union, that had become familiar in Gallup fifteen years earlier.

However, two aspects of the strike were novel. The first was the filming on location of a motion picture about the strike entitled *Salt of the Earth*. A few members of the production team (primarily the producer and writer) were Hollywood radicals blacklisted by the studios in the anticommunist scare brought on by the Cold War.[42] The coincidence of the strike with the outbreak of hostilities in Korea, combined with the film makers' reputations, created a patriotic backlash and made the movie company as provocative as the strike itself.

The second unusual aspect of the strike was gender. Wives and daughters of strikers took over picket lines when the men were arrested, and they conducted many strike-related activities themselves. Much has been made of their role, although their militancy and centrality to the strike may not have been as great as has been claimed.[43] Gender solidarity in mining camps had always been high, however, and perhaps *Salt of the Earth* simply stressed an important aspect of women's role in mining communities that had been previously overlooked.[44] In any case, gender later became an important social issue in American society, and today *Salt of the Earth* is perhaps remembered best as one of the earliest contemporary portrayals of gender-related labor issues.

In January 1952 the Empire strike was ended by a negotiated settlement. Hours were not reduced, wages increased slightly, and benefits were added to the contract. Some strikers were never rehired, however, and the IUMMSW itself ceased operations in 1966 after government prosecution forced its merger with the United Steelworkers.[45] The potent issue of communism in the labor movement made protest decline precipitously after anticommunism became a crusade.

Civil rights became a separate issue. As federal law evolved from the *Brown v. Board of Education* decision of the U.S. Supreme Court in 1954 to the passage of the Civil Rights Act in 1965, the divisive questions of race and radicalism in the labor movement diminished. Hispanics were not covered by early civil rights reform, but until civil rights law was broadened, the greater volume of government spending at the local level allowed federal antidiscriminatory statutes to dominate ethnic issues in New Mexico and to begin addressing a few local issues.[46] In this regard, the Empire strike was more a catalyst for "the evolution of a civil-rights movement among Mexican Americans" than a strengthening of the labor movement.[47]

On a broad front, unions now faced new challenges without the appeal of radical politics or ethnic consciousness in their favor. The state opened employment centers that replaced union halls as the principal arena for labor transactions. Industry, driven by rising costs, adopted an economy of scale that dwarfed unions. One prime area of change was home construction, which evolved from small contractors into large concerns like AMREP. Without regaining control of the industry, craft unions such as that of the United Brotherhood of Carpenters and Joiners streamlined into statewide operations, combining many locals into larger, more efficient units, but at the expense of trade unionism's vital and familiar place at the center of local life.[48]

Younger workers entering the contemporary job market viewed organized labor as another bureaucratic element in their lives, a further obstacle to getting a job. Nonunion labor grew rapidly and made major inroads into all craft-union constituencies, occasionally destroying weaker and entirely Hispanic unions such as the roofers. At state and national levels, labor held on to the principles of New Deal labor legislation with difficulty, often suffering setbacks and unpopularity when they lobbied too vigorously. The Taft-Hartley Act in 1947 was their most serious defeat, and only rarely thereafter did local labor action temporarily reverse this steady decline.

The most successful labor dispute of this later period was the Foodway strike in 1977. Retail clerks hurriedly defended themselves against Winn Dixie's purchase of Foodway stores in the state. The dispute centered on a contract issue concerning unfair labor practices in matters of pay scale and grievance. Of a thousand stores owned by Winn Dixie, only thirteen in New Mexico had a union contract. The strike began in Las Cruces and Carlsbad in June 1977, and spread to Albuquerque, Santa Fe, and Taos in December. The retail clerks' strike arose from a strong sense of ethnicity, since the workforce was largely Hispanic. Community support of the strike was high in southern New Mexico, and the union used good publicity, a positive emphasis on the value of unions, a well-enunciated stress upon services provided by organized labor, a campaign to keep stores in the neighborhoods they served, and a realistic under-standing of the use of gender issues. In the end, Winn Dixie sold its investment to Smiths when it failed to dislodge the union shop.[49]

Gender was important in the Foodway situation, and it remains vital today. Gender issues developed rapidly during the early 1980s, when the coalition of Labor Women was active in Albuquerque and to a lesser extent around the state. Labor disputes involving female workers at Pioneer Wear, Levi Strauss (arbitrated by the National Labor Relations Board), GTE Linkert (which ended in court after women workers were exposed to carcinogens) and Ethicon occurred between 1965 and the present.[50]

Looking back at the short history of labor in New Mexico, we can see that during the first half of the twentieth century, race and radicalism animated labor and troubled ethnic groups as much as any single issue. From the Knights of Labor fiasco onward, Hispanics may have been considered marginal to the labor movement despite their numerical superiority in the state. Anglo racial attitudes forced them into low-paying, difficult work and often excluded them from union membership. Even miners' unions, accustomed to immigrants and persons of color, sometimes hid prejudice and corruption behind militant social and politi-cal ideology.[51] Craft unions were particularly blatant in excluding His-panic workers, and Anglos were sometimes all too willing to take jobs of strikers by becoming strike-breakers in Hispanic-dominated disputes, such as the Empire strike.[52]

The 1922 Gallup conflict, because of Seyfred's militancy, raised expectations to a new level, but Hispanics soon felt that the UMWA minimized their role by failing to appoint Mexicans or Mexican Ameri-cans to responsible positions.[53] As a result, job insecurity and fear of outsiders as strike-breakers generated a millenarian attitude among some Hispanic miners.

Jesús Pallares was a good example. He sought elementary social justice until, failing to receive humane treatment, he finally poured his frustrations into La Liga. La Liga was an unique example of what can be called "primitive rebellion," a movement that sought social justice in the style of a biblical day of judgment, seeking to redress the disasters of the Depression and the inequities of mining-camp society.[54] Pallares's demands and those of La Liga were met instead by INS deportations, a tactic also used fifteen years later, during the Empire strike.[55]

The Communist-dominated NMU accepted Hispanic leadership as a tactic to defeat the UMWA in Gallup. In the long run, however, not even the CPUSA took much interest in the NMU. Had it not been for easterners summering in the "intellectual colonies" of Taos and Santa Fe, the Gallup strike and nightrider incident might have disappeared rapidly from view.[56] The Empire strike in the 1950s was a diminished echo of earlier issues, but labor-union radicalism was already in the process of being curbed by anticommunist legislation. Hispanic protest took other avenues and eventually benefitted from civil rights legislation that attempted to create fair employment practices through federal law. As a result, the labor movement faded as a vehicle of social change in New Mexico. It remains to be seen whether unsolved gender and ethnic issues may someday revitalize it.

Bread-and-butter craft unionism still survives, but it is always on the defensive, protecting what remains of New Deal labor legislation. The single recent union achievement, collective bargaining for public employees (who traditionally have not been a part of organized labor), was a dubious success, despite efforts by the American Federation of State, County, and Municipal Employees (AFSCME) to further develop these clerical unions. But even if public-employee bargaining rights survive repeal attempts, the constraints in dealing with government entities may block vigorous unionization. The same is true of teachers' unions.

In other developments, depletion of mineral resources within the state has greatly decreased the mining unions. In the railway industry, downsizing due to competition from other forms of transportation has reduced the Railway Brotherhoods to little more than social clubs. In addition, the once eagerly awaited relocation of factories to the Sunbelt has proved to be disappointing. New Mexico's decreasing industrial employment, following patterns elsewhere in the United States, illustrates the deindustrialization of America. If this process continues, organized labor, stripped of social and political issues, surely will become a negligible factor in future state politics.

Notes

1. *Engineering and Mining Journal* 34, 9 Sept. 1882, 139. I am grateful to Elizabeth Jameson, Diane Wood, and Howard Rabinowitz for their criticism of this paper.

2. Railway records are imperfect at best. Robert Johnson Rosenbaum, *Mexicano Resistance in the Southwest: The Sacred Right of Self-Preservation* (Austin: University of Texas Press, 1981), 102–3, 115–22, and 130–33, gives some background on the railroad workers of northeastern New Mexico and the Gorras Blancas aftermath. See also Robert W. Larson, "The White Caps of New Mexico: A Study of Ethnic Militancy in the Southwest," *Pacific Historical Review* (May 1975): 181; and Jim F. Heath, "A Study of the Influence of the Atchison, Topeka, and Santa Fe Railway upon the Economy of New Mexico" (M.A. thesis, University of New Mexico, 1955).

3. For activity in New Mexico during the Pullman strike, see *United States Strike Report,* Senate Executive Doc. No. 7, 53rd Cong., 3rd sess.), 138–39; and *Appendix to the Annual Report of the Attorney General of the United States for the Year 1896* (Washington, DC: Government Printing Office, 1896), 42.

4. State Corporation Commission, *First Annual Report* (Albuquerque: Albright & Anderson, 1913), 218–23, lists many of these mutual organizations, the foremost being La Sociedad Unión y Fraternidad Mexicana in Roswell and the Sociedad Hildalgo y Morelos in Gallup. See also, in general, José Amardo Hernández (ed.), *Mutual Aid for Survival: The Case of the Mexican American* (Malabar, FL: Robert E. Krieger Co., 1983), 28, 30–44.

5. On the WFM, see Vernon H. Jensen, *Heritage of Conflict: Labor Relations in the Non-Ferrous Metal Industry up to 1930,* 2d ed. (Westport, CT: Greenwood Press, 1968), 180–200.

6. See Melvyn Dubofsky, *We Shall Be All: A History of the IWW* (Chicago: Quadrangle Books, 1969), 110–12, 115–18, 119.

7. See Sidney Lens, *The Labor Wars: From the Molly Maguires to the Sitdowns* (Garden City, NY: Anchor Press/Doubleday, 1973), 144–55.

8. Gustav Rimlinger, "International Differences in the Strike Propensity of Coal Miners: Experience in Four Countries," *Industrial and Labor Relations Review* 12, no. 3 (Apr. 1959): 389–405. It might be added that this theory today is under strong criticism as the leading explanation of labor militancy.

9. See *State of New Mexico v. Jack Diamond*, 20 *American Law Reports, Annotated*, 1527–50, and *Laws of New Mexico, Legislature of 1919*, chap. 140, for details.

10. Ray Ginger, *Eugene V. Debs: A Biography* (New York: Collier Books, 1962), especially 252–61, and following. The standard contemporary work today is Nick Salvatore, *Eugene V. Debs: Citizen and Socialist* (Urbana, IL: University of Illinois Press, 1982).

11. On Ludlow, see George McGovern and Leonard F. Guttridge, *The Great Coalfield War* (Boston: Houghton Mifflin, 1972), 210–31. On Bisbee, see Michael Casillas, "Mexicans, Labor and Strikes in Arizona, 1896–1917," (M.A. thesis, University of New Mexico, 1979), 116–21.

12. Clinton Jencks, quoted in Jack Cargill, "Empire and Opposition: *The Salt of the Earth* Strike," in Robert Kern (ed.), *Labor in New Mexico: Unions, Strikes, and Social History since 1881* (Albuquerque: University of New Mexico Press, 1983), 194.

13. Foster Rhea Dulles, *Labor in America* (New York: Thomas Y. Crowell Co., 1949), 236–39. A more recent work that should be consulted is Melvin Dubofsky, *Industrialism and the American Worker, 1865–1920* (Arlington Heights, IL: H. Davidson, 1985).

14. See Dulles, *Labor in America,* passim, and the Gamerco materials in the Herbert C. Stacher Collection, Coronado Room, Zimmerman Library, University of New Mexico.

15. A good testimony to these hard times can be found in Joan Jensen, "New Mexico Farm Women, 1900–1940," in Kern, *Labor in New Mexico,* 68–70.

16. Robert Kern (ed.), *Building New Mexico: The Experience of a Southwestern Union* (Albuquerque: United Brotherhood of Carpenters and Joiners/New Mexico Humanities Council, 1984), 52–53.

17. Albuquerque *Journal,* 30 and 31 August, and 1 September, 1922. The dispute came partly in protest to the high number of fatal accidents in the mines.

Dawson suffered mine disasters in 1913, 1920, and 1923, accidents that killed more than six hundred men. Albuquerque *Journal,* 23 October 1913 and 8 February 1923. Arthur Hannett, lawyer for the miners, discusses these catastrophes in his *Sagebrush Lawyer* (New York: Pageant Press, 1964), 126–27.

18.   Harry R. Rubenstein, "Union Activity in the Gallup Mines, 1933–35," (M.A. thesis, University of New Mexico, 1979), 17. See also Richard Stephenson, "The Use of Troops in Labor disputes in New Mexico" (M.A. thesis, University of New Mexico, 1952).

19.   Sheriff Roberts, quoted in the *Gallup Independent,* 15 April 1922.

20.   Henry Brown to Governor Mechem, 13 April 1922, Labor Relations File, Mechem Papers, New Mexico State Record Center and Archives (NMSRCA).

21.   See both Governor Lindsey's and Governor Larrazolo's papers, Subversive Activities File, Special Issues and Events, NMSRCA.

22.   Robert Thompson and Charles Judah, *Arthur T. Hannett* (Albuquerque: Division of Research, Department of Government, University of New Mexico, 1950), 4, 33–34.

23.   See Haven Tobias, "New Mexico Labor Legislation, 1912–1949," in Kern, *Labor in New Mexico,* 277–89. John L. Lewis, future leader of the UMW and CIO, lobbied for labor safeguards in 1911, spending three months in Santa Fe. Melvin Dubofsky and Warren Van Tine, *John L. Lewis: A Biography* (New York: Quadrangle/New York Times Book Co., 1977), 25–26. For the decline in union membership, see Harry R. Rubenstein, "The Great Gallup Coal Strike of 1933," *New Mexico Historical Review,* 53, no. 3 (July 1977): 174.

24.   Thomas R. Brooks, *Toil and Trouble: A History of American Labor* (New York: Dell, 1964), 149–50. The forthcoming study of Hispanic workers in U.S. labor by Juan Gómez Quiñones for the University of New Mexico Press contains the best information on this episode, and I am indebted to him for his stress on this incident.

25.   National Miners' Union, untitled broadside, n.d. [1933?], n.p., in Stacher Collection, UNM.

26.   Richard Melzer, *Madrid Revisited: Life and Labor in a New Mexican Mining Camp in the Years of the Great Depression* (Santa Fe: Lightning Tree Press, 1976), 22–37.

27.   See "La Liga de Habla Española," in Matt S. Meir and Feliciano

Rivera, *Dictionary of Mexican American History* (Westport, CT: Greenwood Press, 1981), 193.

28.   Contemporary comment on this case can be found in Philip Stevenson, "Deporting Jesus," *The Nation,* 143 (18 July 1936). D. W. Dinwoodie, "Deportation: The Immigration Service and the Chicano Labor Movement in the 1930s," *New Mexico Historical Review,* 52 (July 1977), 193–206, develops broader issues concerning the INS.

29.   Harry R. Rubenstein, "Political Repression in New Mexico: Destruction of the National Miners' Union," in Kern, *Labor in New Mexico,* 93.

30.   Ibid., p. 94. For the labor legislation of the period, see William E. Leuchtenberg, *Franklin D. Roosevelt and the New Deal, 1932–40* (New York: Harper, 1963), 106–7.

31.   Rubenstein, "Political Repression," in Kern, *Labor in New Mexico,* 104.

32.   Ibid., 109–12.

33.   Ibid., 116. The best contemporary account is Katherine Gay, "Background of the Gallup Riot," *The Nation,* 142 (May 1935).

34.   Rubenstein, "Political Repression," in Kern, *Labor in New Mexico,* 122–25.

35.   Letter of Governor Tingley to J. Edgar Hoover, May 14, 1935, Governor Clyde Tingley Papers, Subversive Action Files, NMSRCA.

36.   Accounts of the trial can be found in *State of New Mexico v. Juan Ochoa, et al.,* case no. 4220, appeal from District Court, San Juan County to the Supreme Court of the State of New Mexico, Clerk's Office of the Supreme Court of New Mexico, Santa Fe, and *New Mexico Reports: Report of Cases in the Supreme Court of New Mexico, 1936–1937,* 41 (St. Paul, MN: West Publishing Co., 1938), 589–611.

37.   Kern, *Building New Mexico,* 90–94.

38.   See George Norris Green, *The Establishment in Texas Politics. The Primitive Years, 1938–1956* (Westport, CT: Greenwood Press, 1978), 58–62, for charges of the right-to-work's Ku Klux Klan origins and use of scare tactics in advertising it. The Christian Knights, a group active in the 1930s in anti-Semitic and racist campaigns, originally hailed right-to-work, and their messages were broadcast frequently by radio advertisements during the 1946 Legislature.

39.   A summary of these changes can be found in Gerald D. Nash, *The American West Transformed: The Impact of the Second World War* (Bloomington,

Ind.: Indiana University Press, 1985), 122. For Senator Chávez and the origins of fair employment practices, see Roy Luján, "Dennis Chávez and the Roosevelt Era, 1933–1945," (Ph.D. dissertation, University of New Mexico, 1987), 476–542. For general issues concerning mining in Grant County, New Mexico (absent from previous state labor histories), see Christopher J. Huggard's "The Mining Industry and Natural Resource Use and Management: Copper Mining in Grant County, New Mexico, 1870–1980," a portion of which is included in this book.

40.   Jack Cargill, "Empire and Opposition: The *Salt of the Earth* Strike," in Kern, *Labor in New Mexico,* 189–90.

41.   Ibid., 186–8.

42.   Michael Wilson (commentary by Deborah Silverton Rosenfelt), *Salt of the Earth* (Old Westbury, NY: Feminist Press, 1978), 107–9. Even more information can be found in Herbert Beberman, *Salt of the Earth: The Story of the Film* (Boston: Beacon Press, 1965).

43.   See Cargill, "Empire and Opposition," in Kern, *Labor in New Mexico,* pp. 243–6, and Rosenfelt, "Commentary," in Wilson, *Salt of the Earth,* 93–168.

44.   The forthcoming book by Elizabeth Jameson, *All That Glitters: Class, Culture, and Community in Cripple Creek, Colorado* (Urbana: University of Illinois Press), addresses this point. See her "High Grade and Fissures: A Working Class History of the Cripple Creek Gold Mining District, 1890–1905" (Ph.D dissertation, University of Michigan, 1987), especially chap. 7, "Not a White Man's Camp." See also her "Imperfect Unions, class and Gender in Cripple Creek, 1894–1904," *Frontiers* 1: no. 2, (1976).

45.   Bert Cochran, *Labor and Communism* (Princeton, NJ: Princeton University Press, 1977), 294–95.

46.   For Hispanic issues in a local craft union, see Tobias Durán, "Hispanics in the Union," in Kern, *Building New Mexico,* 201–11.

47.   Cargill, "Empire and Opposition," in Kern, *Labor in New Mexico,* 252. For Hispanic politics during this period, see Juan Gómez Quinoñes, *Chicano Politics: Reality and Promise, 1940–1990* (Albuquerque: University of New Mexico Press, 1990), 115–18.

48.   Kern, *Building New Mexico,* 122–34.

49.   Comment from Diane Wood (organizer of the retail clerks' strike), 10 April 1992.

50.   See Guillermo José Grenier, "On Human Relations: Quality Circles,

Control, and Anti-Unionism at a Manufacturing Plant in the Southwest: A Case Study," (Ph.D dissertation, University of New Mexico, 1985).

51. This is a subject of considerable interest for students of labor in the Southwest. Particularly useful is Gunther W. Peck, "Ethnicity and Labor Radicalism in the West: Immigrants and Padrones, 1908–1912" (M.A. thesis, University of Wisconsin, 1989), chap. 3 and 4. A more complete literature on minority exclusion in organized labor exists for other groups. See, for instance, Ralph Emerson Mann, *After the Gold Rush: Society in Grass Valley and Nevada City, California, 1849–1870* (Stanford, CA: Stanford University Press, 1982); A. Yvette Huginie, "Race and Class in Arizona," (Ph.D dissertation, Yale University, 1992); Richard E. Lingenfelter, *The Hardrock Miners: A History of the Mining Labor Movement in the American West, 1863–1893* (Berkeley: University of California Press, 1974); and Rose Hun Lee, *The Chinese in the United States of America* (Hong Kong: Hong Kong University Press, 1960).

52. Cargill, "Empire and Opposition," in Kern, *Labor in New Mexico,* 250.

53. Rubenstein, "The Great Gallup Coal Strike," 175.

54. Eric J. Hobsbawm, *Primitive Rebels: Studies in Archaic Forms of Social Movements in the 19th and 20th Centuries* (New York: W. W. Norton & Co., 1965), especially 74–107.

55. Cargill, "Empire and Opposition," in Kern, *Labor in New Mexico,* 250.

56. See Connie Capers Thorson and James L. Thorson, "Gomorrah on the Puerco: A Critical study of Philip Stevenson's Proletarian Epic, *The Seed,*" in Kern, *Labor in New Mexico,* 147–78.

TEN

COUGHING AND SPITTING AND NEW MEXICO HISTORY

⚜

JAKE W. SPIDLE, JR.

ONE of the conventions of New Mexico's history is the critical role played by ranching and mining in the shaping of the territory and state at the end of the nineteenth and the beginning of the twentieth centuries. Some authorities add railroading as a third factor in New Mexico's development. At least as important as these other three was the care and treatment of tuberculosis (TB) patients, yet this industry does not command the attention enjoyed by the others. Health seekers by the thousands, most of them lung-disease victims, began to flock to salubrious New Mexico in the mid-1800s,[1] and their coughing and spitting reverberated through New Mexico for roughly a century. Even the most casual reader of New Mexico's history must be struck by the powerful impact of these health seekers on New Mexico's society and economy, from the Santa Fe Trail sojourners of the middle of the nineteenth century through the closing of the tuberculosis sanatoria in the mid-twentieth century. Tuberculosis treatment is a prominent theme of New Mexico's heritage and deserving of more careful attention than it has received.

New Mexico's emergence in the 1870s and 1880s as a health seekers' haven was linked to major developments within the world of medicine. As the nineteenth century unfolded, pulmonary tuberculosis—a contagious disease caused by a bacterium—increasingly was seen as the number-one public health problem of modern industrial society. Although its history traces as far back as we are able to see—John Bunyan in the seventeenth century called it "the captain of the men of death"—its epidemic spread through nineteenth-century industrial society, and the frightening futility of western medicine in treating it afforded it the kind of horror and infamy associated with cancer in our own time. It was especially confounding and frightening because it disproportionately afflicted otherwise healthy young adults. No other single disease so captured the public attention in that age as phthisis, consumption, or tuberculosis, to use its various names; one historian calls the nineteenth century "the century of tuberculosis."[2]

Learned physicians confronted with the disease could do little beyond wag their heads and prescribe bleeding, noxious drugs, and other treatments that often hastened the demise of their unfortunate patients. Benjamin Rush, greatest American physician of the premodern age, treated his pulmonary tuberculosis patients by bleeding them two or three times a week, taking 6–8 ounces of blood at a time, then encouraging them to take long journeys on horseback between treatments.[3] In this therapeutic wasteland, two new treatment modalities emerged in the latter half of the 1800s.

The first came to be called "climate therapy," and Swiss and German physicians of the 1850s and 1860s were most influential in its development. The climatologists argued that certain climates were particularly beneficial to TB patients and offered the best chance for their cure, provided treatment began while the disease was still in its early stages.[4] Most of them considered high altitude the single most important element in climate therapy. High altitude supposedly ensured purer air and lower air pressure that were both conducive to the healing of sick lungs. Other climate theorists claimed that the dryness of the air was the critical factor in benefiting TB patients. Still others argued that neither high altitude nor low humidity was so critical as lots of sunshine.

The ramifications of all this for New Mexico history are obvious.

Whether physicians championed altitude, dry air, or sunshine, New Mexico (and the southern reaches of the Rockies in general) had it all. Thus during the last half of the nineteenth century, New Mexico gained national and even worldwide prominence as a health seekers' haven. Soldiers and government officials working in the territory, travelers journeying to and across its terrain, and the scattered occupants of the territory all sang its praises as a specially healthful, or salubrious, place. By the end of the century there was a booster campaign selling the territory's healthfulness. It is no coincidence that territorial New Mexico funded an energetic Bureau of Immigration, and New Mexico's healthfulness was one of the primary properties it sold.[5] This excitement and enthusiasm were captured in an article published in an 1898 issue of the *Journal of the American Medical Association.* Its author, an eminent Boston physician, rhapsodized:

> The climate of New Mexico, though far from ideal, can only be
> understood and appreciated by comparison with that of other
> states and countries. A survey of its climatic conditions, such as its
> altitude, its southerly latitude, its even average temperature, its
> low humidity, the small amount of precipitation, its excess of sun-
> shine, the minute amounts of aqueous vapor contained in its atmo-
> sphere, its isolation from large population centers, its great
> distance from large bodies of water, its immunity from high winds
> and sandstorms [*sic*], and its freedom from unsanitary surround-
> ings, should convince the reader that there does not exist a better
> or more ideal climate for the elimination of disease and the resto-
> ration of health.[6]

It was, then, the climate that brought the health seekers to New Mexico, at least initially. Later on the reputation of its facilities and doctors attracted them, along with the climate.

Simultaneous with the emergence of climate therapy was the development of sanatoria treatment as a major treatment modality for tuberculosis.[7] The first American sanitoria were established in the 1870s and 1880s at Asheville, North Carolina, and at Saranac Lake, New York, where Dr. Edward Trudeau established his famous sanatorium.

The essence of sanatorium therapy for tuberculosis was a belief in the efficacy of rest, more rest, and good food. The claims made for sanatorium therapy and the obvious good work of institutions like Dr. Trudeau's firmly established the sanatorium movement within American health care. Within a decade or two of the founding of the first such institutions, sanatoria for the treatment of tuberculars proliferated. They were particularly prominent in the Rocky Mountain region where ailing "lungers"—the slang label commonly used for TB patients at the time—could hope to capitalize on both treatment modalities at once.

The first "san" in New Mexico was St. Vincent's in Santa Fe, originally founded as a general hospital and hospice in 1865, but sanatoria began to spring up all around the territory in the 1890s, and by 1920 they were liberally sprinkled around the state. As early as 1908 New Mexico, although small in terms of population and economic base, was fifth in the nation in number of beds available for the care of TB patients, in the same league with New York, Pennsylvania, Colorado, and Massachusetts.[8]

By 1922 there were forty-eight officially organized and recognized sanatoria in the state, plus scores of informally organized institutions (many of them called "convalescent homes") and hundreds of private homes renting out one or two rooms to health seekers and their families. Nineteen of the official "sans" were large-scale facilities with more than seventy beds. The Army's Fort Bayard Sanatorium had more than 400 beds, and the U.S. Public Health Service Sanatorium at Fort Stanton housed 250 TB patients. Deming's Holy Ghost Sanitorium had 180 beds, and Southwest Presbyterian Sanatorium and St. Joseph Hospital in Albuquerque had more than 125 beds each devoted to care of tubercular patients. Another half dozen sanatoria around the state at one time or another sheltered more than 100 TB patients. Of the larger institutions—those with more than seventy beds—Las Vegas had two; Santa Fe, two; Albuquerque, seven; Silver City, two; and Alamogordo, Deming, Valmora, and Dulce each had one. Almost every town or community of any size had at least one "san": Las Cruces, Lincoln, Roswell, Aztec, Tucumcari, Carlsbad, Chico Springs, and Laguna. There was even a twelve-bed baby sanatorium in Cloudcroft and a five-bed pavilion at the state penitentiary.[9] By the 1920s sanatorias were big business in New Mexico, and the new state flag might well have had a TB patient's chaise longue emblazoned on it instead of the Zia.[10]

This influx of TB patients undoubtedly had a conspicuous impact on the medical community of New Mexico, resulting in both an enormous increase in the number of physicians and an obvious improvement in their caliber. Many physicians came to the Southwest at the end of the nineteenth century and the beginning of the twentieth as TB patients themselves. Others sought out the salubrious climate of New Mexico in hopes that the health of a sick wife or child or parent might be helped in the new locale. Some, especially physicians interested in pulmonary problems, came because of the number of patients flooding the region. Exact figures are not available, since there were no pollsters asking newcomers the reasons for their migration, but there is abundant evidence to support the generalization that somewhere between a quarter and a third of all physicians in the state in the 1920s and 1930s were either TB patients or their relatives. In many communities their impact was startling. The physician corps of Las Vegas numbered eleven in 1925, all of them tubercular. Thirteen of Roswell's twenty-five doctors in 1926 were tubercular.[11] The daughter of a long-time Santa Fe physician, when asked the reason for her father's selection of frontier New Mexico as the site for his practice in 1915, denied that tuberculosis had anything at all to do with his decision. "But," she said, "every other doctor in town coughed."[12] One obvious effect of this tuberculosis-related physician migration to New Mexico was that New Mexico in the territorial and early statehood periods was something of an over-doctored society. As a thinly populated frontier state New Mexico might otherwise have been short of doctors. But because of the migration of TB patients to the region, the available statistics suggest that New Mexico may have had more doctors than it really needed. In the late 1980s New Mexico had a physician-to-population ratio of approximately 1 physician for every 565 people, a figure considered a good supply of doctors. In 1921 the ratio in the new state was almost as good, at 1 doctor for every 693 citizens. Some towns had such a supply that hard-up doctors may have been reduced to scouting for patients. Tucumcari in 1912 had 1 doctor for every 210 people; Artesia had 13 doctors for its 1,883 residents (a ratio of 1 to 145); and Albuquerque boasted 43 doctors among its population of 11,020, a ratio of 1 for every 256 citizens. Chicago that same year had a physician-to-population ratio of 1 to 580; thus pioneer Albuquerque had twice as many physicians per capita as Chicago.[13]

Alongside this quantitative impact of the migration on the physician community of New Mexico, there was a definite qualitative effect as well. Among the health-seeker doctors flooding the territory and state were some practitioners of national and even international reputation and an even larger number of bright young men (and some women) had originally entertained quite different plans for their medical careers. Young doctors, fresh from distinguished medical schools and top training programs, who were aiming for careers on New York's Park Avenue, near the Loop in Chicago, or in the vicinity of Harvard Yard, instead came down with tuberculosis and suddenly found themselves in Roswell, Albuquerque, or Silver City. Three or four generations of New Mexico physicians were leavened by these involuntary New Mexicans. Dr. William Henry Woolston (1890–1957), for example, had his sights set firmly on the Chair of Surgery at Chicago's distinguished Northwestern University Medical School. He was well on his way toward achieving that objective in 1922 when a series of acute pulmonary hemorrhages and a diagnosis of tuberculosis set him on a train to Albuquerque. Dr. Woolston survived and gave New Mexico thirty-five years of distinguished surgical practice before his death in 1957. Dr. Robert E. McBride (1873–1949) was the proud possessor of a fine medical education and training (Tulane University School of Medicine and New Orlean's Charity Hospital) when in 1904 he abandoned his plans for a distinguished career in internal medicine in

New Orleans and instead hung out his shingle in Las Cruces. Dr. McBride's lungs were sound, but his wife was a TB patient.

Perhaps the best-known example of the lung-ailing young physician forced to "chase the cure" in rough New Mexico Territory was Dr. William Randolph Lovelace (1883–1968). Dr. Lovelace was a Missouri farm boy who apparently intended to return to rural Missouri to set up practice when he finished his medical education in 1905. But his obviously failing health and ominous cough were diagnosed as pulmonary tuberculosis. In the spring of 1906 the young physician found himself heart-and lung-sick in the railroad shantytown of Sunnyside (later Fort Sumner), New Mexico. He, too, got well, and he went on to found what became the famous Lovelace Clinic and later Lovelace Medical Center.[14] These and scores of other distinguished New Mexico doctors spent their careers in New Mexico not by choice but in consequence of their disease. They helped to improve significantly the quality of medical care in the state. New Mexico in the twentieth century possessed a physician corps far better than it might otherwise have enjoyed. It was especially strong in the field of pulmonary medicine, so it was appropriate that the founders of the American College of Chest Physicians held its inaugural meeting in 1935 not in Boston, New York, or San Francisco, but at the Franciscan Hotel in Albuquerque.[15]

The impact quantitatively and qualitatively on the state's physician community of the TB-related migration can be readily demonstrated, but it also affected the state's society at large. It can confidently be argued that the TB-related migration represented a demographic surge. The search for specific numbers is a frustrating one, and all figures cited in discussing this subject are slippery. Contemporary accounts usually settled for vague characterizations such as "large," "numerous," "thousands," and even "enormous" in describing the TB population of the state. No exact records were kept. Possibly the best numerical estimate is that found in a 1913 report by a U.S. Public Health Service doctor and investigator who toured New Mexico and West Texas examining the tuberculosis problem in the region. Dr. Ernest Sweet was cautious with figures but concluded that in almost all New Mexico towns—mining camps were the only exceptions he acknowledged—anywhere from 20 percent to 60 percent of all homes had at least one tuberculosis patient under the roof, and 90 percent of these sufferers were not born in New Mexico.[16] Silver City, Socorro, Las Vegas, Raton, Las Cruces, Roswell, Santa Fe, Deming, and Alamogordo were all heavily affected by the migration; in all these towns a solid majority of families included at least one tuberculosis patient. Albuquerque distinctly bore the impress of the phenomenon, with perhaps as much as 50 percent of its citizenry consisting of TB patients and their relatives.[17] Taking the state as a whole, it's probably safe to conclude that through the 1910s, 1920s, and 1930s, at least 20 percent of all New Mexicans—one of every five people—was there because of this health seekers' influx.[18] Obviously it was an increase of enormous significance.

And, as was true among the physician refugees to New Mexico, within the community of TB patients there were thousands of individuals with great talents and abilities whose sojourn within and contribution to New Mexico markedly improved it. Virtually no sphere of activity—business, the arts, education, and other professions—failed to profit from the immigration. Tuberculosis struck individuals of widely differing educational background, social class, and economic bracket. Thus the social bonanza of the health seekers shaped and accelerated economic, social, and cultural development processes that might otherwise have taken other forms and almost certainly much more time. Whatever sphere of twentieth-century New Mexico life and activity one examines, the contributions of individuals who came to the Southwest as TB patients is clear. I have chosen three areas as examples: politics, education, and the arts.

New Mexico politics of the twentieth century bears indelibly the imprint of the tubercular patients. Political chieftain and President Harding's secretary of the interior, Albert Fall; U.S. senators Bronson Cutting and Clinton P. Anderson; U.S. representative Albert G. Simms and his brother John, Democratic party leader and chief justice of the New Mexico supreme court); and Albuquerque mayor and state governor Clyde Tingley all were TB patients or relatives of TB patients.

In the world of education, France Scholes, scholar of colonial New Mexico, served as dean of the University of New Mexico Graduate School and as the critically important academic vice president of the institution. Dudley Wynn founded UNM's innovative American Studies program and also served as a vice president. Dr. John Weinzirl was a nationally regarded pioneer in bacteriology and climatology. John Milne served as superintendent of the Albuquerque public schools for no less than forty-five years. These are just some of the hundreds of educators who came as involuntary New Mexicans to this part of the world.

In the arts Grace Thompson Edmister was founder and long-time director of the Albuquerque Civic Symphony Orchestra. Kathryn Kennedy O'Connor was cofounder and for decades the guiding spirit of the Albuquerque Little Theater. John Gaw Meem was the most celebrated southwestern architect of the century. Many of the Santa Fe and Taos artists who made New Mexico a prominent force in twentieth-century American art were tuberculosis patients. Within the cultural diversity on which twentieth-century New Mexico prides itself, this nonethnic minority made the state a rich, stimulating place.

The onset of the Great Depression in the 1930s slowed the flood of health seekers to the Southwest, and over the decades of the 1940s and 1950s, the age of coughing and spitting began to disappear. Changes within the world of medicine and in American society generally all but ended the desperate flight of tubercular pilgrims to New Mexico. The economic catastrophe of the 1930s shook the New Mexico tuberculosis industry, for it meant that fewer Americans were able to shoulder the economic burdens required in relocation to the Southwest plus the high costs of long-term care—months and even years—in sanatoria.

More important in the decline of New Mexico's sanatorias, perhaps, was the consensus slowly reached among tuberculosis specialists that the central element of sanatorium care, rest and climate, played a relatively small role in effective treatment. That consensus meant that tuberculosis patients tended increasingly to enter sanatorias in their own home town or state.

The discovery in the late 1940s and early 1950s of effective chemo-therapeutic agents for treatment of tuberculosis—streptomycin in 1944, para-aminosalicylic acid (PAS) in 1950, isonicotinic acid hydrazide (or isoniazid) in 1952—provided the means to treat the disease with speed and safety.[19] The new wonder drugs were a therapy far superior to the old sanatorium regimen, the radical surgical techniques previously employed, or simple good climate. They were so dazzlingly effective that not much time passed before medical textbooks actually preached against the older, time-honored treatments for the problem. A modern textbook states that "chemotherapy is the essential factor in the treatment of tuberculosis—bed rest, nutritional supplements, surgery, and other auxiliary procedures have become unnecessary."[20] More bluntly still, "bed rest, hospitalization, and sanatorium care are not beneficial."[21] In 1950 there were still waiting lists for the beds available in sanatoria around the nation, but within a decade the U.S. Public Health Service was reporting that fewer than half the beds available in the country for TB patients were then in use.[22]

An era of New Mexico and American medicine had passed swiftly. Within the desert Southwest the world of sanatoria, tuberculosis special-ists, and health-seeker migration was transformed into a new one of medical schools, nationally famous clinics and medical centers, and le-gions of young and progressive medical specialists. The coughing and spitting of the lungers faded into the pages of history.

Notes

1. This felicitous phrase belongs to Karen Shane, "New Mexico: Sa-lubrious El Dorado," *New Mexico Historical Review,* 56 (1981): 387–99.

2. Esmond R. Long, MD, "Tuberculosis in Modern Society," *Bulletin of the History of Medicine,* 27 (1953): 301.

3. Julius H. Comroe, "T.B. or Not T.B.? Part II: The Treatment of Tuberculosis," *American Review of Respiratory Disease,* 117 (1978): 379.

4. See, among others, Julius Lane Wilson, "The Western Frontier and Climate Therapy," *The Journal-Lancet* 86 (1966): 564–67; Frank B. Rogers, "The

Rise and Decline of the Altitude Therapy of Tuberculosis," *Bulletin of the History of Medicine,* 43 (1969): 1–16; and Jake W. Spidle, Jr., *Doctors of Medicine in New Mexico: A History of Health and Medical Practice, 1886–1986* (Albuquerque: University of New Mexico Press, 1986), 87–97.

5. Shane, "Salubrious El Dorado," 388–89.

6. Dr. Curtis Bailey, quoted in "New Mexico as a Health Resort," *Journal of the American Medical Association,* 31 (12 November 1898): 1179.

7. For a convenient summary of the development of the sanatorium movement with particular reference to New Mexico, see Spidle, *Doctors of Medicine,* 137–69.

8. Philip P. Jacobs, comp., *The Campaign Against Tuberculosis in the United States* (New York: National Association for the Study and Prevention of Tuberculosis, 1908), 3–143.

9. Penitentiary authorities noted that a "modified" sanatorium regimen was followed in their tuberculosis pavilion, the therapy of "rest, rest, and more rest" being modified by the fact that "some [patients] are sent out to work on the roads." Cited ibid., 167.

10. This discussion of the old tuberculosis sanatoria is more than just ancient history, for after their youthful days as sanatoria, some made the conversion to general hospitals—among them, Presbyterian and St. Joseph in Albuquerque, St. Mary's in Roswell, St. Vincent's in Santa Fe, and St. Anthony's in Las Vegas.

11. The figures for Las Vegas and Roswell come from the testimony of Dr. Carl H. Gellenthien (interview with the author, Valmora, NM, 18 December 1984), a recent medical school graduate who came to the area for his sick lungs in 1925. Dr. Gellenthien survived—and went on to practice sixty-four years in San Miguel County.

12. Mrs. Earlene Brinegar (daughter of Santa Fe physician Dr. Earl LeGrande Ward), interview with the author, Albuquerque, 12 November 1984.

13. Spidle, *Doctors of Medicine,* 35–41.

14. Information on these and more than 1,000 other New Mexico physicians is held in the Medical History Archives of the Medical Center Library, University of New Mexico School of Medicine, Albuquerque. On Dr. Lovelace, see also Jake W. Spidle, Jr., *The Lovelace Medical Center: Pioneer in American Health Care* (Albuquerque: University of New Mexico Press, 1987), especially 1–48.

15.   See *Diseases of the Chest* (later *Chest*) 1, no. 6 (1935), for a full account of that inaugural gathering. The entire issue was dedicated "as a special tribute to the state of New Mexico."

16.   Ernest A. Sweet, MD, "Interstate Migration of Tuberculous Persons, Its Bearing on the Public Health, with Special Reference to the States of Texas and New Mexico," *Public Health Reports,* 30 (1915): 1071, 1066–67. Sweet found the highest concentration of tubercular patients in Silver City where, he judged, a full 80 percent of the families sheltered at least one TB patient. He concluded, "Were all the consumptives to leave . . . Silver City would become a mere spot in the desert" (p. 1250).

17.   Ibid., 1071; and LeRoy Peters, "What New Mexico Needs Most in Tuberculosis Legislation," *New Mexico Medical Journal,* 15 (1915–16): 230.

18.   Spidle, *Doctors of Medicine,* 99.

19.   Selman Waksman, *The Conquest of Tuberculosis* (Berkeley and Los Angeles: University of California Press, 1964), 190–92.

20.   *Current Therapy* (1983): 132.

21.   Ibid., 137.

22.   Waksman, *Conquest of Tuberculosis,* 192.

ELEVEN

HEALTH CARE ACROSS CULTURES:
Public Health Nurses in Hispanic and Native American Communities

Sandra Schackel

LATE in 1922 Augustine Stoll, Red Cross Public Health nurse, began a year-long assignment on the Jicarilla Apache reservation in northern New Mexico. Her first monthly report revealed some of the determination that prompted her decision to take the position.

> I arrived in Dulce November 12, and so far my progress has been so slow that I think it can be compared to the walking here in the mud, you go forward one step and slip back two. There is so much to do and I have absolute faith that some of it can be done. This belief may get a bit battered and hidden because everybody from the janitor up tells me I can't do a thing! But I think I have exhausted some of their probably well-founded pessimism and they are going to let me stop talking and get to work.[1]

Stoll and other women health workers in New Mexico were representative of well-intentioned, middle-class Anglo women nationwide whose efforts to cross ethnic borders were part of a larger cultural movement in the early twentieth century. As a public health reformer, Stoll understood her task to be "corrective, preventive, and educational work." This ethnocentric approach dovetailed with the prevailing social theories that considered all non-Anglo Americans to be somehow defec-

tive or in need of correction and improvement. Of paramount concern to
the reformers in this era was the lack of health care among many
Americans, a problem reflected in the nation's high infant mortality rate.

This chapter examines the role of women health care workers as
agents of change in New Mexico in the first half of the twentieth century.
In particular, it draws on the work of public health workers among New
Mexico's Pueblo, Navajo, and Hispanic communities to show how they
served as cultural conduits between the modern medical world and
cultures in transition. The issue is one of complexity on several levels. The
nurses themselves faced conflicts between their desire to "modernize" the
Native American and Hispanic cultures and also to preserve traditions.
They frequently faced personal conflicts between their basic values and
attitudes and their willingness to suspend parts of their belief systems.
Sometimes there was a contradiction between what the health care agencies wanted and how the nurses met those goals. Finally, there was the
effect of the nurses' actions on their patients. From their letters and
reports, we know how the nurses perceived their actions; hearing the
Indian and Hispanic voices would further enhance our understanding of
the nurses' role as agents of change. I suggest, however, that because the
nurses were sensitive to traditional ways, the changes were not as abrupt
or as intrusive as they might have been.

The voices of the nurses whose accounts have been preserved in
agency reports or letters—those of Augustine Stoll, Agnes Courtney,
Louise Kuhrtz, Molly Reebel, and Elizabeth Forster—revealed a world
view that the nurses shared as middle-class Euro-Americans and as
members of the health profession. All had attended certified nursing
programs, trained in hospitals or clinics, and chosen to work in a public
health setting. Some had served as nurses overseas during World War I
and therefore saw adventure and challenge in a public health assignment
in the American West. Others were drawn to New Mexico for its beauty
and cultural diversity. Not without prejudices and biases, these women
nevertheless were able to suspend judgment of their clients in a way that
fostered harmony and cooperation. More important, they served as facili-

tors of change to a population that was in transition from a traditional to a modern culture.

The nurses shared the late nineteenth-century view of Native Americans as a vanishing race, and they believed that in some small way they could impart knowledge and techniques that would halt that seemingly inevitable process. They were also products of the philosophy of Progressive reform in which the concepts of science, rationality, and efficiency were tools with which to reshape industrial America. Their regular reports were filled with the scientific data of progress: schoolchildren weighed and measured and matched to standardized charts; visits to homes of midwives; number of hours given to class instruction of midwives; children treated for trachoma (a highly contagious eye disease); and medical visits to Indian villages. From this material, I have tried to reconstruct a picture of the nurses' world as they served in ethnic New Mexico communities.

The nurses highlighted in this chapter stood outside mainstream America. Although they shared many of the values typical of middle-class reformers, they also displayed a willingness to suspend cultural judgment regardless of rejection, hardship, or inconvenience. Later in this century, cross-cultural training was provided to such health care workers, but these women were sent directly into the field with little knowledge of the customs or beliefs of the people with whom they would be working. In the ethnocentric thinking of the Progressive Era, health problems did not have a cultural component. Some nurses had difficulty adjusting to a new setting, as Stoll notes:

There is a Miss Reynolds up there [on the Jicarilla Apache reservation] as field nurse. Between you and me she's pathetic. This is her first Indian work and she can't drive a car or ride and she doesn't like the Indian and doesn't want to stay. She asked me to help her but I couldn't do much for her spirit and conception of the work are so wrong. She is utterly Boston! And out of place. But I was so sorry for her.[2]

Most nurses recognized the cultural chasm that separated them from their patients, and some were willing to question their assumptions of difference in an attempt to close the gap. At the same time, sensitivity to differences was a necessary component to successful public health work. For example, when explaining maternity and infant care to Native Americans, Stoll made clear "that we do *not* want to interfere with old customs, dances, religions [sic] observations."[3]

One of the driving forces behind the push for health care services in New Mexico was the extremely high infant mortality rate in the state. In 1929, the first year for which reliable statistics are available, the mortality rate for infants under one year of age was 140 per 1,000. This figure was more than twice the national rate of sixty-one per 1,000; it continued to rise in the 1930s before dropping to 100 per 1,000 in 1940.[4] Several factors accounted for these disturbing statistics. The fifth-largest state at 122,000 square miles, New Mexico had 360,350 citizens in 1920, most of them in rural areas and many in remote reaches where health care was scant or nonexistent. Lack of good roads made it difficult for physicians, nurses, and others to reach the ill. As a result, health care services fell to local *curanderas* (traditional Hispanic healers), medicine men and women, and midwives. These health providers did not meet AMA (American Medical Association) guidelines: they did not possess "formal" training, they did not practice "basic" health techniques, such as sterility and cleanliness; and they were not part of the nation's formal medical establishment.

In response to the lack of services in much of New Mexico, the state department of health began a concerted effort in the 1920s to raise its standard of health care. Although the efforts were directed at all New Mexicans, officials were especially interested in carrying their message to Native Americans and Spanish-speaking citizens.[5] Acting on the belief that scientific, rational medicine offered the best and safest treatment, Anglo reformers began a campaign against traditional forms of health care. Included in their campaign were midwives, especially the Hispanic *parteras* whom they characterized as superstitious, unclean, and uninformed. In singling out midwives, the Anglo caregivers were attempting to alter cultural patterns among the Native American and Hispanic populations. They went among these communities with the highest confidence that by teaching nutrition, cleanliness, and the importance of germ theory, they could effect change.

In many ways, according to Anglo standards, the nurses were successful. In Indian communities, they built dairies to provide fresh milk for children, had wells dug, built laundries and bathhouses; they screened schoolchildren for tuberculosis, treated trachoma, gave inoculations, and provided pre- and postnatal care for mothers.[6] In most cases, these enterprises were successful because they did not conflict with tribal ceremonies or rituals. This was not the case, however, with childbirth which, in many cultures, is surrounded with ritual and secrecy. Here the nurses had the greatest difficulty in bridging the cultural barrier.

Most Indian communities, willingly or cautiously, accepted the nurses and their Anglo ideas. One exception, however, was Santo Domingo Pueblo, one of the most conservative of the Rio Grande pueblos. In one of her last reports from her makeshift home three miles outside the pueblo in 1926, Stoll mused over the traditional faction's rejection of her work.

> For some weeks I have been puzzling over how one can change an attitude of mind or a habit of thinking, particularly when one is held distrustfully and disapprovingly at arm's length. There must be other avenues of approach that we have not found; there must be some way of winning them, for one feels that they are very worthwhile. The village lies so near us, full of customs, traditions, intricate religious ceremonies of which we know nothing.[7]

Yet in the same report she speaks of the Indians at nearby Cochiti, who "are anxious to have us." As at Dulce earlier, Stoll understood she was crossing a prickly cultural barrier when she remarked, "Our work is so very different from anything that has ever been attempted here that in its difference it is a bit puzzling and not to be trusted. Sometimes the newest methods succeed because of their novelty."[8]

One obstacle the health care reformers faced was the power and influence of medicine men and women. To the Bureau of Indian Affairs (BIA), the agency responsible for the welfare of Native Americans, these traditional healers represented all that was wrong in the pueblos and on the reservations. The healers posed a formidable barrier to altering long-held ideas regarding sickness and disease. Until the 1960s agency officials regularly discounted the important role medicine men and women played in health matters and were unwilling to recognize the spiritual and psychological aspects of traditional Indian medicine. The agency attitude of resistance made the nurse's job harder and prolonged the process of health education. The most effective nurses had the cultural sensitivity to recognize that they needed the sanction and approval of local healers, including midwives. At the very least, they knew they must not antagonize the traditional belief structure. Eva Wade Nickolds, working at Newcomb on the Navajo reservation, acknowledged this condition when she noted that "there has been, as in most all pioneer work, all sorts of obstacles to overcome and many things to learn—mainly how to work with the medicine man, rather than against him."[9]

One of the most successful at bridging this cultural gap was Louise Kuhrtz, a Red Cross nurse who spent thirty years (1926–56) at Isleta Pueblo south of Albuquerque. Unusual among the nurses working among Native Americans, Kuhrtz gradually learned their language and endeared herself in many ways to the Isletans. In 1934 she counted the vaccinations of two of the village medicine men as successes in her immunization campaign. In a summary of her work in 1940, she wrote of local beliefs:

> Yes, they have their superstitions and still have their medicine men. It is all more or less pertaining to their religion. The medicine men are like priests. They all cooperate with me in so many ways and they have come to feel and know that I respect their customs and beliefs so that none of it all interferes with my health programs.[10]

Kuhrtz recognized that the practices of the medicine men were part of their religion and, therefore, did not see them as competitors. As a result, she gained their support and her work went ahead unimpeded. Her ability to listen and to respond to Native American cultural preferences was the key to a successful working relationship with the Isleta people. The Red Cross concurred, repeatedly renewing her assignment and commending the "unusually good rapport between the nurse and the Indians."[11]

Elizabeth Forster, a public health nurse among the Navajo in the early 1930s, shared with Kuhrtz some of the traits that allowed her to fit in so well with her Navajo clients. She too remained empathetic and open to Navajo customs and was able to move comfortably between the two cultures. On several occasions Forster had been invited to healing cere-monies, then allowed to take the patient to the hospital for further treatment. This practice, however, displeased the BIA superintendent in the region, who viewed the local healers as an impediment to bringing modern health practices to the reservation. Most agency doctors were suspicious of traditional medicine and saw themselves as competitors with medicine men and women. In their view Forster was perpetuating prac-tices that should be discredited and abolished. As a result, the BIA dismissed Forster after only eighteen months of service, and health care for these Navajos in the remote northeastern corner of the reservation came to a standstill. When Forster next visited the Red Rock region in the early 1950s, she encountered many Navajo friends who had been without medical care since her departure.[12] The lack of sensitivity on the part of Anglo officials had hindered and obstructed the exchange of information that the best nurses, as cultural intermediaries, hoped to promote.

One important facet of the health reformers' work was infant and maternity care, yet the topic of childbirth among Native Americans is noticeably absent or briefly treated in available sources. Among Native Americans, certain ritual ceremonies govern childbirth, the care of the mother, and the dedication of the child to the clan.[13] The nurses recog-

nized that they were outsiders and unless they were welcomed or invited
to take part, they respectfully kept their distance. Yet they were pleased
when they were included in any part of the event. On one occasion, Stoll
reported that a Santo Domingo man invited her "to come to see his sister's
baby. It had attained the advanced age of two days! We were delighted for
it is a rather rare invitation."[14] A few months later Stoll was told she might
attend a birth in Cochiti and was disappointed when she missed the event.
"I was so sorry for I have been told that the rites are very interesting."[15]

In *Denizens of the Desert,* a rich collection of letters Elizabeth Forster
wrote while at Red Rock, she describes a Navajo birth to which she was
invited in June 1932. When she and her interpreter arrived, the hogan was
filled with men, women, and children. They had missed the actual
delivery, but "the old woman who seemed mistress of ceremonies" took
Forster as a pupil and demonstrated how things should be done. The
mother, looking "none too comfortable," was held in a kneeling position
by means of straps extending from the ceiling and attached to each wrist.
After the birth, when the placenta was delivered, Forster was allowed to
release the new mother, apply the umbilical dressing, and rub the baby
with oil. She was then told to hold the baby over a trough of sand on the
hogan floor while an attendant poured first cold then warm water over
the infant, rubbing vigorously all the while. Wrote Forster, "You may
believe it or not, but the result was a fresh pink-tan baby who was then
dressed in swaddling bands with arms pinioned to its sides, as all good
Navajo babies are, and laid in its mother's arms." Meanwhile, other
assistants had prepared cedar tea from pungent foliage for the mother.
Then, reported Forster, "We left peace in the little hogan in spite of the
remaining audience of friends. I couldn't help wondering if there were
still rites to follow, but if there were, I was not invited."[16] Forster appreciated her inclusion in these private events, even for partial rituals, for she
knew it contributed to the Indians' acceptance of her and helped make her
less of an outsider in their culture.

Ethnographies done among the Rio Grande pueblos of Acoma and
Laguna and in the western pueblos of Zuni and Hopi describe similar

birthing ceremonies. Among the Hopi, women of the household care for the mother at birth; the baby is washed in warm water and rubbed with ashes; then the child is laid in a cradle with one or more ears of corn. Lines of cornmeal or ashes are made on each wall to mark the newborn's home.[17] In Picuris Pueblo, near Taos, an ear of corn is laid next to the child to act as its "corn mother" for thirty days, after which the mother takes corn meal to a shrine and offers prayers.[18] At Acoma, a "corn mother" is placed with the child for a four-day lying-in period after which the naming ceremony takes place.[19] A similar ritual occurs at Laguna, where a medicine man arrives on the fourth morning to offer prayers to the Earth Mother and to Father Sun, offering them the child.[20]

At Zuni Pueblo birth is a family and clan matter in which the mother's mother attends the delivery, unless complications ensue; then a midwife is called in.[21] After birth, the father's mother bathes the child, rubs its body with ashes, then places it in a bed of warm sand beside its mother. Naming takes place on the fourth day.[22] These and other rituals normally were not part of the nurses' world, but the nurses accepted the silence that surrounded the birth experience as part of Native American culture that was not meant to be shared with outsiders. For those, who, like Forster, were invited into private ceremonies on occasion, it was still only a partial experience.

There was less silence surrounding the birthing experience among Spanish-speaking New Mexicans. Most Hispanic women wanted and used midwives, women in their communities who had learned birthing skills from their mothers, grandmothers, or other female relatives. These parteras were highly respected women who served as advisers, counselors, and confidantes.[23] They were also targets of the state health system which, between 1920 and 1950, carried out many programs to regulate and license midwives as part of the larger goal of lowering the state's infant mortality rate. When federal funds for infant and maternal health care became available to the states under the Sheppard-Towner Act of 1921, New Mexico was able to hire three public health nurses to conduct maternity and infant care programs.[24] By the end of that decade, twenty public health nurses were working in the state, even after the loss of federal funding in 1928.

Wisely, the New Mexico medical community recognized the need for midwives in rural, isolated villages where few physicians were available. But there were reasons other than isolation that caused Hispanic families to prefer midwives. Courtney noted that because of the "expense of such care and the poverty of some families a doctor would be called only as a last resource."[25] Just as important was the Hispanic families' long familiarity with and dependence on the parteras. Unlike in the native American communities where the birth process was woven into the religious fabric, New Mexico Hispanics viewed birth within the larger framework of Western tradition that accepted "science and reason" as part of their belief system. Hence their views were not unlike those of the Anglo medical community, which made the nurses' task easier. While they had to keep their distance from the birth experience in the pueblos, the nurses were more readily accepted in the Hispanic villages when they arrived to identify and train Hispanic midwives.

Once she had the midwives located, the nurse arranged for a series of ten classes to be held in a woman's home, a school, or another central location. Oral instructions combined with practical demonstrations allowed each woman the opportunity to repeat the action being demonstrated. If the nurse did not speak Spanish, someone in the community would serve as interpreter. The midwives were taught standard obstetrical techniques, procedures for dealing with the most common complications encountered in delivery, and fundamentals in the care of the newborn. They were taught to recognize danger signals and instructed to call a doctor at the first sign of difficulty. Once the delivery was completed, the midwife was required to fill out the birth certificate and mail it to the county health office.

The midwife classes clearly contributed to the steady decline in the infant mortality rate which by 1940 had dropped to 100 deaths per 1,000 births.[26] Equally important, the midwives' willingness to accept instruction from other women prepared the way for a greater acceptance of women physicians later, especially in the specialties of obstetrics and gynecology.[27]

These successes did not come easily as the initial efforts to locate and license midwives in the 1920s were fraught with frustration. The Department of Health could not afford the staff required for the task, and the work was hampered by inaccessibility because many midwives lived in remote mountain villages or isolated rural areas. Since the state was also trying to obtain an accurate count of births and deaths to meet federal census standards, the health care reformers sought out census registrars and subregistrars (local citizens responsible for recording births and deaths) to help in identifying midwives. The midwives were then instructed in filling out birth and death certificates. Many of the women were illiterate, however, and other arrangements had to be made to obtain this important information. Courtney related one experience in Rio Arriba County in 1928:

> The midwives interviewed this week were simply impossible.
> They were all very old and crippled up as well as ignorant. Mrs.
> Gallegos who lives at Los Brazos says that she is using the [eye]
> drops. She does not know how to read or write so can not fill out
> birth certificates but she gives a blank to the family of each baby
> delivered and then collects them and returns them to the sub-
> registrar. She is nearly blind.[28]

This grassroots effort to reach the midwives eventually succeeded. By the mid-1930s, it was determined that between seven hundred and eight hundred midwives were practicing throughout the state, most of them in the Hispanic communities of northern New Mexico.[29] In 1936, with federal funding, the state set up a rural demonstration unit in San Miguel County in northeastern New Mexico where that year midwives attended 701 of 972 births. The project was highly successful, employing as many as ten nurses and engaging the cooperation of several women physicians, including Nancy Campbell of Santa Fe, Gertrude Light of Ranchos de Taos, Mary Lou Hickman of Las Vegas, and later Marian

Hotopp, Edith Millican, and Mary Waddell. One of the most active midwives in northern New Mexico, Jesusita Aragon, was a graduate of the midwife classes and one of the last of the Hispanic midwives to be licensed as part of the state's demonstration project.[30]

The project proved to be a valuable model for providing obstetrical care during World.War II when many doctors were called to the armed services. The local midwife became increasingly important in areas that lacked physicians or other medical professionals. Public officials noted in 1941 that the demand for midwives was likely to increase as more physicians were called into the armed services. In 1942, 273 of 678 of midwives were licensed through the state's midwifery program. The following year the Department of Public Health acknowledged "an awakened consciousness among physicians" that recognized the value of training birth attendants in areas where physicians were not readily available.[31] Not only were the services of the midwife important in the birth experience but

> Since she holds a key position in each little village or crossroads where she lives, the midwife serves as a valuable means of furthering the simple stories told her regarding nutrition, sanitation, and what constitutes safe obstetrical care.... By passing on the lessons she learns she contributes to the overall health program of the state.[32]

Still, the state was determined to reduce the numbers of practicing midwives as part of the medical establishment's overall plan to convince women to give birth in hospitals. Although it seemed a contradiction, the state believed that if women were going to continue to use midwives, then they should be licensed and regulated; at the same time, they expected dependence on midwives to gradually decrease. In 1941 the *New Mexico Health Officer* smugly prophesied that "slowly our problem with midwife service will be solved, and what is now an essential service will in large measure be replaced by more satisfactory assistance at childbirth."[33] So while the licensing program was successful in locating and training midwives, the use of midwives as birth attendants nonetheless gradually declined.

Several factors played a role in this decline, not the least of which was the nationwide movement to transfer birth from the private domain of women and home into the sterile and impersonal world of the hospital. This movement affected both Native American women and Hispanic women, many of whom chose to take advantage of the improved medical procedures and advanced technology that AMA medicine promised. With this form of progress came a loss of autonomy for village parteras and Indian midwives. They no longer controlled the conditions of their trade; the state regulated midwifery by standardizing procedures, requiring examinations, and issuing certificates. Gradually, the numbers of midwives declined as the older parteras died and the younger women failed to take up the profession. Not all midwives followed this route to professionalization nor did they replace their traditional healing practices with the new medical training, which they perceived "as different from but no more reliable than theirs."[34] Because of a shortage of both funds and nurses, the practice of midwifery continued.

The nurses who initiated maternity and infancy care in Indian and Hispanic communities served as cultural agents who helped ease their clients' transition from traditional to more modern methods of health care. We see the results in two ways: the decrease in the infant and maternity mortality rates and the increase in the numbers of women giving birth in hospitals post-World War II. But there were losses in the diminished role of the parteras and in the declining number of practicing midwives. From a high of eight hundred known midwives in 1945, the number fell to less than one hundred by 1965.[35]

As agents of change, the nurses were able to bridge cultural differences because of their empathy and compassion for Hispanic and Native American practices. Yet they were unable to replace traditional childbirth rituals with Anglo methods. Unlike Hispanic women, Native American women resisted adopting middle-class Anglo birthing methods, preferring to keep the birth experience a private, clan-based matter, one shrouded in religious symbolism. These women resisted the nurses' midwifery instructions until after World War II when they more readily accepted the Anglo preference for hospital births.

Why were Hispanic women more accepting of the nurses' instructions than their Native American counterparts? One explanation is that Hispanics are a part of the larger framework of Western tradition while Native American culture has always existed outside this framework. Hispanics, as Catholics, shared ideas and attitudes toward birth, death, and other life experiences with the Anglo community. In contrast, Native Americans' views on these issues were very different. In fact, Native Americans, from long experience, were cautious of Anglo overtures. Stoll put it succinctly when she wrote in 1925 that

> Their fear of losing their racial culture and religion lies at the bottom of their resistance to white man's ways. It would take vast time and rare understanding to comprehend their antipathies and thought. I wonder if a white person will ever do so. It may mean that one of their own race will be the true worker.[36]

If Stoll and others like her were not the "true worker," they nonetheless were important cultural agents in public health work, easing the transition from traditional medicine to modern, and ultimately safer, forms of medical practice. Because of their empathy and sensitivity to cultural beliefs different from their own, the nurses were effective in bringing maternity and infancy education to New Mexico's Hispanic and Native American communities. In retrospect, Stoll's initial determination to "stop talking and get to work" eventually reaped healthy dividends.

NOTES

1. Monthly Report, November 1922, folder 1, Jicarilla Apache Reservation, Augustine Stoll Papers, University of New Mexico Medical Library, Albuquerque, New Mexico.

2.   Augustine Stoll to Elizabeth G. Fox, November 30, 1925, folder 2, Santo Domingo/Northern Pueblos, Augustine Stoll Papers, University of New Mexico Medical Library, Albuquerque, New Mexico.

3.   Augustine Stoll to Anne Fox, January 8, 1926, folder 2, Stoll Papers.

4.   James R. Scott, "Twenty-Five Years of Public Health in New Mexico, 1919–1944," *New Mexico Health Officer* 12 (December 1944), 13–14.

5.   In the census of 1920, the state's population was 60 percent Hispanic, 33.4 percent Anglo, 5 percent native American, and 1.6 percent black. *Fourteenth Census of the United States, 1920,* vol. III, Population (Washington, D.C.: Government Printing Office, 1923) and John L. Andriot, comp. and ed., *Population Abstract of the United States,* vol. I, Tables.

6.   Sandra Schackel, *Social Housekeepers, Women Shaping Public Policy in New Mexico, 1920–1940* (Albuquerque: University of New Mexico Press, 1992), ch. 3.

7.   Monthly Report, April 1926, folder 2, Stoll Papers.

8.   Monthly Report, November 1922, folder 1, Stoll Papers.

9.   Annual Report of Public Health Nursing for 1929, Northern Pueblos, Pre 1950 Annual Reports, Eastern Association on Indian Affairs, box 123, folder Annual Report 1930, American Association on Indian Affairs, Seeley G. Mudd Manuscript Library, Princeton University Archives, Princeton, New Jersey.

10.   This quote is from a draft of a synopsis of her work in Isleta, written in 1940, in possession of her nephew, Robert Mayhew of Santa Fe.

11.   Eric T. Hagberg to Louise O. Kuhrtz, September 6, 1946 and February 18, 1947; William A. Brophy to Louise O. Kuhrtz, September 10, 1949; and Report of Gertrude F. Hosmer, District Supervisory Nurse, n.d., all in the possession of Robert Mayhew of Santa Fe.

12.   Martha Sandweiss, ed., *Denizens of the Desert: A Tale in Word and Picture of Life Among the Navajo Indians* (Albuquerque: University of New Mexico Press, 1988), 18.

13.   Monthly Report, November 1925, folder 2, Stoll Papers.

14.   Monthly Report, January 1926, folder 2, Stoll Papers.

15.   Monthly Report, April 1926, folder 2, Stoll Papers.

16.   Sandweiss, *Denizens of the Desert,* 96.

17.   Fred Eggan, *Social Organization of the Western Pueblos* (Chicago: University of Chicago Press, 1950), 46. To the Hopi, corn is their "mother for they live

on and draw life from the corn as the child draws life from its mother." See Louis A. Hieb, "Hopi World View," in *Handbook of North American Indians,* vol. 9, Southwest (Washington, D.C.: Smithsonian Institution, 1979), 579.

18.   Donald N. Brown, "Picuris Pueblo," in *Handbook of North American Indians,* 272.

19.   Eggan, *Western Pueblos,* 233.

20.   Eggan, *Western Pueblos,* 264.

21.   Edmund J. Ladd, "Zuni Social and Political Reorganization," in *Handbook of North American Indians,* vol. 9, 488.

22.   Eggan, *Western Pueblos,* 191.

23.   Fran Leeper Buss, *La Partera: Story of a Midwife* (Ann Arbor: University of Michigan Press, 1980), 115; Sarah Deutsch, *No Separate Refuge: Culture, Class, and Gender on an Anglo-Hispanic Frontier in the American Southwest, 1880–1940* (New York: Oxford University Press, 1987), 46–48.

24.   Social reformers nationwide had worked for nearly two decades for passage of a federal bill to provide a national form of health care for mothers and children, but their success was shortlived as the influential American Medical Association was able to bring pressure on Congress to discontinue funding by 1928. For a thorough discussion of the Sheppard-Towner Act, see Stanley J. Lemons, *The Woman Citizen: Social Feminism in the 1920s* (Urbana: University of Illinois Press, 1973).

25.   Yearly Report, 1925–1926, Correspondence and Reports Relating to Programs and Surveys, 1917–1954, box 70, folder 20-95-5, Children's Bureau, Record Group 102, National Archives and Records Administration, Washington, D.C.

26.   Scott, "Twenty-Five Years of Public Health," 13–14; also Schackel, *Social Housekeepers,* ch. 2.

27.   Buss, *La Partera,* 118.

28.   Weekly Report, October 1928, folder 4-2-1-2-1, box 266, Central File, Children's Bureau, Record Group 102, National Archives, Washington, D.C.

29.   Greenfield, Myrtle, *A History of Public Health in New Mexico* (Albuquerque: University of New Mexico Press, 1962), 122–23.

30.   In a sixty-year period, Aragon delivered over 12,000 babies in northern New Mexico. Schackel, *Social Housekeepers,* 50, 56.

31.   Annual Report, 1941, New Mexico Department of Public Health, in

New Mexico Health Officer 10 (March 1942), 19–20, 28; Annual Report, 1942, New Mexico Department of Public Health, in *New Mexico Health Officer* 11 (March 1943), 26–28; and Annual Report, 1943, New Mexico Department of Public Health, in *New Mexico Health Officer* 12 (March 1944), 49–51.

32.   Annual Report, 1943, New Mexico Department of Health, 49–50.

33.   Annual Report, 1941, New Mexico Department of Public Health, 19.

34.   Deutsch, *No Separate Refuge,* 186–87.

35.   Interview with Anne Fox, January 14, 1986, Oral History of Medicine Project, University of New Mexico Medical Library.

36.   Monthly Report, November 1924, Stoll Papers.

TWELVE

NEW MEXICO TOURIST IMAGES

❧

WILLIAM E. TYDEMAN

OUTSIDE of New Mexico, no one has ever heard of Joseph Roy Willis or Elizabeth DeHuff, probably with good reason. J. R. Willis was an artist but not a very good one. Elizabeth DeHuff was a lecturer and presenter of slide shows. Both of them dealt in what are now sources for research—commercial visual arts—in which historians have traditionally had little interest—and a subject that historians have neglected—tourism. Nevertheless, any cultural historian of the Southwest should see the popular and commercial arts as important primary sources. An adequate history of tourism in the Southwest demands an integrated history of the making and use of pictures. In this chapter I begin by examining some theoretical issues concerning the most universal form of picture making, photography. I then show how Willis's work and the lantern slide collection of the Indian Detours presented by DeHuff emphasized and stereotyped Native American culture in New Mexico.

In studying the most fugitive of the arts, photography, historians have only within the last two decades begun to develop the methods and tools for analysis. Throughout the history of the medium (now over 150 years) scholars have been fascinated by its verisimilitude and time-freezing capacity. Phrases like "windows on the past" and "mirror with a memory" indicate an early recognition of the photograph's ability to record a forgotten past, but it is only in the 1970s and 1980s that historians and social scientists have taken seriously the possibility of using the photograph as a primary source. The emergence of the so-called new social history, the new western history, popular and material culture study, and cultural history has led to a dramatic surge of methodological and cultural studies that demonstrate ways of utilizing the full potential of photographic sources. To date, however, we still lack a comprehensive account of the place photography holds in American culture,[1] and no one has applied these methods to the Southwest. We have had several recent studies of western painting that pay great attention to the relationship between art and culture[2] but no studies that rely on the full range of visual forms.

A new photographic history of the Southwest[3] would be useful to students of the region, but we also need studies of picture making as part of cultural history. We cannot have a complete history of the Southwest until we have "an integrated history of picture-making."[4] In the Southwest what was pictured often meant as much as what was spoken or written. In tourism, so important to the economy of the region, advertising and image production are closely linked.

The photographic print is only one form of picture making and symbolic representation. Other photographically based sources—the picture postcard and the lantern slide, for example—were equally ubiquitous in the early part of this century. In any of these forms we must accept the premise that writing history and making pictures are ways of making propositions and comparisons. Both posit ideas and symbols about the possibility of a world.[5] The historian's method and concerns about point of view, bias, and frame of reference apply to photographs and to all symbolic forms of expression.

The usefulness of photographic images in understanding New Mexico's past can be demonstrated by looking at the individuals who worked with the pictorial traditions of the tourist trade. J. R. Willis worked in a variety of formats. Through the proliferation of his imagery and the distribution of the picture postcard, he became a major entrepreneur in

New Mexico's twentieth-century tourist industry. Illustrator, cartoonist, photographer, muralist, and painter, he was born in Sylvania, Georgia, on 24 November 1876. His formal education began in the public schools, and he later attended Hilton Academy in Sylvania. After high school he worked briefly in the mining industry. He was studying art in Atlanta when the Spanish American War began in 1898 and was also employed illustrating war stories for several area newspapers. Even though the technological innovation of the half-tone screen-printing process had made photographic reproduction commercially feasible in 1888, it had yet to replace illustrator recreations of war scenes. Work with the *Atlanta Constitution* followed. With the money he had saved from these ventures, Willis enrolled at the Chase School of Art in New York. On the faculty of the Chase School of Art was the famous realist and leader of what later became the Ash Can School, Robert Henri. This brief work with Henri was decisive. Willis absorbed the lessons of realism and effectively used the genre in his photography and painting.

Willis arrived in the Southwest in 1917. In the ten years between his training at the Chase School and the opening of his tourist business in New Mexico, he dabbled in a variety of picture-making enterprises. He also appeared in vaudeville, and at Chautauqua meetings he gave "chalk talks," one of the little-studied American popular expressions in the period before movies. At these shows he entertained his audience by drawing on the blackboard while delivering a continuous monologue. He painted theatrical scenes for Balboa Film Company in Long Beach, California, and there he became infatuated with film. He tried his hand at producing animated cartoons. His cartoon creation, *Rastus Fraid-o-Nothin,* was not successful, and he worked only briefly in the film studios at Universal City in California with little success. On his way to New York from California to discuss a pending contract, Willis made his first stop in the Southwest. In Arizona at the Hopi reservation he discovered the region's magic. Seeing the potential for marketing his imagery, he set up his business in 1917 in "the heart of Indian Country"—Gallup, New Mexico.[6]

Willis remained at Gallup through 1931. His art studio, as he called his curio shop, became a fixture in the Gallup commercial scene, and he became a successful entrepreneur of the tourist trade. He continued to paint in oils, and his portraits and mountain scenes sold well. But always with an eye to the commercial possibilities, he also photographed the Southwest, frequently turning his photographs into the most popular form of tourist art, the postcard.

Willis's early years reflect the period near the end of the century that was marked by the decline of such forms of depiction as steel engraving, the chalk talk, photoplay (still photos arranged to tell a story), and lantern slide shows, and the emergence of new photographic technologies—the half-tone screen photographic process and cine film. Willis's work in the film industry and theatrical design can be understood partially as a struggle to find commercial possibilities in these emerging technologies. Displaced by photography like the portrait artists of the mid nineteenth century, many artists of the early twentieth century turned to the new technologies and to advertising and the tourism industry as a way of making a living. Willis was one of the more successful of these artists-turned-entrepreneurs.

The tourist industry, created in part by these new technologies, helps explain the careers not only of J. R. Willis but also Charles Fletcher Lummis, George Warton James, Carlos Vierra, Jesse Nussbaum, and Karl Moon. They are part of a much larger group who combined photography with other visual and written formats to promote New Mexico in those transitional decades of the twentieth century. In fact, the linkage of art, commerce, and local boosterism typified an entire generation of New Mexicans who helped shape the cultural life of the state.

One of New Mexico's boosters was Elizabeth DeHuff, who made a career of presenting illustrated lantern-slide lectures. In the evenings, three to six times a week, at La Fonda Hotel in Santa Fe, she lectured to the tourists visiting Santa Fe as part of the Fred Harvey Company's tour promotion known as the Indian Detour.[7] From 1926 to 1941 in a remarkable record of endurance, DeHuff offered tourists a perception of the cultures of the Southwest. Remarkably, these lantern slides still exist, and their fine hand-colored hues transport us to the lost world of New Mexico tourism between the wars.[8]

The lantern-slide show is the equivalent of the modern slide show. Rather than on cardboard or plastic, the image and the mounts were on glass. The glass photograph was protected with another glass cover, and both were bound together with an opaque paper to create a commercial format 3¼ by 4 inches. Then one at a time, the slides could be placed in a metal carrier and slipped before the lens of the "lantern," a powerful arc light projector. The photograph etched on glass, combined with delicate hand coloring, produced an image of remarkable clarity and tone.

By the turn of the century, lantern slides were widely available. The educational uses included every conceivable subject, from the wonders of agriculture to the problems of New York tenement life. At La Fonda, DeHuff used hundreds of lantern slides to show tourists the major attractions in the area surrounding Santa Fe.

Slides used the visual power of color to transport tourists from a darkened room to a new cultural world. T. C. McLuhan explains: "The Santa Fe Railroad used the language of color aggressively and imaginatively. Color was one of its greatest assets. The campaigns to promote travel on the Santa Fe evoked a golden age when color glowed and image flowered."[9]

What the tourist wanted to see, and what the Indian Detours shamelessly promoted, was Native American culture. As Paul Horgan reminds us, Santa Fe tourism was fundamentally about exhibiting the Indian:

> Both the ancient and modern life of Santa Fe and its *ambiente* were brought into a state of high organization for the entertainment of the tourist. Until World War II, the tourist trade was the largest annual business of New Mexico. If there was much to show the tourist, it had to be made presentable for him by way of exhibits, natural or arranged, and his comfort had to be insured

through hotels, transportation, and good roads. Efforts in all these concerns were designed at Santa Fe to bring him face to face with the leading exhibit of all which was the Indian.[10]

The lantern slides presented and explained by Elizabeth DeHuff offered a view of New Mexico Native American culture drawn to please the consumer. They emphasize Pueblo culture, and they demonstrate what historian Richard Frost has called "the romantic inflation of Pueblo culture."[11]

In a swirl of color, and completely removed from their original ethnographic context, the slides of the Indian Detours reinforced the cultural stereotypes of Pueblo peoples. They glossed over the differences among Pueblo groups and concentrated on aspects of their domestic life that highlighted the differences between middle-class European Americans and Pueblo families. Because the images were grounded in the ordered materiality of the economics of family production, tourists could easily see cultural differences. The slides reinforce a timeless vision of the Pueblo Indians centered on craft production in a civil but primitive environment. The overall effect is to suggest that, although Indians are different from them, tourists have nothing to fear from them. While producing goods for a European American economy, Pueblo people are gracious, smiling, trusting, civil, nonthreatening, and family centered.

The images from the DeHuff Indian Detours collection—more than 200 in all—did not concentrate exclusively on the Pueblos. Centering on the Rio Grande Pueblos made economic sense because they were nearby, but the presence of many slides of Hopis and Navajos indicates that the representation of Native American groups had more to do with products for the tourist trade than it did with easy geographic access and driving distance. Hopi-land exercised great allure, but tourists did not have to travel that far to purchase Hopi pottery and Navajo rugs. These crafts could easily be purchased at Fred Harvey Company's "Indian rooms" in Santa Fe and Albuquerque.

The presentation of native life in the slides was astonishingly simplistic and ethnocentric. Pueblo and Hopi peoples occupied the highest cultural order, followed by Navajo and Apache. This hierarchy suited the prevailing European-American middle-class norms for "good" and "bad" Indians. The Navajo produced rugs and silver jewelry of astonishing beauty, but in the lantern slides Navajos gambled and engaged in such raucous pursuits as chicken pulls. The warlike Apache had little to offer the tourist. The image of the fierce Apache warrior had softened by the 1920s, but two of the few Apache images in the collection show a diapered, dirty baby wailing and a poverty-stricken family living in a wickiup. According to her taped reminiscences, Elizabeth DeHuff's presentation that accompanied the slides informed the audience, "Apaches don't dress carefully." When the obligatory scene of women making baskets appears, we learn that the Apache make baskets just like the Hopi, except that they are flat and less durable.[12]

The lantern slides incorporate several stereotypes. As the "noble savage" the Navajo man is depicted in romantic silhouette. Slides of a war dance for visitors at Santa Clara and Tesuque pueblos are replete with the dancers in the feathered headdresses of the Plains Indians. At Taos Pueblo we see more transported Plains Indian dress with buckskin costumes and headdresses. Women are depicted as Indian princesses or as Indian madonnas. Hopi maidens prepare bread in their finest jewelry and dresses.[13]

The Pueblo-centrism of Indian Detours was an attempt to limit the tourist's view of New Mexico's multiculturalism. There was little economic utility in selling the Anglo aspects of New Mexican culture except as a guarantee of the first-class amenities in hotels and other tourist accommodations. The Hispanic tradition had to be handled with great care. The solution of Indian Detours was to emphasize the architectural and mission tradition of New Mexico life, to promote a celebration of the ties to the grand tradition of Spain, but to avoid any reference to New Mexico Hispanics or village life. The racism and class consciousness of eastern tourists made it hard to turn New Mexico's Hispanic life into a commodity.

The promotion of New Mexico from the colonial capital of Santa Fe,

in the La Fonda hotel with its Spanish furniture and Old World trap-
pings, spoke to the selective cultural appropriation of the Spanish tradition. It was safe to promote the clean, pristine images of mission churches
and to emphasize a craft tradition derived from Spain, but it was not safe
to show New Mexico's Hispanic people or to suggest their Mexican roots.
The Indian Detour lantern-slide collection, filled with portraits of Indians
and Indian life, contains not a single slide of a Hispanic. However, to
promote effectively the fifty miles surrounding Santa Fe, other Hispanic
images had to be included: churches, archaeological sites, and homes
festooned with chili peppers and ristras. There were photographs of
wood wagons and the standard imagery of the wood-bearing burro, but
never—except for one image of Penitentes carrying a cross—a Hispanic
face. While this avoidance of Hispanic people may be surprising, it is not
exceptional. The same stereotyping and racism are found in the conventional written sources of the period.

Distorted cultural assumptions were also at work in motion pictures
of the silent era made on location in New Mexico. In 1898 the Edison
Studios made the first film in New Mexico, *Indian Day School,* a 40-second
assimilationist fantasy. Young Indian pupils in dresses and trousers parade
in and out of their classroom under the watchful eye of their teacher.
Made at Isleta Pueblo, *Indian Day School* focused on the triumph of
European ideals of regimentation and order. By contrast nearly thirty
years later when the Indian Detours were launched, it was the enduring
traditions of the Pueblo and Navajo and their failure to assimilate that
stimulated tourist interest.

D. W. Griffith's *A Pueblo Legend* (filmed at Isleta in 1912) starred
Mary Pickford as an orphan maiden from Hopi. The film shows Pickford
falling in love with a Pueblo warrior who fights the evil Apache, saves his
tribe from their clutches, and, aided by Pickford, finds a blue sapphire. *A
Pueblo Legend* is consistent with the pattern of Pueblo-centrism and the
stereotype of the evil Apache found in the lantern slides. However, the
theme of the warrior suggests that by 1912 the notion of the peaceful,
cooperative Pueblos had not yet triumphed.

Other silent films made in New Mexico also included racial stereotypes. The lazy Mexican taking his siesta wearing a large sombrero was one of the popular stereotypes of the period. In *The Rattlesnake* (1917) Hispanics were portrayed as evil Mexican banditos.

These characterizations stand in marked contrast to tourist films, such as *Adventures in Kit Carson Land* (1917). This film was the first piece produced by the New Mexico Tourist Promotion Bureau. It showed absurd scenes of members of the Taos Society of Artists in Indian head-dresses painting in the Taos plaza. In recognition of the growth of automobile touring, the viewer is led by map along the emerging road network to tourist sites in northern New Mexico. The use of the legend of Kit Carson is another example of the avoidance of Hispanic themes. The title suggests the ideology of adventure associated with the frontier. Creators of tourism propaganda relied on the exotic, primitive fascination of frontier and Indian and avoided negative images of New Mexico's Mexican past.

Both the lantern-slide imagery of Indian Detours and the early silent films demonstrate the selective portrayal of the past. The choice of images and captions offers only one-dimensional views of Hispanic and Indian culture. There is no mention of social problems—no poverty, disease, alcoholism, or marginalization. What these tourist promotions created was "a romantic and one-dimensional view of Indian life and the Southwest landscape," as T. C. McLuhan put it. "What the Detours did succeed in creating, however, was a horde of urban consumers. The Indian was promoted as an item to be "consumed" by the tourist."[14]

The tourist consumption that the Indian Detour program promoted is indicated by letters from that era. In March 1927, less than one year after the Indian Detours began, Frederic Snyder, superintendent of Carson Indian School and Agency in Nevada, wrote to the Northern Pueblo Agency. He asked whether a nice collection of Pueblo pottery could be loaned for the Transcontinental Highway Exposition to be held in Reno. Superintendent C. J. Randall replied:

Since the advent of the Harvey Detours among the Pueblos, all
pottery manufactured by these Indians is readily sold for cash
and there is even a greater demand than supply. Things are different since the influx of tourists and travelers. Seven large buses
have been known to visit Puye Cliffs in one day. Each bus carries
from a dozen to 20 people. When Indians can sell their products
for cash, they are not inclined to take a chance shipping it on
prospect.[15]

The files of the Northern Pueblo Agency are replete with tourist requests
for information about and prices of Pueblo pottery.[16]

Tourists discovered the great distance between the romantic ideal of
the lantern slide and their own experience. One government report
observed:

It was interesting to listen to the comments of the automobile
tourists who were passing through Pueblo country. A considerable
number of them evidently were disappointed because what they
saw on the way did not square with the alluring advertising pictures and what they read about these Indians. They had kept eager eyes open for Indians dressed picturesquely in robes or
blankets, feathered and painted, dancing and posing and generally
making fascinating spectacles of themselves. Instead they found
men on their farms and in their fields. It was lambing time and
the Indians were too busy with their ewes and new born lambs to
bother with passing tourists.[17]

The later career of J. R. Willis illustrates the importance of the one
other medium central to this examination of tourist imagery—the picture
postcard. In 1931 Willis moved to Albuquerque and opened his business
on Central Avenue. In 1938, recognizing the commercial possibilities in
the completion of Route 66 and the emergence of the Old Town area, he
moved his operation from downtown to Old Town. Willis continued his
artistic work and devoted more attention to oil painting. His local fame

increased, and so did his sales. By the 1940s the Willis property included his shop, studio, and a sixteen-apartment complex, called El Mirador. El Mirador was on the periphery of Albuquerque's choicest real estate, the Country Club, and was often referred to as one of the most attractive areas of Albuquerque.⁓

From the establishment of El Mirador to his retirement in the 1950s, Willis continued to promote Southwest tourist art. But the most intriguing aspect of his Albuquerque years is his regional distributorship of southwestern postcards for the Chicago-based Curt Teich Company. Founded in 1898 Teich printed postcards until 1974, when it was bought out by Europeans. Over the span of seventy-six years, Curt Teich Company became the largest volume producer of postcards in the world.[18] During these years the company produced more than 100,000 picture postcards of the Southwest. In the 1940s and 1950s many of these images were distributed by J. R. Willis. The Teich postcards are a fascinating glimpse into the popularity of Indian views in New Mexico, and they demonstrate the essential link between the romantic aesthetic of the Pueblos and tourist consumerism.[19]

Some postcards are duplicate images of the slides in the Indian Detours collection. A young Navajo child festooned in a squash-blossom necklace, Hopi maidens, and an Indian woman with two children on cradleboards all bear the distinct hand of the Santa Fe Railroad colorists. However, the scope of New Mexico postcards is much broader. They provide ways for tourists to verify their experience, to prove they were there. Orders from J. R. Willis cover hotels and tourist facilities, landscapes, monuments, churches and shrines, roadway scenes, local townscapes, and booster sites.

Orders to the Curt Teich Company from Willis's rival, the Fred Harvey Company, include titles such as "A Primitive Indian Village," "Navajo Blanket Wearers," "Indian Building Santa Fe Station," and "A Navaho Papoose." J. R. Willis ordered cards with such titles as "Pueblo Indian Women Baking," "Call of the Clan," and "Pueblo Indian Turquoise Driller."[20]

David J. Kammer, who has made the most extensive study of southwestern postcards, highlights one postcard of a Pueblo ceremonial dance and suggests that "the final evidence to the tourist that he would not be disappointed with a visit to New Mexico is this image of fellow tourists covering the rooftops of the Pueblo itself. Here the verification of having achieved the quest for the exotic and different becomes complete as the tourists have seemingly taken possession, at least for the duration of the feast, of an entire Indian village."[21]

Hispanic stereotyping also occurs. In one stylized image produced and copyrighted by Willis ristras hang from the eaves rather than the door lintels of an adobe home, and a faceless Hispanic woman clad in black robes has her back to the viewer. This Spanish Pueblo Revival–style adobe home bears the caption "Quaint Mexican Home, Old Colonial Spanish Influence." The text explains, "Whether you are in San Diego, Calif., Tucson, Ariz., El Paso, Tex., Albuquerque, Santa Fe or Taos, N.M. you cannot help but observe the influence of the beautiful simplicity of our old Colonial Spanish settlers, associated with the care-free existence of these descendants of the Spanish Conquistadors."[22]

The images of Native Americans and Hispanics in popular arts, such as the postcard and the lantern slide, offer useful evidence to verify written sources. However, visual sources are not a direct reflection of American values during a given period. Each visual form reflects the desire to communicate with an audience, the potential consumers or tourists. The necessity to create an illusion of a culture leads the sources to make a statement of desire rather than reality. When we remove these images from their original contexts, their original meanings are less clear. In cine film the relationship of the final product to the audience is even more uncertain. Overall, we have little information about the effects of all these products on their viewers.

It is a mistake, however, to demand a higher test of visual sources than of conventional written accounts. As much as we would like to believe that novels, speeches, and newspapers reflect social reality, we still cannot determine the effect they had on readers of their day. We should bear in mind the dangers in inferring meaning from content, whatever the form. As we move toward an integrated history of visual forms, the likelihood of verifying our reading increases. Finally, we should compare these findings with the conventional written sources. In reconstructing the history of tourism in New Mexico visual sources should be placed on the same level as written sources, not above them.

Visual material and the work and activities of lesser known artists, such as J. R. Willis, provide additional channels for verifying hypotheses based on written documents. The infatuation with Pueblo peoples and the lack of interest in Hispanic people shown in the materials suggest a tendency of tourist promotion in New Mexico before World War II. Photography and related commercial arts can be primary sources in deciphering the meaning of tourism. They not only verify myth and stereotype but suggest that image makers and distributors played a significant role in creating the cultural contradictions of twentieth-century New Mexico.

NOTES

1. Daniel Boorstin, *The Americans: The Democratic Experience* (New York, 1973), 389.

2. See, for example, Barbara Novak, *Nature and Culture: American Landscape and Painting, 1825–1975* (New York, 1980).

3. For the geographic definition of the Southwest used here, see Donald Meining, *Southwest: Three Peoples in Change* (New York, 1971).

4. See Carl Chiarenza, "Notes Toward an Integrated History of Picture Making," in Thomas F. Barrow et al., eds., *Reading into Photography* (Albuquerque, 1982), 209–36.

5. Ibid., 213.

6. I have relied on Frank Reeve's *History of New Mexico*, vol. 3 (New York, 1961), 76–78, for these and subsequent biographical facts.

7. The Indian Detour was a cooperative effort of the Fred Harvey Company and the Atchison, Topeka and Santa Fe Railroad to operate a rail and bus system. It concentrated on the fifty mile area surrounding Santa Fe from Las

Vegas to Albuquerque. Longer day coach trips would be arranged to the Hopi reservation and Canyon De Chelly.

8. These slides are part of the DeHuff Family Papers, 1833–1981, located at the Center for Southwest Research, University of New Mexico, Albuquerque.

9. T. C. McLuhan, *Dream Tracks: The Railroad and the American Indian* (New York, 1985), 39–40.

10. Paul Horgan, *Three Centuries of Santa Fe* (New York, 1963), 318.

11. Richard H. Frost, "The Romantic-Inflation of Pueblo Culture," *The American West,* 17 (1980): 5–9, 56–60.

12. Cassette tapes accompanying the lantern slide collection, DeHuff Family Papers, 1883–1981, Center for Southwest Research, University of New Mexico, Albuquerque.

13. The depiction of Indian women in the lantern slide collection coincides with the stereotypes identified in Patricia C. Albers and William R. James, "Illusion and Illumination: Visual Images of American Indian Women in the West," in *The Women's West,* Susan Armitage and Elizabeth Jameson, eds. (Norman, 1987), 35–50.

14. McLuhan, *Dream Tracks,* 44.

15. C. J. Randall to Frederic Snyder, 29 March 1927, Bureau of Indian Affairs, Record Group 75, Northern Pueblo Agency, Decimal File No. 1912-38, box 81, file 963, Manufacturing, Federal Records Center, Denver, CO.

16. Ibid. See also box 17 in the same subseries.

17. Ibid., box 17, folder 092.

18. *Post Card Journal* 3 (Spring/Summer 1986): 3.

19. The business record of the Curt Teich Company are part of the Curt Teich Postcard Archives of the Lake County Museum in Wauconda, Illinois.

20. Albuquerque, New Mexico Subject File, Curt Teich Postcard Archives, Lake County Museum, Wauconda, Illinois.

21. David J. Kammer, "Indian Imagery in Southwest Post Cards," unpublished paper presented at the Western History Association Annual Meeting, Los Angeles, CA, 10 October 1987.

22. J. R. Willis postcard in author's collection.

THIRTEEN

CASUALTIES OF CAUTION AND FEAR:
LIFE IN SANTA FE'S JAPANESE INTERNMENT CAMP, 1942–46

RICHARD MELZER

A mysterious twelve-car passenger train with drawn shades and a unique manifest of passengers pulled into Santa Fe, New Mexico, at 7:20 A.M. on March 14, 1942. From this train 425 Japanese "alien enemies" were led between rows of armed guards, the U.S. border patrol, and New Mexico state police. In clothes from overalls to business suits, these Japanese Americans represented occupations from fishermen and farmers to ministers and businessmen. Unaccustomed to the morning chill of northern New Mexico, several men wrapped towels around their necks. Most remained expressionless as the white shipping tags tied to their shirts were checked for identification. Most of the prisoners (euphemistically called internees) were middle-aged Californians; all were resident aliens. An older internee pointed to the sun as it rose over the Sangre de Cristo Mountains. A new day had dawned on a new, constrained life for these domestic prisoners of World War II. Within two hours all 425 men had been transported by truck to their new wartime home, a concentration camp (euphemistically called an internment camp) on the western outskirts of Santa Fe.[1]

An additional 401 prisoners arrived from California in the next month and a half. These 826 men in Santa Fe had been abruptly taken from their homes soon after the Japanese attack on Pearl Harbor on

December 7, 1941. More than 3,000 other West Coast Japanese-Americans were shipped to similar camps, including one in Lordsburg, New Mexico. All were suspected members of a fifth column that many Americans feared might assist in a Japanese invasion of the West Coast or engage in industrial sabotage. Many were detained on spurious charges. Some had been branded as dangerous because they had been trained in such Japanese martial arts as sumo wrestling and kendo, an ancient form of fencing using bamboo sticks. Several were considered an immediate threat to national security because they belonged to Japanese martial arts clubs, including Butokukai, although the latter was more of a social group than a military clique. Others were picked up by federal authorities because they were known to keep "weapons"—including a carved ceremonial bow in one case and a supply of rope in another—in their homes or businesses. Some businessmen had engaged in the sale of strategically important goods to Japan before the war. Others were said to have maintained close ties to the Japanese military, if only by entertaining Japanese officers when their ships visited West Coast ports in the 1930s. Fishermen were especially feared for their extensive knowledge of the American coastline and because they possessed shortwave radios on their Pacific Ocean fishing vessels. A majority were Issei, members of a generation that had migrated to the United States from Japan but had remained intensely loyal to their motherland, its emperor, and its ancient culture. All had been classified by the U.S. government as Group A suspects long before the war broke out, meaning that they were "known dangerous" and required the closest scrutiny.[2]

Unlike other Japanese men, who were allowed to remain with their families at War Department relocation camps elsewhere in the West, these men were considered to be such high security risks that they had to be isolated in Santa Fe or at similar Justice Department facilities until decisions were made regarding their individual destinies. Forced to abandon their businesses and personal property, the Japanese suffered huge financial losses. Forced to relinquish their private lives and civil liberties, they were victims of what John Hersey has called "a mistake of terrifically horrible proportions."[3] Only wartime hysteria and a longstanding racist fear of the "yellow peril" can explain how such an unjust policy could be implemented by the U.S. government and condoned by large segments of the American population.[4]

When the internees arrived, the Santa Fe facility had just recently been refurbished as a makeshift prison. A Civilian Conservation Corps (CCC) camp in the 1930s, the property had passed to the control of the New Mexico State Penitentiary by 1941. The state penitentiary in turn granted the U.S. Immigration and Naturalization Service (INS) free use of the eighty-acre area for wartime needs. Using an abandoned CCC camp offered several advantages, especially because internment camp officials had less than two weeks to prepare for the first internees' arrival in mid-March 1942. Existing structures, including eight barracks and a mess hall, were put to good use, although much was left to be done with the assistance of 150 quickly hired local laborers. The camp's electrical system and plumbing facilities were restored to working order, and utilities were turned on with the cooperation of the Santa Fe city government. Prefabricated Victory Huts were shipped in for additional housing, and food and supplies were hurriedly procured. Two hundred spools of wire were strung on 10 foot wooden posts. The fences were topped with an additional 2 feet of barbed wire. Spotlights were installed, and lookout towers were erected every hundred yards. Finally, permanent camp personnel were hired, including twenty guards drawn from a list of twenty-five submitted by Santa Fe County sheriff Tom Delgado. Each applicant was carefully screened, partly to help calm an increasingly jittery local population that considered the "holding of a large number of enemy aliens . . . [to be] far more dangerous than the detention of criminals at the state penitentiary."[5]

Local fear was mixed with a large dose of racial hatred. Racist portrayals in Hollywood movies, government propaganda, and the wartime press reinforced the prevailing distrust of Japanese from outside the state.[6] News of American military defeats in the Philippines, where over 1,800 New Mexicans served in the U.S. Army, raised emotions to a fever pitch. Reports of a private plan to colonize 60,000 West Coast Japanese in New Mexico caused a public outcry seldom equaled in New Mexico history. Angry letters, telegrams, and petitions poured into Governor John E. Miles's office in March and April 1942. Just as the Santa Fe camp received its first internees, New Mexicans from Chamber of Commerce officials to state district court judges were denouncing all Japanese as treacherous "rats" and "skunks" while declaring the colonization plan "utterly repugnant" and inevitably disastrous.[7] New Mexicans grew even less tolerant with news of the fall of Bataan on April 9.[8] Newspaper editorials were usually more rational, but no less adamant in their opposition to the proposed migration.[9] With Governor Miles's opposition, the unpopular plan died by early summer.

Internees spent much of their time in Santa Fe at government hearings to determine the extent of their loyalty to the United States. Major cultural differences and serious language barriers made these hearings difficult, frustrating, and often unfair. Kenko Yamashita's case was sadly typical. An Issei, Yamashita later recalled that he was asked "strange questions" by his five-person hearing board, including questions about his membership in Butokukai. Asked to translate the word *Butokukai* into English, Yamashita replied that he did not think a direct translation was possible. Unsatisfied with this response, the hearing board called in a Korean student who attempted to decipher the word's meaning by looking up its parts in a pocket-sized Japanese dictionary. *Butokukai* was found to mean "military virtue association," a translation that "disgusted" Yamashita because in his opinion the group was a cultural society that "had nothing to do with the military." As a result of this hearing, Yamashita was classified as an "undesirable enemy alien."

Of the camp's original 826 men, 303 received classifications similar to Yamashita's, and by the fall of 1942 they were turned over to the U.S. Army for internment elsewhere. The remaining 523 were given lesser classifications and were either reunited with their families in one of the ten relocation camps built west of the Mississippi or simply released inland from the West Coast military zone. By September 24 the Santa Fe camp had been evacuated with the assumption that it had fulfilled its wartime mission.[10]

But news of the camp's demise was premature. After a winter of inactivity, the facility was reopened. The federal government ordered the INS to detain "undesirable enemy aliens" on a more permanent basis. The camp was therefore refurbished a second time, this time for the arrival of 375 new internees on March 23, 1943. By June 30 the camp's population had climbed to 1,894.[11]

Internees of the reopened camp were much like their predecessors of 1942, but there were some significant differences. With greater numbers came a greater variety of professions, including doctors, actors, reporters, and college professors. They also had greater experience with internments. Men like Suikei Kuruya had been transferred to as many as five camps before arriving in Santa Fe. Some were moved so often that their personal letters were returned to their families covered with forwarding addresses that never quite caught up with them.

Hearings led one camp commander to conclude that "some internees are rabid pro-Japanese. . . . others appear to be staunchly American, while the majority . . . view the war between Japan and the United States in the same light as a son would view a fight between [a] father and mother" in which neither side could be favored and neither side could be opposed.[12] Files were kept on each prisoner with exact notes regarding his behavior and attitude as well as his overall "parole risk." To help keep peace, camp officials separated internees in barracks based on their predominant political views regarding the war.[13]

State and national origin constituted the greatest difference between those who had been interned in 1942 and those who arrived from 1943 to the end of the war. In 1942 the internees came primarily from California. Of those who came later, approximately 25 percent were apprehended outside the contiguous forty-eight states, in such places as Hawaii, Alaska, and twelve Central and South American countries. The largest number of Central and South American Japanese came from Peru, where hundreds of the "humbler classes" had been rounded up. The Peruvian Japanese were sent to Santa Fe and similar camps for possible prisoner exchanges with the enemy.[14]

Like prisoners in all wars, those in Santa Fe coped with their incarceration by staying as busy as possible within the confines of their suddenly shrunken world. Camp officials encouraged internee activities because they believed that active internees would have less time to ponder their fate and cause trouble.[15] Local workers were scarce in any case, and there was much work to be done in camp. Described as an "industrious lot," the internees served as carpenters, plumbers, mechanics, bakers, barbers, tailors, and firemen.[16] Others worked on a small truck farm adjacent to the camp's exterior fence. This operation proved so productive that it helped feed internees at a considerable savings to the federal government. Surplus vegetables were often traded to Bruns General Hospital in Santa Fe in exchange for much-needed fish, to the state penitentiary in exchange for canned fruits and vegetables, and to a supermarket chain in exchange for valued foods of all kinds.[17]

Small groups of internees were also used as laborers in a Tesuque apple orchard, at the Santa Fe municipal golf course, and at Fort Stanton when the German internment center there was demolished. Unfortunately, as the first survivors of Bataan began arriving home in March 1945 with fresh stories of atrocities committed against Americans in Japanese prisoner-of-war (POW) camps, an "unfavorable public reaction" set in against these Japanese work crews.[18] Outside labor was therefore discontinued. Japanese internees who remained at their jobs in camp were eventually paid 80 cents a day in accordance with the Geneva Convention. When praised by a representative of the International YMCA for his camp's fine physical condition, a Santa Fe commander replied that his Japanese internees "would make any . . . commander look good. . . . They do all the work that has to be done . . . and they're very good at it."[19]

But with only 400 jobs available, no more than one in every four internees could count on work as a regular means of diversion. They had to be resourceful to fill their days with meaningful—or at least distracting—activities. Some broke the monotonous routine of prison life by keeping small pets or by growing vegetables and flowers "in every available space."[20] A large percentage attended informal internee-taught classes in subjects from English to engineering.[21] Many read magazines, newspapers, and books from the camp's small library, well aware that these materials were carefully censored to avoid all literature that "could tend to incite the internees against the [U.S.] Government and its policies."[22] Several clubs were organized, including a poetry-writing group known as the Santa Fe-shisha Tanka Poetry Club.[23] Internees wrote letters to their distant families, although each man was limited to one letter of thirty lines per week. A team of four censors checked all correspondence.[24] The few who protested this policy faced rather harsh punishment. One particularly disgruntled internee, Henry Hideo, wrote to a friend in Chicago that "rights and freedoms are restricted so I am having an awful time . . . in here. . . . Our desire is to see those damn fool censors . . . destroyed."[25] He received a twenty-day sentence in the camp's small jail for his imprudent remarks.[26]

As at many Japanese internment and relocation camps, internees in Santa Fe also occupied their time by printing their own newspaper. The single-paged Santa Fe *Jiho* (or *Times*) was mimeographed daily with general news on one side of each sheet and camp news on the opposite side. Written mostly by internees who had served as reporters before the war, stories ranged from the practical (such as what one might expect if repatriated to Japan) to the literary (including internee poems) to the trivial (such as a list of which items were most popular at the camp canteen). As might be expected, the censor's black pen blocked out all questionable stories, although some—such as Japanese prime minister Hideki Tojo's prediction that Japan would win the war in 1944—slipped by, undoubtedly to the surprise of local readers and the chagrin of camp officials.[27]

A great many Japanese filled their time diligently working on arts and crafts, such as the carving of ornate walking sticks or the painting of scenes depicting the camp and its surrounding southwestern landscape. Escaping into the freedom afforded by their art, men like Kango Takamura painted for as many as ten hours a day. Stone polishing was undoubtedly the most popular craft practiced in camp. Using stones and petrified wood found in camp or purchased from local ranchers at 10 cents a pound, the men often took "several weeks . . . to grind [each] stone to the desired shape and luster."[28] Completed crafts were sold at swap meets.[29]

Athletic internees engaged in more vigorous activities. Internees chosen by lottery were permitted to hike in the open country north of camp as long as they were accompanied by guards on horseback. This privilege was discontinued when an elderly internee became lost on an outing and because "anti-Japanese feelings exhibited by residents of this vicinity" persisted.[30] Back in camp, internees played tennis on two courts and golf on a small course they had built themselves. Many also played baseball on the camp's four diamonds.[31]

Movies were shown twice a week in the camp's recreation hall with Japanese projectionists often called upon to serve as translators as well as technicians. Traditional storytellers were also popular. A controversial one drew crowds of listeners with his sensational tales of "romantic love and underground heroes."[32] Internees read novels aloud on the camp's small radio station each evening.[33] Large audiences attended Kabuki performances, the most popular entertainment in camp. Performed in an outdoor theater constructed as a small replica of Tokyo's famous Imperial Theatre, these highly stylized Japanese plays ranged from traditional stories about Samurai warriors to original scripts written by the internees themselves. Performances lasted as long as six hours. Actors were held in such high regard that some were exempted from all menial camp chores.[34]

Despite these diversions, the men in Santa Fe were hardly free of personal problems. Many suffered psychological effects of captivity not unlike combat prisoners. Above all, they suffered from the prolonged separation from their families. The average internee remained isolated from his family for eighteen months.[35] Internees continually pleaded their cases before government boards in hopes that they would one day be reunited with their loved ones and resume their roles as the heads of traditional households.[36] Frustrated and discouraged by late 1943, 350 of the camp's internees demanded that they be reunited with their families by the new year or they would call for the forced separation of American families interned by Japan in the Far East. Nothing came of this hollow yet telling threat.[37] Some internees were eventually reclassified and granted permission to rejoin their families, though only in family relocation camps scattered throughout the West.[38]

The less fortunate prisoners resorted to other means in coping with their deepening anxiety. Suikei Furuya of Hawaii became "mentally exhausted" and longed "to be alone in a quiet atmosphere." To his great pleasure, Furuya eventually discovered a "quiet grass field" within the camp's confines where he could gaze with delight "at the endless view of [the] Santa Fe Plateau."[39]

Other internees turned to religion. According to one estimate, 65.5 percent of the men were Buddhists, 19.5 percent were Christians, 8.5 percent were Shintoists, and the remaining 6.5 percent professed no faith or belonged to one of the "less known denominations." With many religious leaders in the internee population, religious services were held regularly.[40]

Still others turned to alcohol. A good many drank homemade sake manufactured with rice, raisins, and sugar pilfered from camp stock. Once fermented, as much as a hundred gallons of this brew was poured into empty soda bottles, stored in large underground holes, and covered with dirt. Frustrated in their attempts to discover the owners of these "wine cellars," authorities finally relented and allowed the drinking of beer in the camp canteen. Cases of public drunkenness were nevertheless rare and seldom tolerated by the internees.[41]

Unfortunately, some internees dealt with their anxieties in a far more aggressive manner. Frustrated by their plight, these men "became irritable and quarreled over trivial matters," according to internee leader Yoshiaki Fukuda.[42] A victim of such aggression, Fukuda was once attacked by a sumo grand champion when the two disagreed over a minor issue. Similar "fights and disputes occurred among internees almost everyday,"[43] making fights "the offense committed most often within the camp," according to camp commander Ivan Williams.[44] When the camp was closed in 1946, workers found homemade weapons of all kinds buried in underground caches.[45] Although knives and hatchets had occasionally been discovered, and a pistol was lost among the prison population in 1945, officials hardly appreciated the extent of this potential for violence. According to Williams, "As a rule, any encounters between internees is not brought to the attention of the officers unless it becomes serious, as apparently the Japanese believe that they should handle their own affairs, and in case of violations of this sort attempt to keep it from the officers."[46] Reluctance to report altercations was understandable, especially given the internees' strong sense of personal honor, their hatred of informers (called *inus,* or "dogs"), and their overriding desire not to imperil their individual cases for early release.

Most internees were simply bored by their prolonged passive existence in Santa Fe. After active, productive lives before the war, nothing could replace their lost freedom and sense of purpose. In Fukuda's words, restraining these men behind barbed-wire fences was as cruel as "fencing a thousand free-spirited mustangs."[47] Nowhere was this feeling of lost freedom and wasted time better expressed than in the internees' short, quietly powerful poems called *tankas.* Keiho Soga of Hawaii bore witness to the harsh impact of inactive lives in Santa Fe:

> Many a friend
> Who is incarcerated
> Ages visibly.
> Summer is passing by.[48]

Though bored, frustrated, and eager to leave their prison world, few internees broke under the strain, and only one attempted an escape.[49] Camp officials had prepared for possible escapes by developing an elaborate recapture plan in conjunction with the New Mexico state police, the state guard, the civil air patrol, the border patrol, and sheriffs from counties within a 250- to 300-mile radius. In the event of a breakout, roads were to be blocked, search dogs deployed, and constant radio contact maintained.[50] In addition to these measures, camp officials had another potent weapon: the local populace. Antagonism toward the Japanese interned at what locals called the "Jap trap" was so great that most internees believed they were much safer within their fenced-off compound than in the New Mexico countryside. One internee probably spoke for the majority when he told an officer that if the camp's gates were left wide open one morning, he might leave for a short time, but he would undoubtedly be back seeking protective custody by nightfall.[51]

Under these circumstances, the only attempted escape resembled an attempted suicide far more than a flight to earthly freedom. At 10:45 P.M. on November 14, 1945, Otomatsu Kimura boldly scaled the exterior fence near a guard tower. Ordered to get down, Kimura (who had attempted suicide on at least three occasions at another camp) called for the guard to shoot him. When the guard refused to comply, he fell from the fence and injured himself in the fall. Guards assisted Kimura to the camp hospital for physical, if not psychological, care.[52]

Serious internee escapes were unheard of partly because conditions in Santa Fe—though hardly ideal and sometimes below the standards of the Geneva Convention—were better than at many other camps. Food was normally adequate in quality, if not always in quantity, given frequent wartime shortages. An average of 39 cents a day was spent to feed each internee. In an effort to conserve food and save money, camp officials studied trash reports to determine how much food was wasted in the internees' mess hall. In 1945 they reduced rations based on these reports and on their assertion that the average Japanese man on a "passive diet" required less food than prescribed by the Geneva Convention.[53] Barracks housing was also spartan, with each internee limited to little more than a bed and a shelf. Overcrowding became so serious that in 1943 the space allotted to each man was reduced from the Geneva Convention standard of 60 square feet to a far less comfortable 44 square feet.[54]

Medical care was provided by internee physicians, Santa Fe doctors, and U.S. Health Service nurses at the camp's hundred-bed hospital. On average, 502 men were treated at the hospital's clinic each month until December 1945. Santa Fe's Bruns General Hospital was available for more complicated cases. Internees were vaccinated for typhoid and smallpox but occasionally suffered other diseases, including the flu in a minor epidemic in the fall of 1943. Dysentery, described as a "seasonal health menace due to location," was so prevalent that the Japanese called it "Santa Fe-itis." A separate ward of the camp hospital was provided for victims of tuberculosis, a group normally shunned and feared (along with the mentally unstable) by their fellow internees even after they were discharged as cured. Because of its generally older population, the camp experienced a rather high number of deaths: thirty-five in forty-three months. A majority of the thirty-five internees who died had succumbed to tuberculosis, cancer, heart disease, and cerebral hemorrhage.[55] At least one former internee has argued that the Santa Fe camp's "unnatural life . . . took its toll and seems to have shortened the life of many [men]."[56] This conclusion may well be true, although without the individual medical records of those who died, it may never be confirmed or refuted.

The Santa Fe internment camp faced two major crises in its three-and-a-half-year history. The first of these occurred at 2 A.M. on Wednesday, June 23, 1943, when a fire of unknown origin swept through the camp. Despite "prompt action on the part of . . . Guards and internees alike," wind helped spread the destructive flames. Several buildings, including all kitchen and mess facilities, were destroyed.[57] Fortunately, no one was killed or injured. The destruction, however, "taxed the ingenuity" of camp officers left to feed over 1,800 internees "with no indoor kitchen or mess hall facilities whatsoever."[58] Meals prepared at the state penitentiary were trucked into camp until an outdoor kitchen was set up with field equipment lent by the Kirtland Army Post in Albuquerque.[59]

Camp officers took pride in the fact that their prisoners never missed a meal while new facilities were under construction.[60] The internees were not as impressed. When Yoshiaki Fukuda and 290 other Japanese arrived in camp shortly after the June 23 fire, many complained about conditions. With the loss of several barracks, sixty men were forced to reside in barracks built for no more than forty, Fukuda claimed. Meals shipped from the state penitentiary were said to have arrived in containers resembling garbage cans. The camp's water and sewage systems were considered "so inadequate that mosquito larvae was found in our drinking water."[61] Irate over these conditions, Fukuda and a group of his fellow internees formed a protest committee and drew up a petition. Fukuda was so critical that camp officials finally prohibited him from making any further statements regarding conditions at the camp.[62]

The camp's second, far more violent, crisis occurred on March 12, 1945. Over the preceding several months 366 Japanese American men had been transferred to Santa Fe from the Tule Lake Relocation Center in California where officials had identified them as troublemakers who needed to be closely watched. The vast majority were twenty- to thirty-year-old Kibei, born in the United States but so militantly pro-Japanese that they had renounced their American citizenship, sought repatriation to Japan to enlist in the Japanese armed forces, shaved their heads in the style of Japanese soldiers, and joined such radical groups as the Sokuji Kokoku Hoshi Dan, or Organization to Return to the Homeland to Serve. Once in Santa Fe, these young men intimidated internees they considered insufficiently loyal to the Japanese cause and threatened camp censors with "bodily harm" in a note signed by a "Suicide Squad." Much to the displeasure of camp officials and most older internees, the Tule Lake rebels organized quasi-military drills, blew bugles, and brazenly waved homemade Japanese flags.[63]

In a final act of defiance, the new internees painted rising-sun emblems on white sweatshirts to create makeshift Japanese "uniforms." When the Tule Lake internees ignored orders to surrender these contraband garments, camp commander Williams planned a camp-wide search, called for reinforcements, and contemplated swift action against the youths' principal leaders. Thirty border patrol officers from El Paso arrived within hours to participate in a thorough search that led to the confiscation of several dozen sweatshirts and the isolation of several important ringleaders. Williams notified three of the group's most radical leaders that they were about to be transferred to a special isolation compound at Fort Stanton, New Mexico.[64]

News of their leaders' imminent departure caused between 250 and 300 Tule Lake internees to gather at the fence opposite the camp's main office at about 9 A.M. on Monday, March 12. Armed with billy clubs and tear gas grenades, camp guards and their border patrol reinforcements fell into formation outside the gates. The camp's chief surveillance officer, Clifton Monroe, ordered the internees to disperse. After issuing two such warnings with no response, he ordered his guards to fire tear gas into the crowd. The young Japanese retreated about a hundred feet while shouting and hurling stones. A squad of sixteen border patrol officers responded by entering the camp's main gate and proceeding "into the thick of the group."[65] Although most internees scattered, some fought back, throwing rocks and using iron pipes as weapons in hand-to-hand combat. The better armed patrol officers soon prevailed, squelching the riot in about ten minutes. Four internee combatants were hospitalized with cuts and bruises from the fray, and the entire Tule Lake group was quickly segregated in a fenced-off part of the camp.[66] With seventeen of the group's leaders exiled to Fort Stanton and later deported to Japan, a high INS official Willard F. Kelly, could report that the "general situation" was showing such "steady improvement" by March 21 that he expected "no further trouble."[67] Kelly was overly optimistic in his appraisal (the Tule Lake group continued to be an "unruly element" on a smaller scale), but overall peace was restored, and camp life had returned to normal by the summer of 1945.[68]

The restoration of peace in Santa Fe was largely due to the calming influence of older internees and the prudence of camp officials. Having refused to participate in the March 12 riot, the older Issei were eager to recreate the modus vivendi they had established over many months with cooperative camp officials, such as Williams and Loyd H. Jensen. As one observer put it, the "delicate balance" in the older internees' relationship with camp officials had "trembled but held firm" during and after the March 12 disturbance because the Issei "had much to lose and little to gain in any form of rioting."[69] The Isseis' individual conduct records would be damaged by violent behavior. Violence would also threaten the group's favorable treatment by an administration that normally tolerated their ethnicity in the interest of camp peace and, ultimately, camp control. Led by INS veterans, such as Williams, Bundy Avant, and Abner Schreiber, camp officers and many of the facility's forty-six border guards had years of experience in dealing with groups of varying backgrounds and cultures.[70] Unlike officers at other internee camps, these officers had little desire to interfere with Japanese ways—either to strip internees of their dignity or to Americanize them. On the contrary, camp commanders often supported Japanese customs. Within days after the camp's opening in 1942, and later within two months after the camp's brief riot of 1945, officials allowed internees to observe Emperor Hirohito's birthday with daylong celebrations. Traditional wrestling matches were permitted, as were Asian religious services and the well-attended Kabuki plays. Although initially rejected as unsanitary, Japanese baths were eventually constructed in camp latrines. Special efforts were made to include favored foods in mess-hall meals. Indeed, one internee recalled that commander Williams once went as far as Colorado to retrieve rare varieties of rice and fish traditionally eaten in Japanese New Year celebrations.[71] The camp's internee-operated canteen stocked Japanese delicacies, such as squid and *ajinomoto* (monosodium glutamate). Canteen profits were used to help finance the camp's Japanese-language newspaper. Internees also subscribed to Japanese-language publications from outside the camp, though not from Japan.[72]

Camp officers displayed their respect for their prisoners' dignity in other ways as well. In deference to the internees' sense of honor, head counts were normally made at night while the men slept, rather than in demeaning daytime proceedings.[73] Camp officials "granted wide latitude in the matter of visits [by] friends and relatives," resulting in as many as forty-five visitors a day, including at least one son who had served in the U.S. Army in Europe and "was pretty badly shot up."[74] Internee suggestions, as presented by elected spokesmen, were respectfully listened to, if not always acted on by camp officers.[75]

Outside observers may have called such treatment "coddling," but Williams rejected this term in a 1946 interview with the *Santa Fe New Mexican.*[76] Cultural cooperation had simply served to elevate internees' self-esteem while effectively averting cultural conflict in camp. Only aggressive acts, such as threatening camp censors or exhibiting military behavior could not be tolerated by those in charge. Although this hands-off policy reflected the tolerance of high-caliber officers, it was also a means of prisoner control. Camp officials recognized that granting small privileges, especially as they related to Japanese culture, had "the psychological effect of creating high internee morale and a desire ... [by] the internee group to show their appreciation by cooperating wholeheartedly with the camp administration" on nearly every issue.[77]

Hardly ignorant victims of manipulation, internees often couched their concerns in terms of the Geneva Convention and defended their interests with appeals to Spanish and Swiss legations representing the Geneva accords.[78] Many internees undoubtedly made the most of the camp's system of small privileges with the realistic resignation, ready cooperation, and stoicism characteristic of their culture.[79] At least one historian of the internment period has argued that the internees used cultural expression, and religion in particular, as a subtle means of resistance.[80]

While factions existed and fights were common, the generally similar age and experience of the men as first-generation immigrants greatly reduced the animosity that led to serious division and internal strife in other camps.[81] Late in arriving and never fully assimilated, the young internees of Tule Lake seldom appreciated the camp's well-established way of life. Their behavior in March 1942 was a clear exception to the general rule of peaceful coexistence in Santa Fe.

News of the dropping of the atomic bomb and the end of World War II produced mixed reactions in the Santa Fe camp. Camp officials received word with an understandable degree of apprehension. Despite overall good relations in camp, Williams wrote to his superiors in Washington regarding "the remote possibility of a banzai charge by the [facility's]

radical element" in the days following Hiroshima's destruction on August 6, 1945.[82] Although the sale of beer was temporarily banned and
plans were made to evacuate all camp personnel in the event of an
emergency, no attack occurred. Indeed, the internees appeared divided
over whether to believe later reports of Japan's unconditional surrender.
While some welcomed peace, others believed rumors that a large Japanese
fleet was en route to Pearl Harbor to renew the fighting.[83] On August 14,
the day of Japan's official surrender, many internees reportedly heard wild
celebrations in Santa Fe and secluded themselves in camp barracks fear-
ing mob attacks.[84]

In an effort to calm fears and stem internal unrest, Williams released
a bulletin to all internees on the following day. He asserted that after a
conflict that had "caused many . . . hardships and heartaches," peace had
"again settled over the . . . world. Above all," Williams wrote, "we do not
want demons of any kind. I personally assure each of you the same fair
treatment will prevail as heretofore."[85]

Despite these reassuring words, tension remained high, as demonstrated by two internees who fought over the war's outcome on the very
evening that Williams released his announcement.[86] The same violence
that had previously erupted as a result of family separations and divided
loyalties now erupted as a result of anxiety regarding the internees'
impending release and possible repatriation to defeated Japan. Some
internees were reluctant to accept their long-awaited paroles because, as
Williams put it, they were "afraid of public opinion," worried about
securing employment, and concerned about "any place to live."[87] Suikei
Furuya feared that his young daughter might be frightened of him after
four long years of separation.[88] Others, including an elderly cook, a
gardener, and a chimney sweep, resisted parole out of a sense of duty
toward a prison community that still required their services.[89] Most
internees, however, celebrated in their barracks when their names appeared on camp bulletin boards signifying that they were free to leave at
last.[90]

The Santa Fe camp served as a holding center and clearinghouse for internees as the INS shut down similar facilities in the West. The internee population thus reached a record 2,100 just before the bombing of Hiroshima and was still over 2,000 two months after Japan's surrender.[91] Population figures fell quickly thereafter. Nearly half the camp's population departed in November 1945 alone.

Only 224 men remained by mid-April 1946. Of these men, 60 percent were finally reunited with their families at a relocation camp in Crystal City, Texas, while the remaining 40 percent were deported to Japan, voluntarily repatriated (some still believing that Japan had won the war), or, in the case of thirteen Peruvians, returned home overseas. All left by train, the same way every one of the camp's 4,555 internees had arrived since 1942. The final group departed in late April.[92] These last few internees may have bowed to the rising sun on their last day in camp. However, unlike the first internees of 1942, those of 1946 could greet the sun as the symbol of a new life of potential rather than one of confinement as the tragic casualties of caution and fear.

NOTES

1. *Santa Fe New Mexican,* 12 March 1942; *Albuquerque Tribune,* 14 March 1942; Tom I. Yamamoto interview, 9 September 1976, in Paul F. Clark, "Those Other Camps: An Oral History Analysis of Japanese Alien Enemy Internment during World War II" (unpublished master's thesis, California State University at Fullerton, 1980), 164. According to the census of 1940, 73.8 percent of all Japanese Americans in the United States lived in California. John Modell, ed., *The Kikuchi Diary: Chronicle from an American Concentration Camp* (Urbana: University of Illinois Press, 1973), 5, table. On the use of euphemisms in the U.S. government's Japanese relocation program, see Raymond Y. Okamura, "The American Concentration Camps: A Cover-Up Through Euphemistic Terminology," *Journal of Ethnic Studies,* 10 (Fall 1982): 95–109. Though the internment was unjust, American camps hardly compared to the brutal concentration camps of Nazi Germany or the Japanese POW camps in Asia.

2. Kenko Yamashita interview, 10 August 1978, in Clark, "Those Other Camps," 184; Toby Smith, "Barbed Wire and Kabuki: The Story of an Intern-

ment Camp," *Impact Magazine* (31 March 1981): 7–8; Yoshiaki Fukuda, *My Six Years of Internment: An Issei's Struggle for Justice* (San Francisco: Konko Church, 1990), 7–11, 24n; Bob Kumamoto, "The Search for Spies: American Counterintelligence and the Japanese American Community, 1931–42," *Amerasia Journal,* 7 (1979): 45–75; Suikei K. Furuya, *Haisho Ten-Ten* (Honolulu, 1964), 416. I am grateful to Minoru Ohuchi for assistance in translating much of Furuya's wartime journal.

3.   John Hersey, "A Mistake of Terrifically Horrible Proportions," in John Armor and Peter Wright, *Manzanar* (New York: Random House, 1988), 1–66. See also Eugene V. Rostow, "The Japanese American Cases—A Disaster," *The Yale Law Journal,* 54 (June 1945): 489–533. On the mass Japanese relocation program based on President Franklin Roosevelt's Executive Order 9066 of 19 February 1942, see Roger Daniels, *Concentration Camps USA: Japanese-Americans and World War II* (New York: Holt, Rinehart & Winston, 1971); and, most recently, Gerald Stanley, "Justice Deferred: A 50-Year Perspective on Japanese Internment Historiography," *Southern California Quarterly,* 74 (Summer 1992): 181–206. For a rare defense of the treatment of Japanese Americans, see Lillian Baker, *American and Japanese Relocation in World War II* (Medford, OR: Webb Research Group, 1990).

4.   See Roger Daniels, *The Politics of Prejudice: the Anti-Japanese Movement in California and the Struggle for Japanese Exclusion* (New York: Atheneum, 1968), especially chap. 5, "The Yellow Peril," 65–78.

5.   *Santa Fe New Mexican,* 7 March (editorial), and 4, 6, and 12 March 1942; *Albuquerque Tribune,* 2 March 1942; *Albuquerque Journal,* 3 March 1942; Jettie Avant Sullegner, *These Hands: The Bundy Avant Story* (Albuquerque, 1990), 397–405; John W. Nelson, "Alien Enemy Detention Program," a speech presented in Roswell, New Mexico, 2 August 1976, Record Group (RG) 83-131, Rio Grande Historical Collections, New Mexico State University Library, Las Cruces (Nelson was an INS official involved in alien enemy camps located in New Mexico and elsewhere during World War II); [Ivan Williams], "Memorandum to Mr. Jerre Mangione," [Santa Fe, 14 October 1943], p. 1, File #1300/L, Records of the U.S. Immigration and Naturalization Service, RG 85, National Archives, Suitland, MD (hereafter cited as RG 85); H. H. Barnes to Immigration and Naturalization Service, Albuquerque, 20 March 1942, File #1303, RG 85; Loyd H. Jensen to W. F. Kelly, Santa Fe, 20 January 1944, p. 8, File #1300G, RG 85; Ivan Williams to W. F. Kelly, Santa Fe, 9 August 1945, pp. 1–2, File #1300, RG 85. The last

three reports are hereafter cited as Williams, October 1943 Report; Jensen, January 1944 Report; and Williams, August 1945 Report.

6. See Roger Daniels, *Asian America: Chinese and Japanese in the United States since 1850* (Seattle: University of Washington Press, 1988), 29–185. For contrasting anti-Allies propaganda in Japan, see Gordon Daniels, "Japanese Domestic Radio and Cinema Propaganda, 1937–1945" in K. R. M. Short, ed., *Film and Radio Propaganda in World War II* (Knoxville: University of Tennessee Press, 1983), 293–318. Japanese Americans living in New Mexico at the outbreak of World War II were generally treated as far more trustworthy than the internees. Indeed, community leaders in towns like Gallup, Grants, and Belen made concerted efforts to prevent the relocation of Japanese families that had lived in their respective communities for some time. See Art Togami interview with the author, 30 December 1991, Los Lunas, New Mexico; *Albuquerque Journal,* 17 October 1990; Richard Chalfen, *Turning Leaves: The Photographic Collection of Two Japanese American Families* (Albuquerque: University of New Mexico Press, 1991), 58.

Less assimilated Japanese and those with railroad jobs in New Mexico were discriminated against, much like those of Japanese ancestry on the West Coast. In the most tragic case of this kind, ten Japanese American railroad workers and their families were forced to move from Clovis to the Baca Ranch Camp (twelve miles from Fort Stanton) largely for protection from local citizens; *Albuquerque Journal,* 31 January 1942. These families remained at the Baca Ranch Camp until December 1942 when they were moved to Japanese relocation camps in Utah and Arizona. See John J. Culley, "World War II and a Western Town: The Internment of Japanese Railroad Workers of Clovis, New Mexico," *Western Historical Quarterly,* 13 (January 1982): 43–61; Nelson, "Alien Enemy Detention Program," 9–11.

7. See, for example, P. Cooper, executive chairman, Deming Chamber of Commerce, to John E. Miles, Deming, 9 April 1942; District Judge James B. McGhee to John E. Miles, Roswell, 10 April 1942, Governor John E. Miles Papers, New Mexico State Records Center & Archives, Santa Fe.

8. For New Mexicans fighting in the futile Battle of Bataan in early 1942, see Dorothy Cave, *Beyond Courage: One Regiment Against Japan, 1941–1945* (Las Cruces: Yucca Tree Press, 1992), 1–166.

9. See, for example, the *Santa Fe New Mexican,* 7 March 1942.

10. Yamashita interview, 184–85; Williams, October 1943 Report, 2; Jensen, January 1944 Report, 2; John J. Culley, "The Santa Fe Internment Camp and the Justice Department Program for Enemy Aliens," in Roger Daniels, Sandra C. Taylor, and Harry H. L. Kitano, eds., *Japanese Americans: From Relocation to Redress* (Salt Lake City: University of Utah Press, 1986), 59. Santa Fe's 826th internee died of cancer before he could be transferred from the New Mexico camp. For the controversial nature of government loyalty hearings and questionnaires, see Daniels, *Concentration Camps,* especially, chap. 6, "A Question of Loyalty," 104–29.

11. Jensen, January 1944 Report, 2. Ironically, the highly sensitive Manhattan Project at Los Alamos (within thirty-five miles of Santa Fe) began less than a month after the reopening of the Santa Fe camp with its supposedly high-risk internees. According to a high-ranking camp official, no special efforts were made to link security in the two facilities; Abner Schreiber interview with the author, 28 January 1987, Los Alamos.

12. Williams, August 1945 Report, 28; Furuya, *Haisho Ten-Ten,* chaps. 1–11; Yoshiko Uchida, *Desert Exile: The Uprooting of a Japanese-American Family* (Seattle: University of Washington Press, 1982), 82.

13. N. D. Collaer to Officers in Charge of Camps, Philadelphia, 14 January 1944, File #1300/0-1, RG 85; Williams, August 1945 Report, 28.

14. C. Harvey Gardiner, *Pawns in a Triangle of Hate: The Peruvian Japanese and the United States* (Seattle: University of Washington Press, 1981); P. Scott Corbett, "Quiet Passages: The Exchange of Civilians Between the United States and Japan during World War II" (Ph.D. dissertation, University of Kansas, 1983), 267–72; Furuya, *Haisho Ten-Ten;* Gary Y. Okihiro, *Cane Fires: The Anti-Japanese Movement in Hawaii, 1865–1945* (Philadelphia: Temple University Press, 1991), 195–276; Claus-M. Naske, "The Relocation of Alaska's Japanese Residents," *Pacific Northwest Quarterly,* 74 (July 1983): 124–32. A total of 2,118 Japanese were brought to the United States for these purposes during World War II. Eighty percent were from Peru. Reference to the "humbler classes" of Japanese in Peru was made by the U.S. ambassador to Peru, R. Henry Norweb, in a 1943 letter quoted in Corbett, "Quiet Passages," 267.

15. Abner Schreiber interview, 19 March 1979, in Clark, "Those Other Camps," 93; Williams, October 1943 Report, 13.

16. Williams, August 1945 Report, 29. Camp jobs were listed in Ivan

Williams to All Department Heads, Santa Fe, 20 November 1944, File #1300, RG 85.

17.   Williams, October 1943 Report, 8–9; Williams, August 1945 Report, 20–21; *Santa Fe New Mexican,* 21 March 1946; Sullegner, *These Hands,* 436–45. Crops included onions, cabbage, lettuce, cucumbers, radishes, carrots, and turnips. The camp's farm reportedly grew as much as $9,000 worth of crops per year. Gardiner, *Triangle of Hate,* 98–99. Bruns General Hospital, named after tuberculosis specialist Earl Harvey Bruns, served as a military medical facility off Cerillos Road in Santa Fe from 1942 to 1947.

18.   Ivan Williams to W. F. Kelly, Santa Fe, 1 March 1945, File #13400, RG 85; Williams, August 1945 Report, 22; *Santa Fe New Mexican,* 15 March 1945; Gardiner, *Triangle of Hate,* 99; Gene Dale, John Morrett, and Bert Schwarz, "We Lived to Tell," *Collier's,* 101 (17 March 1945): 24, 37–39. On the German camp at Fort Stanton, see Nelson, "Alien Enemy Detention Program," 2–9, 13–15.

19.   Loyd H. Jensen quoted in Jerre Mangione, *An Ethnic at Large: A Memoir of America in the Thirties and Forties* (New York: G. P. Putnam's Sons, 1978), 341; Williams to All Department Heads, Santa Fe, 20 November 1944, File #1300, RG 85; Fukuda, *My Six Years of Internment,* 15–16. Jerre Mangione was involved with publicity for the INS camps. For additional praise of the camp by visitors, see the *Santa Fe New Mexican,* 31 July 1942, and 16 February 1945.

20.   Williams, August 1945 Report, 18; Schreiber interview in Clark, "Those Other Camps," 93.

21.   Katsuma Mutaeda interview, 22 May 1975, in Clark, "Those Other Camps," 80.

22.   W. F. Kelly to Officer in Charge, Washington, D.C., 6 September 1945, File #13400, RG 85; Jensen, January 1944 Report, 7, 11. Approximately 950 books were donated to the camp by the Japanese Red Cross. Most books were fiction or dealt with religious or philosophical themes. Furuya, *Haisho Ten-Ten,* 317.

23.   Jiro Nakano and Kay Nakano, eds., *Poets Behind Barbed Wire* (Honolulu: Bamboo Ridge Press, 1983), 2.

24.   Censors read an average of 2,000 pieces of mail per day. Williams, August 1945 Report, 3–5; Smith, "Barbed Wire and Kabuki," 6; Donald Nakahata and Violet de Cristoforo interviews in John Tateishi, *And Justice for All: An Oral History of the Japanese American Detention Camps* (New York: Random House, 1984), 34, 130.

25. Quoted in Williams to Kelly, Santa Fe, 1 September 1945, File #1300, RG 85.

26. Ibid.

27. Subscriptions cost ten cents a month. Two hundred issues of the newspaper are now housed in the Powell Library at the University of California at Los Angeles. Fukuda, *My Six Years of Internment,* 17; Furuya, *Haisho Ten-Ten,* 295, 328; Williams, August 1945 Report, 18; Smith, "Barbed Wire and Kabuki," 5–6. Also see John D. Stevens, "From Behind Barbed Wire: Freedom of the Press in World War II Japanese Centers," *Journalism Quarterly,* 48 (Summer 1971): 279–87.

28. Williams, August 1945 Report, 18, 29; Furuya, *Haisho Ten-Ten,* 310–11; Smith, "Barbed Wire and Kabuki," 7; Deborah Gesensway and Mindy Roseman, *Beyond Words: Images from America's Concentration Camps* (Ithaca, NY: Cornell University Press, 1987), 120–22.

29. Williams, August 1945 Report, 29. Once polished, stones were used for such things as paper weights and doorstops.

30. Ibid., 31; Furuya, *Haisho Ten-Ten,* 310.

31. Ibid., 334; Williams, October 1943 Report, 9; Williams, August 1945 Report, 16; Yamamoto interview in Clark, "Those Other Camps," 163; *Santa Fe New Mexican,* 21 March 1946; Gardiner, *Triangle of Hate,* 99.

32. Williams, August 1945 Report, 17; Fukuda, *My Six Years of Internment,* 17.

33. Furuya, *Haisho Ten-Ten,* 295–96. Apparently, the camp's radio station was so small that it was not considered a security risk in the war.

34. Williams, October 1943 Report, 10; Williams, August 1945 Report, 17; Furuya, *Haisho Ten-Ten,* 334; Mangione, *Ethnic At Large,* 339–40. Photos of an acting group and the camp's outdoor stage are included in Mangione, *Ethnic at Large,* photo-insert section.

35. Williams, October 1943 Report, 11. For the effects of captivity on POWs, see Pat Reid and Maurice Michael, *Prisoner of War* (New York: Beauford Books, 1984), 150–69.

36. Fukuda, *My Six Years of Internment,* 51. For the tragic experiences of three wives whose husbands were interned in Santa Fe, see Tazuko Uchida to Isamu Uchida, Newell, California, 4 July 1945, File #1300/P-1, RG 85; Violet de Cristoforo interview in Tateishi, *And Justice for All,* 130–32; Michi Weglyn, *Years*

of Infamy: The Untold Story of America's Concentration Camps (New York: Morrow Quill, 1976), 213. Also see Valerie Matsumoto, "Japanese American Women During World War II," *Frontiers,* 8 (1984): 6–14.

37. Culley, "Santa Fe Internment Camp," 62.

38. See, for example, Fukuda, *My Six Years of Internment,* 22.

39. Quoted in Okihiro, *Cane Fires,* 261–62.

40. Williams, October 1943 Report, 10; Williams, August 1945 Report, 28; Gardiner, *Triangle of Hate,* 138, table 10; Fukuda, *My Six Years of Internment,* 14–16 (including a photo of Japanese ministers in Santa Fe on p. 16).

41. Furuya, *Haisho Ten-Ten,* 334–35; Sullegner, *These Hands,* 418–20; Williams, August 1945 Report, 35; Mutaeda interview in Clark, "Those Other Camps," 78; Julian P. Langston, chief internal security officer, to Ivan Williams, Santa Fe, 9 May 1945, File #1300/P, RG 85.

42. Fukuda, *My Six Years of Internment,* 18.

43. Ibid., 18–21. See also Furuya, *Haisho Ten-Ten,* 332.

44. Williams, August 1945 Report, 34. Williams served as camp commander throughout the camp's history, with the exception of the period April 1943 to October 1944 when Loyd H. Jensen served.

45. Sullegner, *These Hands,* 417.

46. Williams, August 1945 Report, 34. On the lost gun incident, see Ivan Williams to W. F. Kelly, Santa Fe, 7 August 1945, File #1300, RG 85.

47. Fukuda, *My Six Years of Internment,* 18.

48. Nakano and Nakano, *Poets Behind Barbed Wire,* 52.

49. Williams, August 1945 Report, 27, 32; Fukuda, *My Six Years of Internment,* 68.

50. State Police Chief Frank Young to Jensen, Santa Fe, 6 April 1943, File #1303, RG 85; State Guard Lt. Col. J. R. Guild to Jensen, Santa Fe, 13 April 1943, Files #1303, RG 85; Williams to Kelly, Santa Fe, 2 November 1944, File #1303, RG 85; Williams, October 1943 Report, 4; Williams, August 1945 Report, 30–31.

51. Williams, August 1945 Report, 35.

52. Ivan Williams to W. F. Kelly, Santa Fe, 11 July 1945, File #1300, RG 85; Herbert C. Davy, guard, to C. M. Monroe, chief surveillance officer, Santa Fe, 11 November 1945, File #1303, RG 85; Abner Schreiber to N. D. Collaer, Santa Fe, 14 November 1945, File #1300, RG 85. Shootings of internees occurred at camps in Lordsburg, New Mexico, and Fort Sill, Oklahoma. See Tetsuden

Kashima, "American Mistreatment of Internees during World War II: Enemy Alien Japanese," in Daniels, Taylor, and Kitano, *Japanese Americans,* 53–54; John J. Culley, "Trouble at the Lordsburg Internment Camp," *New Mexico Historical Review,* 60 (July 1985): 225–48.

53. Williams, August 1945 Report, 7, 9. German POWs in the United States also experienced reductions in their food rations in 1945. Arnold Krammer, *Nazi Prisoners of War in America* (New York: Stein and Day, 1979), 240–42. For conditions in New Mexico's Roswell and Lordsburg POW camps, see Jake W. Spidle, "Axis Invasion of the American West: POW's in New Mexico, 1942–46," *New Mexico Historical Review,* 49 (April 1974): 93–122.

54. Williams, October 1943 Report, 14; Jensen, January 1944 Report, 2. Also see Fukuda, *My Six Years of Internment,* 44. Space allocations for internees were to be based on similar space allocations for U.S. troops during the war.

55. Jensen, January 1944 Report, 11; Williams, August 1945 Report, 14–15; Hospital Medical Officer's Monthly Reports, File #13248/B, RG 85; Abner Schreiber to Brigadier General Larry B. McAfee (Bruns General Hospital), Santa Fe, 24 February 1945, File #1280, RG #85; Furuya, *Haisho Ten-Ten,* 410.

56. Fukuda, *My Six Years of Internment,* 69. Fukuda listed the names of sixteen of those who died in Santa Fe, along with their ages and death dates. The average age of those listed was fifty-seven. For a photo of an internee's grave in Santa Fe's Rosario Cemetery, see John Sherman, *Santa Fe: A Pictorial History* (Norfolk, VA: Donning, 1983), 166.

57. Williams, October 1943 Report, 12; Jensen, January 1944 Report, 2; Williams, August 1945 Report, 8, 32.

58. Williams, August 1945 Report, 8.

59. *Ibid.;* Williams, October 1943 Report, 12.

60. Williams, October 1943 Report, 12.

61. Fukuda, *My Six Years of Internment,* 44–45.

62. Ibid., 45.

63. Ivan Williams to W. F. Kelly, Santa Fe, 11 July 1945, pp. 3–5, File #1300, RG 85; Schreiber interview with the author; John Christgau, *"Enemies": World War II Alien Internment* (Ames: Iowa State University Press, 1985), 156–57. For an example of an internee threatened by this group, see Seikaku Takesono to Ivan Williams, Santa Fe, 5 April 1945, File #1300/P, RG 85. Tule Lake experienced more than its share of internal strife before the transfer of these 363 rebels

to Santa Fe. See Weglyn, *Years of Infamy,* 229–45; Gary U. Ohihiro, "Tule Lake under Martial Law," *Journal of Ethnic Studies,* 5 (Fall 1977).

64.   Ivan Williams to W. F. Kelly, Santa Fe, 11 July 1945, File #1300, RG 85; Sullegner, *These Hands,* 429–31; Furuya, *Haisho Ten-Ten,* 358; Clark, "Those Other Camps," 36–37.

65.   Schreiber interview with the author; Sullegner, *These Hands,* 432–33.

66.   Furuya, *Haisho Ten-Ten,* 358–61; Schreiber interview with the author; Schreiber interview in Clark, "Those Other Camps," 37–38; Nelson, "Alien Enemy Detention Program," 13.

67.   Quoted in Clark, "Those Other Camps," 38. Also see Furuya, *Haisho Ten-Ten,* 361–65; *Santa Fe New Mexican,* 20 March 1946.

68.   W. F. Kelly to Ivan Williams, Washington, D.C., 3 July 1945, File #1300/0-1, RG 85; *Albuquerque Journal,* 21 March 1946; *Santa Fe New Mexican,* 21 March 1946; Culley, "Santa Fe Internment Camp," 63–66. For examples of other riots in Japanese relocation and internment camps, see Norman R. Jackman, "Collective Protest in Relocation Centers," *American Journal of Sociology,* 63 (November 1957): 264–72; George Wada, "Riots and Rioters [at Manzanar]," *Western Political Quarterly,* 10 (December 1957): 864–74; Arthur A. Hansen and David A. Hacker, "The Manzanar Riot: An Ethnic Perspective," *Amerasia Journal,* 2 (Fall 1974): 112–57; Ohihiro, "Tule Lake."

69.   Clark, "Those Other Camps," 39.

70.   Jensen, January 1944 Report, 3. By 1946 Williams had served a total of twenty-one years in the border patrol. *Santa Fe New Mexican,* 21 March 1946. To compare Santa Fe's officers and guards to those at New Mexico's less tolerant Japanese internment camp in Lordsburg, see Fukuda, *My Six Years of Internment,* 40–44; Culley, "Trouble at the Lordsburg Internment Camp," 225–48.

71.   Williams, August 1945 Report, 8–9; Furuya, *Haisho Ten-Ten,* 334; Mutaeda interview in Clark, "Those Other Camps," 78–79.

72.   Jensen, January 1944 Report, 9, 12; Williams, August 1945 Report, 17; Yamamoto interview in Clark, "Those Other Camps," 176n; Furuya, *Haisho Ten-Ten,* 306, 333–34; Gardiner, *Triangle of Hate,* 99.

73.   Williams, October 1943 Report, 4.

74.   Ibid., 14; Togami interview with the author. Minoru Yasui's mother traveled by bus from Denver to Santa Fe to visit her interned husband once a month over a period of three years. Minoru Yasui interview in Tateishi, *And*

Justice for All, 84–85. The 100th Battalion and the 442nd Regimental Combat Team, consisting of Japanese American soldiers, were among the most decorated U.S. Army units in World War II, earning a total of 18,000 individual and unit awards, including a Medal of Honor. Williams, August 1945 Report, 27; Daniels, *Concentration Camps,* 151–53; David I. O'Brien and Stephen S. Fugita, *The Japanese American Experience* (Bloomington: Indiana University Press, 1991), 66–67. One hundred sixteen WACs of Japanese ancestry also served during the war. Edward N. Barnhart, "The Individual Exclusion of Japanese Americans in World War II," *Pacific Historical Review,* 29 (May 1960): 121n.

75. Williams, August 1945 Report, 2–4; Fukuda, *My Six Years of Internment,* 15.

76. *Santa Fe New Mexican,* 21 March 1946 (reprinted as Will Harrison, "The Santa Fe Internment Camp," *INS Monthly Review* [April 1946]: 298–300). New Mexico's newspapers usually respected the Justice Department's request "that as little as possible be said about the arrest and detention of alien enemies." Mangione, *Ethnic at Large,* 322; Jerre Mangione to Ivan Williams, Washington, D.C., 11 September 1945, File #13400, RG 85. This censorship curtain was lifted on 20 March 1946.

77. Williams, August 1945 Report, 6, 26; Schreiber interview with the author.

78. Fukuda, *My Six Years of Internment,* 45.

79. See, for example, Takaichi Saiki to Ivan Williams, Santa Fe, 25 April 1945, File #1300, RG 85, regarding events planned to celebrate the emperor's birthday in 1945.

80. Gary Y. Okihiro, "Japanese Resistance in America's Concentration Camps: A Re-evaluation," *Amerasia Journal,* 2 (Fall 1973): 20–34; Gary Y. Okihiro, "Religion and Resistance in America's Concentration Camps," *Phylon,* 45 (September 1984): 220–33.

81. For examples of tension between generations at other camps, see Modell, *Kikuchi Diary,* 54, 59, 61, 65–67, 70–71, 100, 197, 239.

82. Ivan Williams to W. F. Kelly, Santa Fe, 7 August 1945, File #1300, RG 85.

83. Mutaeda interview in Clark, "Those Other Camps, 79–80, 83n. Also see Furuya, *Haisho Ten-Ten,* 389, 392–93, 404–5.

84. Ivan Williams interview in the *Santa Fe New Mexican,* 21 March 1946.

85.   Ivan Williams to All Internees, Santa Fe, 15 August 1945, File #1300, RG 85.

86.   Julian P. Langston to Abner Schreiber, Santa Fe, 15 August 1945, File #1300, RG 85.

87.   Williams, August 1945 Report, 27. Also see Furuya, *Haisho Ten-Ten,* 417. Otomatsu Kimura's attempted escape (or suicide) of November 14, 1945, may well have been caused by anxiety associated with the end of the war. For violence among Peruvian internees in the weeks following Japan's surrender, see Gardiner, *Triangle of Hate,* 127. Some men, like Chiye Tomihiro's father, never fully recovered from their internment in Santa Fe. "The saddest thing that happened," said Tomihiro, "was when my father came out of internment, after being idle for four years. . . . He never was able to get back on his feet in the real sense of the word." Chiye Tomihiro interview in Tateishi, *And Justice for All,* 240.

88.   Furuya, *Haisho Ten-Ten,* 416.

89.   *Santa Fe New Mexican,* 21 March 1946. On the problems of Japanese resettlement after World War II, see Sandra C. Taylor, "Leaving the Concentration Camps: Japanese American Resettlement in Utah and the Intermountain West," *Pacific Historical Review,* 60 (May 1991): 169–94.

90.   Christgau, *"Enemies",* 176; Furuya, *Haisho Ten-Ten,* 418–19.

91.   Monthly Reports, Santa Fe, File #13430/10, RG 85.

92.   Monthly Reports, Santa Fe, File #13430/10, RG 85; Ivan Williams to Officer in Charge at Terminal Island, San Pedro, California, Santa Fe, 22 April 1946, File #13430/10, RG 85; Abner Schreiber to F. G. Gurley, President, Santa Fe Railroad, Santa Fe, 12 February 1946, File #1280, RG 85; *Santa Fe New Mexican,* 29 December 1945, 21 March 1946, and 22 April 1946; Gardiner, *Triangle of Hate,* 124–27. The camp's property reverted to the New Mexico State Penitentiary in 1946. It was later sold and used to create a housing subdivision. Smith, "Barbed Wire and Kabuki," 5. On U.S. government restitutions to Japanese internees long after the war, see William Minoru Hohri, *Repairing America: An Account of the Movement for Japanese-American Redress* (Pullman: Washington State University Press, 1988). Unfortunately, most of Santa Fe's internees did not survive to benefit from the restitution payments awarded each former internee by Congress in 1988.

NOTES ON SOURCES

SPENCER WILSON

THERE is a great deal of material available to the serious reader of New Mexico history in the twentieth century, ranging from traditional academic studies to publications of state and local historical societies.

A set of bibliographies has recently been published by the Center for the American West in the History Department at the University of New Mexico under the general editorship of Richard W. Etulain. This series of five volumes starts with *Women and Family in the Twentieth-Century American West: A Bibliography,* Occasional Paper Number 1 (1990), compiled by Pat Devejian and Jacqueline J. Etulain. This is followed by *Environment in the Twentieth-Century American West; A Bibliography,* Occasional Paper Number 2 (1990), compiled by Thomas Jaehn. Jacqueline Etulain also compiled *Mexican Americans in the Twentieth-Century American West,* Occasional Paper Number 3 (1990). Richard W. Etulain compiled *Religion in the Twentieth-Century American West,* Occasional Paper Number 4 (1991). Most recently Joe Hummer compiled *A Selective Bibliography of New Mexico History,* Occasional Paper Number 5 (1992). The last volume is of the most interest, of course.

Another valuable bibliographic source is "Book Talk," the publication of the New Mexico Book League of Albuquerque. The publication's five issues a year, "irregularly published," include articles on New Mexico and southwestern authors as well as book reviews. This is an important reference tool.

Several general histories include chapters covering the twentieth century. Among the many recent general histories of New Mexico are Marc Simmons, *New Mexico: An Interpretive History* (W. W. Norton, 1977; Albuquerque: University of New Mexico Press, 1988); and Calvin A. Roberts and Susan A. Roberts, *New Mexico* (Albuquerque: University of New Mexico Press, 1988). While neither of these books deals in detail with the twentieth century, they do provide an overview. A good geographic study of the state with short sections on various aspects of New Mexico history is provided in Jerry Williams, ed., *New Mexico in Maps,* 2nd ed. (Albuquerque: University of New Mexico Press, 1986). There are also good population figures in Williams's work. A fine short but interpretive history is Myra Ellen Jenkins and Albert H. Schroeder, *A Brief History of New Mexico* (Albuquerque: University of New Mexico Press, 1974 and later editions), first published as a part of the Historic Preservation Plan by the State Planning Office in 1973.

Most of the secondary literature on twentieth-century New Mexico is found in western or southwestern regional studies, such as Robert W. Larson, *New Mexico's Quest for Statehood, 1846–1912* (Albuquerque: University of New Mexico Press, 1968). For a traditional view of "tricultural" New Mexico, see D. W. Meinig, *Southwest: Three Peoples in Geographical Change, 1600–1970* (New York: Oxford University Press, 1971). David F. Myrick, *New Mexico Railroads* (Golden: Colorado Railroad Museum, 1970; and Albuquerque: University of New Mexico Press, 1990), traces the railroads from their arrival in the territory in about 1880 to the present. Don E. Alberts, *Balloons to Bombers: Aviation in Albuquerque, 1882–1945* (Albuquerque: Albuquerque Museum, 1978) contains helpful information on the construction of Oxnard Field and its transfer to the U.S. Army.

Much of the history of New Mexico in the twentieth century is now available in general interpretations of the West. Two works by Gerald D.

Nash, *The American West in the Twentieth Century: A Short History of an Urban Oasis* (Albuqerque: University of New Mexico Press, 1977) and *The American West Transformed: The Impact of the Second World War* (Bloomington: University of Indiana Press, 1985), discuss the evolution of the relationship between New Mexico and the rest of the United States. Another particularly good discussion of how New Mexico fits into the West of the twentieth century is Michael P. Malone and Richard W. Etulain, *The American West: A Twentieth-Century History* (Lincoln: University of Nebraska Press, 1989).

The Historical Society of New Mexico and the University of New Mexico Press entered into a joint publication program in 1980. This program has resulted in twenty-some volumes devoted to various topics of New Mexico history, with more in the works. Several of these studies treat subjects in the twentieth century. Robert R. White edited and annotated *The Taos Society of Artists* (1983). White discovered the original constitution, by-laws, and minutes of the meetings of that society and fixed July 1915 as the founding date. Michael R. Taylor edited and annotated *Along the Rio Grande: A Pastoral Visit to Southwest New Mexico in 1902* (1986), which was translated by Mary W. de Lopez. This publication recounts the visit of Monsignor Henry Granjon, bishop of Tucson to the churches in Las Cruces, Mesilla, Alamogorodo, Tularosa, and El Paso. It provides social history, accounts of daily life, and photographs of people and places seen by Bishop Granjon. In 1951 the Dutch doctor J. Peter Voute and his family emigrated to New Mexico to start a new life. Dr. Voute was a resistance worker in Holland during World War II, and wrote of his experiences in *Only a Free Man: War Memories of Two Dutch Doctors, 1940–1945,* with the Journals of Henry Rynders (Santa Fe, NM: Lighting Tree Press, 1982). After retiring from medical practice, he wrote another memoir of the family experiences in New Mexico, *Strangers in New Mexico: A Doctor's Journey, 1951–1968* (1987). Another in the same series is Joe Chew, *Storms above the Desert: Atmospheric Research in New Mexico, 1935–1985* (1987). Chew and his fellow students at New Mexico Institute of Mining and Technology put together an excellent, and sometimes funny, history of the research that is currently carried out atop the Magdalena Mountains at Langmuir Laboratory.

Hispanic life is detailed, also with considerable humor as well as scholarship, by Nasario García in two works in the Historical Society-UNM Press series: *Recuerdos de los Viejitos: Tales of the Río Puerco* and *Abuelitos: Stories of the Río Puerco Valley* (1992). Garcia was born in the Rio Puerco Valley and later recognized the rich resource in the tales of relatives and friends from the area. The stories tell of life in remote villages, using the Spanish vernacular, translated into English opposite the Spanish original. Some of the tales are from the later nineteenth century, but most are of the twentieth century, up to the final abandonment of those Puerco villages. There is touching bitterness in the final tales about government agents forcing people to destroy their cattle to comply with government regulations. Most of the inhabitants moved to Bernalillo and Albuquerque, where García later conducted his interviews. The books include photographs.

Two final examples of this Historical Society-University of New Mexico Press collaboration: In *Creator of the Santa Fe Style: Isaac Hamilton Rapp, Architect* (1988), Carl D. Sheppard seeks to develop the story of the "true originator" of the architectural tradition referred to in story and ordinance as the Santa Fe style—fighting words in some quarters. Martha A. Sandweiss, then curator of photography for the Amon Carter Museum in Fort Worth, came across letters and some previously unpublished photographs of Laura Gilpin and her close friend Elizabeth W. Foster. *Denizens of the Desert: A Tale in Word and Pictures of Life among the Navaho Indians* (1988) contains the letters of Foster to Gilpin from the Navaho lands when Foster was a public health nurse in the 1930s. The photographs were taken by Gilpin.

Works on cultural life in New Mexico include Alice Lee Marriott's *Maria: the Potter of San Ildefonso* (Norman: University of Oklahoma Press, 1968), a study of one of the most famous potters.Georgia O'Keeffe figures in two studies: Laurie Lisle, *Portrait of an Artist: A Biography of Georgia*

O'Keeffe (Albuquerque: University of New Mexico Press, 1986); and Roxanne Robinson, *Georgia O'Keeffe: A Life* (New York: Harper and Row, 1986). Sharyn Rohlfsen Udall's *Modernist Painting in New Mexico, 1913–1935* (Albuquerque: University of New Mexico Press, 1984) covers another aspect of the state's rich artistic traditions. The origins and development of the Santa Fe Opera are presented by Eleanor Scott, *The First Twenty Years of the Santa Fe Opera* (Santa Fe: Sunstone Press, 1976).

U.S. government agency publications do not receive wide distribution usually due to budgetary limitations, but they should not be overlooked. As previously mentioned, David Myrick's book, *New Mexico Railroads,* gives a general treatment of the subject. However, more detailed studies are found in documents from the Cultural Resource Management office of the U.S. Forest Service. Vernon J. Glover wrote three such studies. *Logging Railroads of the Lincoln National Forest,* Report Number 4 (1984), covers the Sacramento Mountain lumber and tourist operations from Alamogordo to Cloudcroft and beyond. This is complemented by Dorothy Neal Jensen's *The Lodge, 1899–1969* (Alamogordo: Alamogordo Printing, 1969), the story of a hostelry built by the railroad to stimulate traffic and one that still operates although the rails are long gone. Glover's next study, *Zuni Mountain Railroads: Cibola National Forest,* Report Number 6 (1986) covers the lumber roads going south from the Grants area. Finally, he wrote *Jemez Mountains Railroads; Santa Fe National Forest,* Report Number 9 (1989). Glover's books were given wider dissemination through the Historical Society of New Mexico, the Railroad Club of New Mexico, and the Friends of the Cumbres & Toltec Scenic Railroad. Otherwise, these studies are buried in government files for in-house use only.

The field of historic preservation has attracted growing interest in recent decades. The *New Mexico Historic Preservation Plan,* II Volumes, was published in 1973. Pre-dating that set is *New Mexico Architecture Magazine.* This journal was a project of the New Mexico chapter of the American Institute of Architects and was published from 1959 to 1990. The series is a treasure trove of histories of towns, buildings, preservation projects, preservation failures, and some special topics of New Mexico history. The magazine has unfortunately ceased publication.

Another fruitful source which, like governments publications, is limited in dissemination and often overlooked, is the output of state and local historical societies. These societies produce books, articles, pamphlets, and newsletters that are often well-researched, well-written, and reviewed by an editor or board. Most of this body of information is privately printed, which limits distribution. The writers of this material are often dismissed as history buffs or amateur historians. However, much local history is researched and recorded by these groups. At one time the *New Mexico Historical Review* belonged to the Historical Society of New Mexico, a private, non profit organization. The *Review* is now owned and published by the University of New Mexico. It is well known for scholarly articles and reviews. Also, *New Mexico Magazine* presents both popular and scholarly articles.

The New Mexico Bureau of Mines and Mineral Resources, located at New Mexico Institute of Mining and Technology, publishes mostly for geologists and mines. It also publishes some works of history. The bureau has a first rate archive of mining history from the late nineteenth and twentieth centuries. Mining camps played a vital role in New Mexico. Also on the subject of mining is the Historical Society of New Mexico-University of New Mexico Press publication of Jim Berry Pearson's *The Red River-Twining Area: A New Mexico Mining Story* (1986). The story is of mining in the last century, but it continues into the tourist era of our own time.

The atomic bomb was a development of the twentieth century and New Mexico was a center of that development. An excellent work on the subject is Ferenc Morton Szasz's *Day the Sun Rose Twice: The Story of the Trinity Site Nuclear Explosion* (Albuquerque: University of New Mexico Press, 1984). He describes the persons involved in the development of the bomb, the events leading up to the explosion, and the reactions of witnesses. Four other works add to the story of New Mexico in the Atomic Age. They are James W. Kunetka, *City of Fire: Los Alamos and the Atomic*

Age, 1943–1945 (Albuquerque: University of New Mexico Press, 1979); Necah Stewart Furman, *Sandia National Laboratories: The Postwar Decade* (Albuquerque: University of New Mexico Press, 1990); Hal Rothman, *On Rims and Ridges: The Los Alamos Area since 1880* (Lincoln: University of Nebraska Press, 1992); Peggy Pond Church's classic, *House at Otowi Bridge* (Albuquerque: University of New Mexico Press, many reprints, 1973).

Water and water resources are of primary importance in New Mexico. Ira G. Clark has written the monumental study on the subject, *Water in New Mexico: A History of Its Management and Use* (Albuquerque: University of New Mexico Press, 1987). There are also subtopics. For example, *A Guide to the Elephant Butte Irrigation District Records* by John W. Grassham, Darlis A. Miller, and Ira G. Clark was published as a technical report of the New Mexico Water Resource Research Institute in Las Cruces, June 1985. Another work is Douglas K. Boyd and Meeks Etchieson, *Historic Resources Related to Construction Actvities at Elephant Butte Reservoir*, a Department of Interior, Bureau of Reclamation Report, Southwest Region, Amarillo, TX, August 1986.

The U.S. Forest Service also put out several volumes on a specialized but intriguing subject. Cultural Resources Management reports numbers 7, 8, 11, and 12 are collected under the general heading of *Lookouts in the Southwest Region,* most of which apply to the current century. They are a history of the fire watchers in the national forests.

The coming of the railroad to New Mexico had a profound and permanent effect on events in the territory, and much of that impact extended into the twentieth century. In addition to the U.S. Forest Service publications mentioned earlier, much research and writing is found in other non-academic sources. Too often the topic is left to the railroad "buff," but this is a serious misunderstanding of sources. There is a vast amount of literature that includes New Mexico published by the Colorado Railroad museum of Golden, the New Mexico Railroad Club, and the Friends of the Cumbres & Toltec Scenic Railroad, Inc. Commercial publications are also a continuing source of articles pertinent to railroads and related topics in New Mexico. *Trains Magazine,* a general journal of railroad subject in the United States, and *Railroad and Railfan* are noted for treating history and historic preservation as well as current events. A more recent magazine is *Locomotive & Railway Preservation,* which is devoted wholly to preservation projects and practices in the United States and has featured New Mexico prominently in several issues. Several publishers devote their lists almost solely to railroading. There are standard histories of the Santa Fe and the Denver & Rio Grande railroads, but they are concerned with corporate developments and corporate rivalry rather than local concerns. Academic sources are also available, of course. Peggy Pond Church's *House at Otowi Bridge* should be mentioned again for the railroad connection. Vernon J. Glover and Spencer Wilson have written *The Cumbres & Toltec Scenic Railroad Preservation Study,* 4th ed. (Albuquerque: University of New Mexico Press, 1980).

This review is intended as a selective guide to the sources available to the student of New Mexico history, particularly to publications not usually found in university libraries. There is a great deal of good research and writing out there, and I urge the serious student or general reader to widen the search.

CONTRIBUTORS

Judith Boyce DeMark received the Ph.D. in American History from the University of New Mexico. She is an assistant professor of history at Northern Michigan University.

Joan M. Jensen has recently retired from the Department of History, New Mexico State University. She has numerous publications in the field of women's history to her credit, including *Promise to the Land: Essays on Rural Women*.

Ira G. Clark is Professor Emeritus at the department of history, New Mexico State University. He continues to write and research on management and use of water in the arid areas of the Southwest. His major works include *Water in New Mexico: A History of Its Management and Use* and *Then Came the Railroads: The Century from Steam to Diesel in the Southwest*.

Susan E. Perlman received the M.A. in American History from New Mexico State University. She currently owns a contract ethnographic and history research company in Albuquerque.

Steve Cormier completed his M.A. in American History from Wichita State University. He is a doctoral candidate in American Studies at the University of New Mexico and is an adjunct instructor of history at Albuquerque Technical-Vocational Institute.

Robert Kern is professor of Iberian and modern European history at the University of New Mexico. One of his research fields is international labor history, which he reviews regularly for *Choice* magazine. His local labor publications include *Labor in New Mexico: Unions, Strikes, and Social History Since 1881* and *Building New Mexico: The Experience of a Carpenters Union in the Southwest.*

Christopher J. Huggard is a doctoral candidate in history at the University of New Mexico. His research interests concentrate on the impact of mining on the environment in the American West.

Arthur Goméz received the Ph.D. in history from the University of New Mexico. He is a staff historian for the U.S. Park Service. His major research interest is the twentieth-century West.

Judith R. Johnson is an assistant professor of history at Wichita State University where she teaches twentieth-century American history. She received the Ph.D. in American history at the University of New Mexico.

Sandra Schackel is an associate professor of history at Boise State University. She received the Ph.D. in history from the University of New Mexico. She writes and publishes in women's history and the American West.

Jake W. Spidle, Jr. is associate professor of modern European history and the history of medicine at the University of New Mexico. He has published several works on New Mexico medical history including *Doctors of Medicine in New Mexico; A History of Health and Medical Practice, 1886–1986* and *Lovelace Medical Center: Pioneer in American Health Care.*

Barron Oder received the B.A. and M.A. in history at the University of San Diego. He is currently completing the Ph.D. in American history at the University of New Mexico. He has worked as a contract historian for the U.S. Air Force Phillips Laboratory, History office.

William E. Tydeman is the State Archivist at the Idaho State Historical Society. He received the Ph.D. in American Studies from the University of New Mexico. His current research involves a history of Route 66.

Richard Melzer completed the Ph.D. in Latin American history at the University of New Mexico. He is assistant professor of history at the University of New Mexico-Valencia campus. His major research interest is twentieth-century social history of New Mexico.

Spencer Wilson is professor of history at New Mexico Institute of Mining and Technology. He is a past president of the Historical Society of New Mexico and a member of the Cumbres & Toltec Scenic Railroad Commission. His research interests include New Mexico, Socorro, and railroad history.

John W. Grassham received an M.A. in history from New Mexico State University. He is currently president of the Historical Society of New Mexico. He is employed as the Curator of History at the Albuquerque Museum.

INDEX